Legal Responsibilities
of Real Estate Agents

Rosemary Bocska
Martin K.I. Rumack

LexisNexis®
Butterworths

Legal Responsibilities of Real Estate Agents
© LexisNexis Canada Inc. 2006
April 2006

Members of the LexisNexis Group worldwide

Canada	LexisNexis Canada Inc, 123 Commerce Valley Dr. E. Suite 700, MARKHAM, Ontario
Argentina	Abeledo Perrot, Jurisprudencia Argentina and Depalma, BUENOS AIRES
Australia	Butterworths, a Division of Reed International Books Australia Pry Ltd, CHATSWOOD, New South Wales
Austria	ARD Betriebsdienst and Verlag Orac, VIENNA
Chile	Publitecsa and Conosur Ltda, SANTIAGO DE CHILE
Czech Republic	Orac, sro, PRAGUE
France	Éditions du Juris-Classeur SA, PARIS
Hong Kong	Butterworths Asia (Hong Kong), HONG KONG
Hungary	Hvg Orac, BUDAPEST
India	Butterworths India, NEW DELHI
Ireland	Butterworths (Ireland) Ltd, DUBLIN
Italy	Giuffré, MILAN
Malaysia	Malayan Law Journal Sdn Bhd, KUALA LUMPUR
New Zealand	Butterworths of New Zealand, WELLINGTON
Poland	Wydawnictwa Prawnicze PWN, WARSAW
Singapore	Butterworths Asia, SINGAPORE
South Africa	Butterworth Publishers (Pty) Ltd, DURBAN
Switzerland	Stämpfli Verlag AG, BERNE
United Kingdom	Butterworths Tolley, a Division of Reed Elsevier (UK), LONDON, WC2A
USA	LexisNexis, DAYTON, Ohio

Library and Archives Canada Cataloguing in Publication

Bocska, Rosemary
    Legal responsibilities of real estate agents / Rosemary Bocska, Martin K.I. Rumack.

Includes text of Real Estate and Business Brokers Act, 2002 (Ontario) and applicable code of ethics.
Includes index.
ISBN 0-433-45142-4

    1. Real estate business—Law and legislation—Ontario. 2. Real estate agents—Ontario. 3. Real estate agents—Professional ethics—Ontario.
I. Rumack, Martin K.I. II. Title.

KEO502.R4B62 2006   346.71304'3   C2006-901233-4
KF2042.R4B62 2006

Printed and bound in Canada.

ABOUT THE AUTHORS

Rosemary Bocska, of the Ontario Bar, is a research lawyer. She provides in-depth legal research on a broad range of topics for small and mid-sized law firms across Canada. Alongside her research practice, she has also worked both in-house and on a freelance basis for various legal publishers, performing research and manuscript writing, and providing consulting services in connection with online legal information and its related technology.

Rosemary has written for numerous law publications, legal newspapers and current-awareness services. She is the author of *Ontario Limitation Periods (2d ed.)*, and is the updating author of *Ontario Residential Real Estate Practice Manual*, a looseleaf publication.

Martin K. I. Rumack has been practising real estate law for over 33 years, acting for a wide variety of clients, including purchasers, vendors, lenders and developers. He has run his own law firm specializing in this area since 1978. He has taught credit courses for real estate agents with the Toronto Real Estate Board, and has presented a number of seminars for real estate companies for the benefit of real estate agents. This is his first book.

PREFACE

This book is intended to be a readily-accessible source of information, and is designed to provide an easily-understood educational reference guide. In my experience, the field of real estate involves not only the law of real estate, but also the daily intricacies, practicalities and realities of handling various transactions on an on-going basis, whether they are of a residential or a commercial nature. My philosophy has always been that in a real estate transaction, you the real estate agent, and myself the lawyer, will work as a team to facilitate the completion of the transaction in as smooth and effortless a manner as possible for the benefit of our mutual client, the Seller or the Buyer of the Property.

This book is a compilation and refinement of seminar materials which I have prepared on a variety of real estate and other topics. Some have never been presented in a seminar. My co-author, Rosemary Bocska, has worked with me for a number of years in helping to research, prepare, draft and re-draft material for my presentation. Rosemary is a lawyer whose practice is restricted to research for other lawyers on a wide variety of legal matters. Her focus is on the area of real estate law, and she regularly writes for publications dealing primarily with real estate topics.

Based on Rosemary's legal research and writing, and based on my 33 years of practice, we have come to the conclusion that there is a need for this book in order to help you, the real estate professional, assist your client to the best of your ability; and at the same time, help you to prevent and avoid problems and mistakes before they arise. This in turn, will hopefully assist you to avoid incurring personal liability and financial repercussions, thereby helping you to keep the money you have worked so hard to earn! We have attempted to make this book enjoyable, easily readable and most of all, practical. In addition, this book includes the full text of the new *Real Estate and Business Brokers Act, 2002*; the new *Code of Ethics Regulation* and the new *General Regulation*, all of which are in force as of March 31, 2006.

I would also like to thank some of the people who have helped to influence, educate and assist me over the years: my Real Estate Law Professor, Arnold Weinrib, University of Toronto, Faculty of Law; my principals when I initially graduated from the Bar Admission Course, Saul and Paul Merrick; various real estate agents, managers and brokers who over the years have been of assistance and provided a guiding light; Allan C. Rosen, a true friend from the first day of law school and always there as a friend, support, *"confrère"*, resource and back-up; and to another good friend, Douglas A. Hendler who has been there as a mentor, and has provided guidance and support throughout the years. I also want to acknowledge the thousands of clients who over the years, have entrusted their real estate transactions to me. Finally, I would be remiss in not acknowledging the support, friendship and encouragement provided to me by the agents, managers and brokers throughout the years, particularly those people who suggested that I share my knowledge through the mediums of teaching and writing.

I would also like to acknowledge the encouragement, love and support throughout the years of my parents, Murray and Sylvia Rumack and my brothers, David and Norman. To my co-author, researcher, sounding board *"par excellence"*, for her many years of insight, sharing of knowledge, and many re-writes based on my idiosyncratic demands, a big thank you Rosemary and congratulations on a job well done!

To my dedicated, loyal and supportive office staff, Anita, Luisa, and Sue, for your contributions over the years to my real estate education, and for being there through thick and thin, for doing re-writes and proofreading, many thanks. Lastly, to my wife, Judi and son, Darren, who against my advice is now in law school, thank you for always being there, through rain or shine, snow or sun, providing late dinners and your constant support, love, understanding and devotion... a big hug and kiss!!!!!!

Martin Rumack
April 2006

Although I have worked on many legal publications over the years, the experience of writing this one was by far the most pleasant for me, both professionally and personally. For that I want to thank my friend and co-author, Martin Rumack, for his inspired ideas, his sharing of knowledge, his gentle critiquing, and his always-cheerful demeanor.

I'd also like to thank my parents, Rose and Steve Bocska, for their unwavering encouragement, love, and support over the years, and for their continuing pride in my little accomplishments. I extend particular gratitude to my ever-supportive husband Joe Garvey, whose love, patience and assistance make the elusive balance between work and homelife not only a possibility, but a very successful and satisfying reality. And lastly, I want to thank my two young children, Benjamin and Alexandra, for occasionally leaving Mommy alone long enough to get her work done.

Rosemary Bocska
April 2006

TABLE OF CONTENTS

INTRODUCTION

By definition, the modern housing marketplace is a fast-paced, unpredictable environment: it involves an inherently volatile, high-stakes game, and its participants are often emotionally invested in the outcome. When you add various complicating factors into the mix, such as (so-called) "buyer's/seller's market" phases, bidding wars, and the potential to "flip" properties, it is really no surprise that problems and misunderstandings can abound.

As a real estate professional, you already know that the process of marketing, listing, and helping a client to buy or sell a home can be fraught with pitfalls for even the most careful amongst you — and naturally, this handbook can only cover the "tip of the iceberg" in this regard. But prevention is still the best strategy, and you can avoid many difficulties by using a little common sense. Indeed, if there is a prevailing theme throughout this book, it is one of simple *awareness*. In a nutshell, this involves:

- Knowing who your client is.
- Knowing what your duties are to that client (and potentially to non-clients, too).
- Knowing all the facts.
- Knowing what makes the particular property — and/or your client — unique.
- Knowing when you are approaching morally/ethically murky territory, and steering clear of these situations.

With these general guidelines in hand, we turn to the more complex task of helping you foresee and prevent problems on a day-to-day basis, and in a variety of transactions.

CHAPTER 1

THE ROLE OF A REAL ESTATE AGENT

A. Agency Explained
B. What is an "Agent", Anyway?
C. "Ratification"
D. The "Undisclosed Principal"

The first step is to understand precisely what is involved in your role as real estate agent.

In a typical buyer/seller scenario, it may be tempting to simply view your job as being that of a *liaison* between those parties. However, the situation is far more complex, and involves the well-established legal concept known as "agency".

A. AGENCY EXPLAINED

"Agency" and "agent" are common terms that are used in modern conversation — we often hear the phrases like "employment agency", "real estate agent", "player's agent", and "double agent", to name just a few.

However common these terms may be, few people realize that the concept of "agency" is actually strictly defined, in a legal sense. In fact, there are several different types of agency, each with its own characteristics. In the context of everyday legal relationships — such as the purchase and sale of real estate — the distinction can be important.

B.   WHAT IS AN "AGENT", ANYWAY?

In the plainest of terms, an "agent" is someone who has the authority to act on behalf of someone else as their representative. By becoming someone else's agent, that person assumes certain important duties, including the duty to act in good faith and only in the other person's best interests.

Let's use a very simple example: "Agnes" has been authorized by "Paul" to purchase a sports car. Agnes will go to the dealership, will negotiate the deal, and will sign the contract on Paul's behalf. In the end, the sports car belongs to Paul, and Paul has the obligation to pay for it. Agnes was merely exercising the authority she had been given by Paul, to conclude Paul's deal with the car dealership for him.

In this scenario, Agnes is known as the "agent", while Paul is the "principal". A relationship of "agency" has been established. More-over, from a legal standpoint, the contract for the sale of the car will be between Paul and the dealership, rather than between Agnes and the dealership. Agnes merely acted as Paul's representative.

Now let's complicate the scenario somewhat. Let us imagine that Agnes goes to the dealership to negotiate the deal for Paul's sports car. However, while Agnes is surveying the sports cars in the lot, she notices a nifty little motorcycle. Rather than purchase a car for Paul, she decides to purchase a motorcycle for him, thinking it will better suit Paul's personal style.

In this situation, Agnes has acted beyond the scope of her authority. Her assignment was to purchase a sports car on Paul's behalf, but she bought a motorcycle instead. Assuming she did not receive Paul's permission in advance to buy a motorcycle (and despite her good intentions), Agnes cannot ask Paul to be responsible for the cost of the motorcycle, since Paul did not authorize its purchase.

In our example, the authority that Agnes has to negotiate and conclude the transaction on behalf of Paul can come in many different forms, and the law recognizes different nuances between them. For example, Agnes might have express authority — *e.g.*, Paul's verbal or written permission to buy *either* a sports car or a motorcycle. Or, Agnes' authority might be implied by the circumstances — for example, Paul has allowed Agnes the blanket authority to arrange for Paul's transportation needs. In such cases, Agnes might be authorized to buy a range of things, such as plane tickets, vehicles (including a motorcycle), or skateboard. Alternatively, Agnes might have a certain amount of authority because it is usual or customary (*e.g.*, where she is a particular type of agent, like a real estate agent).

Whether or not an agent has the requisite authority from his or her principal can be a very important issue — it can determine whether the contract made on the principal's behalf is a valid one.

C.   "RATIFICATION"

Getting back to the car-purchase scenario, it is important to point out that even if Agnes bought Paul a motorcycle without his permission, there is a concept known as "ratification" that might save the day. Despite the fact that Agnes failed to adhere to the scope of her authority (*i.e.*, the purchase of a sports car), Paul may decide that the motorcycle actually suits him better, and may decide to confirm the contract Agnes entered into with the dealership, after-the-fact. In this situation, Paul's ratification makes the contract with the dealership as good as if Agnes had been authorized to buy a motorcycle in the first place.

D.   THE "UNDISCLOSED PRINCIPAL"

The concept of "undisclosed principal" can also be important — particularly in real estate transactions where the identity of the parties to the deal might matter. Assume that "Carlos" owns two condominium units side-by-side, and lives in one of them but decides to put the other one up for sale. Whoever purchases the unit from Carlos will also become his neighbour, so Carlos is hoping to find someone who shares his fondness for peace and quiet.

"Delilah", who looks like the quiet type, approaches Carlos with an offer. Delilah leads Carlos to believe that she is interested in the condominium personally, *i.e.*, that Delilah is the potential buyer.

Unbeknownst to Carlos, however, the offer put forth by Delilah is actually from Hector, who is a determined (but hopelessly untalented) novice trombone player. In this situation, Delilah is Hector's agent, and Hector is what is known as an "undisclosed principal".

If Carlos accepts the offer to purchase, mistakenly believing that it comes from Delilah, is Carlos out of luck? Generally speaking, there is nothing to prevent an agent from entering into a valid contract on behalf of an undisclosed principal. There is an exception, though, if the true identity of the buyer of the condominium is important to Carlos as seller, or if Delilah the agent somehow exceeded her authority from Hector. In these instances, there may be no valid contract between Carlos and Hector at all.[1]

Fortunately, in most typical real estate transactions, there is no real confusion as to whom the agent acts for, because the agency relationship arises through the signing of a contract (*i.e.*, the seller signs an agreement with the listing agent). And yet, some circumstances give rise to what is known as a dual agency, or else an agency relationship can arise without a written contract being signed — either through the consent between the agent and the seller, or by their mere conduct. This will be discussed in Chapter 7.

---

[1]   In this example, if it was important that Carlos did not want to sell to Hector, then he would have to instruct his agent accordingly, and/or would have to ensure that a condition to this effect is put into the offer.

CHAPTER 2

THE SOURCE AND NATURE OF AGENTS' DUTIES

A. Statutory Duties
B. Contractual and Tort Duties
C. Fiduciary Duties
D. The Duty to Disclose Information
E. Other Assorted Duties
F. Chart of Agents' Duties

Before we begin to catalogue potential problems, the next step is to understand precisely where your *duties* as an agent originate in the first place.

In Ontario, the *Real Estate and Business Broker's Act, 2002*[1] and its regulations[2] are the primary sources for all agents' general obligations. Essentially, these legislative enactments collectively govern general conduct and procedure in relation to dealing with clients and trading in real estate, as well as matters such as the registration of agents, advertising, and commissions.

Additional restrictions are imposed by two other sources:

• the Real Estate Council of Ontario's *Code of Ethics Regulation*, which covers agents' ethical behaviour, financial disclosure, confidentiality, *etc.*; and

---

[1] S.O. 2002, c. 30, Sched. C, in force March 31, 2006. This Act replaced the former version of the legislation, namely the *Real Estate and Business Broker's Act*, R.S.O. 1990, c. R.4.

[2] Specifically, *Code of Ethics Regulation*, O. Reg. 580/05; and *General Regulation*, O. Reg. 567/05. Both are in force as of March 31, 2006.

- by agents' own governing boards and associations, such as the Ontario Real Estate Association ("OREA"), the Canadian Real Estate Association ("CREA"), and the Toronto Real Estate Board ("TREB").

Finally, decisions from the courts also provide guidance to agents as to what their duties and liabilities are.

Despite this wide array of sources, your duties as an agent can essentially be grouped into a small number of categories, namely:

- statutory duties;
- contractual duties;
- duties of disclosure; and
- fiduciary duties.

These will be discussed in turn.

A. STATUTORY DUTIES

The duties imposed by statute are simple to itemize, and are probably the easiest to understand. As an agent, the *Real Estate and Business Brokers Act, 2002*[3] and its regulations[4] impose an extensive set of requirements on agents, including the requirement to:

- Account to your client;
- Deliver listing agreements;
- Deliver offers, acceptances and related materials;
- Deliver statements on the sale of a business;
- Avoid inducing a breach of contract;
- Avoid making certain promises;
- Disclose relevant information; and
- Deal honestly, fairly, and with integrity.

Note that this list is just a summary; the statutory duties placed on agents are quite lengthy. A copy of the *Real Estate and Business Broker's Act, 2002* and its relevant regulations are found in the Appendices.

---

[3]   S.O. 2002, c. 30, Sched. C, in force March 31, 2006. This Act replaced the former version of the legislation, namely the *Real Estate and Business Broker's Act*, R.S.O. 1990, c. R.4.

[4]   *Code of Ethics Regulation*, O. Reg. 580/05; and *General Regulation*, O. Reg. 567/05. Both are in force as of March 31, 2006.

All of the requirements in this legislation are extremely important; however it is particularly noteworthy that section 32 of the Act imposes a specific *disclosure* obligation on agents in defined circumstances; namely, any time you are contemplating making an offer to purchase or otherwise obtaining an interest in the seller's property for yourself. In this situation you must disclose, in writing, your status as broker or salesperson (as the case may be). If the seller has listed the property with the firm that employs you, then there are added requirements: — namely full disclosure to the seller of all the facts within your special knowledge that affect the resale value of the property, and disclosure of the specifics of any negotiation or agreement by you for the sale of the real estate to a third party. In either case, the seller must provide written acknowledgment of having received such disclosure from you.

Although section 32 of the Act is quite straightforward, some agents have had difficulty complying with it, and the legal consequences have been predictable. For example, in one decision by the court named *Beaver Lumber Co. v. 222044 Ontario Ltd.*,[5] a sales agent and a broker bought the seller's property without making the required disclosure under the Act, and then re-sold the property for $500,000 more than they had paid. The agent and broker were found to be collectively liable to the seller for that amount, and had their licences revoked as well.

B.   CONTRACTUAL AND TORT DUTIES

As compared to the statutory duties, the non-statutory duties imposed on you are a little more complex, because they can arise either expressly or by implication. In particular, they stem from an oral or written contract between you and your client, or from tort law principles, or both.

These duties can be summarized as requiring you to:

- Perform the contract of agency;
- Maintain a duty of loyalty;
- Obey your client's lawful instructions;
- Act in person;
- Exercise reasonable skill and care;
- Maintain confidentiality;

---

[5]   [1996] O.J. No. 1132 (Gen. Div.).

- Disclose relevant information; and
- Comply with the duty to account.

On paper, most of these duties are quite straightforward, and several of them echo the statutory duties described above. In practice, however, they may be difficult for you to identify in specific factual contexts, and indeed some agents have found themselves liable for what is little more than a poor judgment call.

For instance, in a Manitoba case called *Krasniuk v. Gabbs*[6] a seller's agent had to forfeit her commission because she did not advise the sellers that a *verbal* offer had been made to buy their property. Her decision stemmed from the fact that under Manitoba law, all real estate offers must be in *writing* or else they are invalid. The sellers later sold to someone else for an amount lower than that verbal offer, and they sued the agent for the difference. In evaluating the agent's conduct, the court found the legislation governing written real estate contracts was irrelevant to determining what *disclosure* obligations the agent had to her clients; her overriding duty was simply to disclose *all* material information to the sellers, and this she had failed to do.

Likewise, conduct that complies with your duty to exercise "skill and care" can be hard to identify with precision, mainly because there is no single, absolute standard that applies to all scenarios and transactions. Instead, the proper standard of care is judged in light of the particular circumstances at hand, and will be even higher than usual for agents who hold themselves out as having particular skills or special expertise that is not normally found in the average member of the profession. All of this means that the precise degree of skill and care that you need to exercise will be difficult to ascertain, and may vary from one deal to the next.

The specific fact scenario will often determine the precise scope of your duty. One example of this is found in the Ontario case called *Mohn v. Dreiser*,[7] which involved the sale of a motel business. The seller had claimed that net annual operating profits were about $60,000, but in reality the motel had been losing money for at least four years straight. The seller's agent had prepared a profit statement for the buyer's review, unwittingly relying on the false information provided by the seller. The agent made no other inquiries as to the motel's financial health and indeed

---

[6]   [2002] M.J. No. 13 (Q.B.).

[7]   [2002] O.J. No. 4989, 119 A.C.W.S. (3d) 352 (S.C.J.), supp. reasons [2003] O.J. No. 462 (S.C.J.), affd [2004] O.J. No. 4444 (C.A.).

failed to provide the buyer with the additional financial documentation required by the *Real Estate and Business Broker's Act*. When the true state of affairs came to light, the buyer sued both the seller and the agent. In that particular fact scenario, the court found that the agent: (1) should have realized that the seller's information was inadequate to provide an accurate picture of the motel's financial status; and (2) should have taken positive steps to obtain proper financial statements prepared by chartered accountants. The average, reasonably competent agent faced with the same scenario would have done so, the court found.

C. FIDUCIARY DUTIES

The third category of duty arises because the connection between you and your client is of a special character known as a "fiduciary relationship" (which means, loosely speaking, a relationship based on trust). Because in the role of agent you are able to exercise some *discretion or power* that can affect your client's interests, there is a legal presumption that a fiduciary relationship exists, and accordingly additional protections and prohibitions apply. Under this heading, all agents must:

• Disclose any conflicts of interest;

and must not:

• Act for parties on both sides of a transaction;
• Make a secret profit;
• Sell your own property to the client;
• Secretly purchase the client's property for yourself; and
• Misuse information.

As compared to other duties, this fiduciary duty — also known as the "duty of loyalty" — is probably the most onerous. The overriding philosophy behind it is that, as an agent, you are never allowed to place yourself in a situation where there is a temptation to do something that is not best for your client.[8]

The reason behind these prohibitions is readily illustrated by a hypothetical situation. Let's say you wanted to secretly buy the seller's property for yourself; the seller would naturally be aiming to attain the highest price for the property, while you would want to encourage him

---

[8]   *Stahl v. Miller* (1918), 40 D.L.R. 388 (S.C.C.).

or her to accept the lowest price possible. These interests are in direct conflict with each other, and it places you in a position where you cannot both properly protect the seller's best interests, and yet minimize the price you pay for the property. Therefore, both the common law and legislation (in the form of the Ontario *Real Estate and Business Brokers Act, 2002*[9] and its regulations)[10] impose a positive legal obligation on you to disclose to the seller all relevant facts within your knowledge that would reasonably influence the seller in deciding whether or not to sell to you, and at what price.[11] Moreover, as was established long ago in a court decision named *D'Atri v. Chilcott*,[12] the price you pay for the property in such circumstances must be as advantageous to the seller as any other price that you could have obtained from someone else.

In essence, these fiduciary obligations dictate that you must conduct yourself scrupulously, and with the utmost honesty when dealing with clients and non-clients alike. Unfortunately, some agents have failed to adhere to this rather straightforward principle, and have faced extensive and costly litigation to untangle the resulting legal dispute.

One example is the case of *Soulos v. Korkontzilas*,[13] which went all the way to the Supreme Court of Canada. There, a buyer's agent did not tell his client that the seller would accept the client's offer on a particular property; instead, the agent bought the property for himself. The client sued the agent for breach of fiduciary duty, and asked that the property be conveyed to him. Interestingly, the value of the property had actually *declined* in the interim, so the client did not suffer a loss and the agent did not truly "benefit" from his actions. Nonetheless, the Supreme Court of Canada found there had been a breach of the agent's fiduciary duty to disclose to his or her client *all* the relevant facts in connection with the transaction, particularly where the client's decision may be affected if all the facts are not provided. The court ultimately determined that the agent could not "in good conscience" retain the property, and ordered him to re-convey it back to the client, subject to appropriate adjustments.

Not surprisingly, similarly rigorous requirements apply in cases where an agent wants not to *buy* the seller's property, but rather wants

---

[9]   S.O. 2002, c. 30, Sched. C, in force March 31, 2006.
[10]   *Code of Ethics Regulation*, O. Reg. 580/05; and *General Regulation*, O. Reg. 567/05. Both are in force as of March 31, 2006.
[11]   *Lunt v. Perley* (1916), 35 D.L.R. 214 (N.B.S.C.).
[12]   (1975), 7 O.R. (2d) 249 (H.C.J.).
[13]   [1997] S.C.J. No. 52, [1997] 2 S.C.R. 217.

to *sell* property to his or her own client. In a 1910 decision called *Johnson v. Birkett*[14] the court said:

> It has never been doubted that the agent may sell to his principal property of his own, if it be proved that no advantage was taken by the agent of his position, and that the transaction was entered into in perfectly good faith and after full disclosure. But the onus of proving all this lies upon the agent.

More specifically, agents in this situation will be in breach of their fiduciary duties unless it can be established that:

- the agent did not take advantage of the special relationship with the client;
- the transaction was in all respects fair;
- the agent's ownership interest in the property or in the transaction was fully disclosed to the client; and
- the client was advised to obtain, and was given the opportunity to obtain, independent advice respecting the transaction.

As with the other types of duties outlined already, the precise nature and extent of your fiduciary duty to your client depends on the particular facts of the transaction, and there are many Canadian court decisions that consider this. However, a few are particularly worth noting.

In *Knoch Estate v. Jon Picken Ltd.*,[15] the Ontario Court of Appeal had to determine whether a fiduciary relationship arises automatically in the course of *all* agency relationships, and — fortunately for real estate agents — concluded that it did not. In that case, the court was considering whether a selling agent should be found liable to the seller if he was involved in the negotiations between buyer and seller but failed to tell the seller the buyer's highest price. The court concluded that fiduciary duty did not arise where the seller had no real contact with the selling agent before the agreement of purchase and sale was presented to the seller, and did not rely on the selling agent's skill.

This duty of loyalty becomes particularly key whenever you are acting in a situation involving a *dual* agency, *i.e.*, where you simultaneously act for both buyer and seller, and have defined duties to both. In *Vokey v. Edwards*,[16] the buyers had retained the real estate agent to assist

---

[14] [1910] O.J. No. 135, 21 O.L.R. 319 (H.C.J.).

[15] [1991] O.J. No. 1394, 4 O.R. (3d) 385 (C.A.).

[16] [1999] O.J. No. 1706 (S.C.J.).

them in finding a new home with a swimming pool in good condition. The agent found a suitable property and brought the prospective buyers to see it; however, due to the weather the buyers were unable to inspect the pool themselves. The agent assured them that a pool warranty clause, attesting to the good condition of the pool, would be added to the offer. Moreover, the agent recommended *against* a home inspection, since he felt it was not worth the cost. The seller provided a disclosure statement indicating the true extent of the annual repairs needed to the pool, but the agent for some reason did not show it to the buyers. The deal closed, and upon learning that the pool was in an unusable condition, the buyers sued their own real estate agent for breach of fiduciary duty and negligence. The court found that the buyers had placed special confidence and trust in the agent, and had made clear to him their precise needs respecting the condition of the pool. It went on to find that the agent's recommendation against a professional inspection, his insertion of a "weak" warranty clause in the offer, and his failure to show the disclosure statement to the buyers, were all breaches of his duty to the buyers and grounds upon which his liability to them could be based.

See Chapter 7 for a further discussion of dual agency situations.

D.   THE DUTY TO DISCLOSE INFORMATION

The disclosure duty placed on all agents is also quite fundamental, and arises from a variety of sources. First of all, it can arise by way of statute, in the form of the *Real Estate and Business Brokers Act, 2002* and its regulations. This is discussed in Part A of this chapter.

Secondly, the duty to disclose information may legally arise in a more general sense, firstly because you and your client have entered into a contract with each other, and secondly, because the relationship between you and your client is one of a fiduciary nature, which has been discussed above. As a result, the law imposes a strict duty on you to make full disclosure:

- whenever you have gained an advantage in the transaction;
- where the information may affect the value of the property; or
- where a conflict of interest exists.

Unfortunately, the determination of when an "advantage" has been gained, when "conflict" exists, or when "value" is affected will all be difficult for the average person to determine definitively on a day-to-day basis. Still, as a rule of thumb, you have a positive obligation:

- to always act in your client's best interests; and
- to make full disclosure of everything you know respecting the sale of the property that would likely influence your client's conduct.[17]

A prime example of what *not* to do is found in the decision of *Raso v. Dionigi*,[18] which involved a buyer whose husband's brother was an agent. She approached him to find her an income-generating property. He in turn approached the sellers, and presented them with an offer signed by the buyer using her maiden name, as a means of concealing the fact that they were related by marriage. The deal was to proceed as planned until the sellers learned of the relationship between the agent and the buyer; they then refused to close. The court found that the agent was a dual agent for both seller and buyer, and had conflicting fiduciary duties to both of them, including a duty to try to get the seller the best price. In the circumstances, the deal could only proceed if the agent made full disclosure of all relevant information to the sellers, which included the fact that he was the buyer's brother-in-law.

E.   OTHER ASSORTED DUTIES

Your obligations are certainly not limited to the four categories discussed above — indeed, there are many additional obligations to which agents are subject. Among these are the duty of confidentiality (which requires you to keep confidential any information respecting your client that you have acquired during the course of the relationship) and the duty not to profit unlawfully at your client's expense. This last rule dictates that you may not:

- Use information you have acquired in the performance of your function as agent;
- Purchase your clients' properties or sell your own properties to the client; or

---

[17] *Ocean City Realty Ltd. v. A.M. Holdings Ltd.*, [1987] B.C.J. No. 593, 36 D.L.R. (4th) 94 (C.A.).
[18] [1993] O.J. No. 670, 12 O.R. (3d) 580 (C.A.).

- Receive secret commissions or payment from persons other than your clients (unless those payments are fully disclosed and acknowledged to your clients).

The last prohibition against the receipt of secret profits or commissions is worth a comment: these can include referral fees, or gifts from contractors, lending institutions, other brokers, or lawyers, to name just a few. Although these types of payments have proven irresistible to a small number of agents, it goes without saying they must be scrupulously avoided. Problems can arise, however, where the facts obscure the impropriety of taking the fee, and/or where the agent is wholly unaware of the resulting conflict.

For example in *Klingspon v. Royal Lepage Real Estate Services*,[19] the seller had a farm to sell, and listed it with a real estate brokerage. The interested buyer wanted to sell her own cottage first before buying the farm, and received a referral from the same agent to list with the same brokerage. This entitled the agent to a $453 referral fee if the cottage was to sell. As difficulties in the sale between the buyer and seller unfolded, the issue arose as to whether it was proper for the agent to profit from this transaction from another source entirely, *i.e.*, from the brokerage. The court decided it was not, confirming that in order to safeguard against a conflict of interest, the law does not allow an agent to receive commission or any other remuneration from any person other than his or her principal.

F.   CHART OF AGENTS' DUTIES

The following is a chart that conveniently summarizes some of the various statutory and common-law duties imposed on agents.[20]

---

[19]   [1993] O.J. No. 1439 (Gen. Div.).

[20]   Chart content inspired in part by the text of Paul M. Perell's "The Duties of Real Estate Agents" (2004) 19 R.P.R. (4th) 20.

AGENT FOR THE SELLER	Duties to the seller	General duties		
		Abide by the requirements under the *Real Estate Brokers Act, 2002* and its regulations	*Code of Ethics Regulation*, O. Reg. 580/05, s. 2, under the *Real Estate and Business Brokers Act, 2002*, S.O. 2002, c. 30, Sched. C
		Deal fairly, honestly, and with integrity	*Code of Ethics Regulation*, O. Reg. 580/05, s. 3, under the *Real Estate and Business Brokers Act, 2002*, S.O. 2002, c. 30, Sched. C
		Provide conscientious service, and demonstrate reasonable knowledge, skill, judgment and competence	*Code of Ethics Regulation*, O. Reg. 580/05, s. 5, under the *Real Estate and Business Brokers Act, 2002*, S.O. 2002, c. 30, Sched. C
		Determine the material facts, and disclose them to the client	*Code of Ethics Regulation*, O. Reg. 580/05, s. 21, under the *Real Estate and Business Brokers Act, 2002*, S.O. 2002, c. 30, Sched. C
		Follow the seller's instructions	*Len Pugh Real Estate Ltd. v. Ronvic Construction Co.* (1973), 1 O.R. (2d) 539 (Co. Ct.), vard 6 O.R. (2d) 454 (C.A.)
		Confirm certain information provided by the vendor (*e.g.*, title, size, zoning)[21]	*Posthumus v. Garner*, [1995] O.J. No. 3362, 48 R.P.R. (2d) 286 (Gen. Div.)
		Draft an agreement that is not vague, unenforceable, or contrary to the seller's instructions	*Academy Aluminum Products Ltd. v. Mchernney Realty Ltd.*, [1980] A.J. No. 660, 113 D.L.R. (3d) 289 (C.A.)

---

[21] In some circumstances.

AGENT FOR THE SELLER	**Duties to the seller**	General duties	Aim to obtain as high a price as possible for the seller's property
			Raso v. Dionigi, [1993] O.J. No. 670, 12 O.R. (3d) 580 (C.A.)
			Advise the seller promptly if the buyer's cheque is non-negotiable
			Morton v. Francis, [1994] O.J. No. 1664 (Gen. Div.)
		Fiduciary duties	Conform to the duty of loyalty, which includes a duty to: (1) not breach confidences; (2) disclose material information; and (3) avoid conflicts of interest
			Hodgkinson v. Simms, [1994] S.C.J. No. 84, [1994] 3 S.C.R. 377; *Raso v. Dionigi*, [1993] O.J. No. 670, 12 O.R. (3d) 580 (C.A.)
			Avoid making any profit not agreed to
			Midcon Oil & Gas Ltd. v. New British Dominion Oil Co., [1958] S.C.R. 314
	Duties to the buyer		Avoid making negligent or fraudulent misrepresentations (*i.e.*, false information or wrong advice)[22]
			Hercules Management Ltd. v. Ernst & Young, [1997] S.C.J. No. 51, [1997] 2 S.C.R. 165
AGENT FOR THE BUYER	**Duties to the buyer**	General duties	Abide by the requirements under the *Real Estate and Business Brokers Act, 2002* and its regulations
			Code of Ethics Regulation, O. Reg. 580/05. s. 2, under the *Real Estate and Business Brokers Act, 2002*, S.O. 2002, c. 30, Sched. C
			Provide conscientious service, and demonstrate reasonable knowledge, skill, judgement and competence
			Code of Ethics Regulation, O. Reg. 580/05, s. 5, under the *Real Estate and Business Brokers Act, 2002*, S.O. 2002, c. 30, Sched. C

[22] Although this is not a "duty" to the buyer *per se*, the seller's agent can face liability to the buyer in the right circumstances.

AGENT FOR THE BUYER	Duties to the buyer		
	General duties	Determine the material facts, and disclose them to the client	Code of Ethics Regulation, O. Reg. 580/05, s. 21, under the Real Estate and Business Brokers Act, 2002, S.O. 2002, c. 30, Sched. C
		Confirm the information provided by the seller[23]	Winsham Fabrik Canada Ltd. v. RE/Max All Stars Realty Inc., [2001] O.J. No. 1478 (S.C.J.)
		Follow the buyer's instructions	Wemyss v. Moldenhauer, [2003] O.J. No. 38, 7 R.P.R. (4th) 124 (S.C.J.)
		Draft terms of the agreement that protect the buyer and reflect his or her instructions	Vokey v. Edwards, [1999] O.J. No. 1706 (S.C.J.)
		Disclose information that is material to the buyer's decision whether to sign or complete the agreement	Vokey v. Edwards, [1999] O.J. No. 1706 (S.C.J.)
		Avoid making negligent or fraudulent misrepresentations	Various cases such as Nielson v. Watson (1981), 33 O.R. (2d) 515 (H.C.J.)
	Fiduciary duties	Avoid secret purchase of property, and/or any methods of obtaining a secret profit	Soulos v. Korkontzilas, [1997] S.C.J. No. 52, [1997] 2 S.C.R. 217

[23] In some circumstances, depending on the facts.

AGENT FOR THE BUYER	*Potential* **duties to the seller**[24]	Avoid deceiving or misleading the seller	*Knoch Estate v. Jon Picken Ltd.*, [1991] O.J. No. 1394, 4 O.R. (3d) 385 (C.A.)
		In some circumstances, to disclose to the seller any material information about the identity, character, or plans of the buyer.	Various cases such as *Harland v. Fancsali*, [1994] O.J. No. 3171, 21 O.R. (3d) 798 (Div. Ct.), affg [1993] O.J. No. 961, 13 O.R. (3d) 103 (Gen. Div.)
DUAL AGENT	**Duties to both the buyer and the seller**		
	General concerns	Be alert to whether an unintended dual agency situation exists	*489212 Ontario Ltd. v. Participactive Dynamics Inc.*, [1994] O.J. No. 780, 38 R.P.R. (2d) 32 (Gen. Div.), affd [1997] O.J. No. 3856, 13 R.P.R. (3d) 32 (C.A.)
	Contractual, tort and fiduciary duties	If a dual agency situation exists, be aware of the potential pitfalls inherent in having duties to both buyer and seller	*Raso v. Dionigi*, [1993] O.J. No. 670, 12 O.R. (3d) 580 (C.A.)
	Disclosure duties	If a dual agency situation exists, make full disclosure to both buyer and seller, and obtain both parties' consent to act	*Raso v. Dionigi*, [1993] O.J. No. 670, 12 O.R. (3d) 580 (C.A.)

---

[24]   These are duties of a fiduciary nature that may arise, depending on the facts. Note that the mere fact that the seller pays the buyer's agent's commission does not give rise to a fiduciary duty between the agent and the seller, however; see *Knoch Estate v. Jon Picken Ltd.*, [1991] O.J. No. 1394, 4 O.R. (3d) 385 (C.A.).

AGENT AS A BUYER/SELLER			
Agent who personally buys the seller's property	Fiduciary duties, where agent has an existing duty to the seller	Advise the seller that the agent personally intends to buy the property (whether directly or indirectly)	*Real Estate and Business Brokers Act, 2002,* S.O. 2002, c. 30, Sched. C, s. 32
		Advise the seller of all material information relevant to the transaction	*Remax Creative Realty Inc. v. Daltrey,* [1990] O.J. No. 1849, 13 R.P.R. (2d) 292 (Dist. Ct.); *D'Atri v. Chilcott* (1975), 7 O.R. (2d) 249 (H.C.J.)
Agent who sells his or her own property to the buyer	Fiduciary duties, where agent has a duty to the buyer	Advise the seller of all material information relevant to the transaction, work to obtain a favourable price, and avoid making a secret profit	Various cases such as *Rankin v. Menzies,* [2002] O.J. No. 51, 47 R.P.R. (3d) 265 (S.C.J.)

CHAPTER 3

COMMISSION

Listing agreements are of key significance to every agent, since they are the vehicle by which the agent gets paid a commission for his or her services. It is important to remember that they are legal contracts, which means (among other things) that they must be validly executed, must conform to the relevant legislation, and — as with all other kinds of contracts — can certainly be breached.

This chapter aims to highlight some of the issues that arise in connection with listing agreements, namely:

- the content and form of the agreement;
- whether it complies with the *Ontario Real Estate and Business Brokers Act, 2002*;
- limitations involving the amount of, and entitlement to, commission;
- the prerequisites involved in connection with an agent bringing a lawsuit to collect commission owed; and
- how entitlement to commission can be lost.

A. THE FORM AND CONTENT OF THE COMMISSION AGREEMENT — LEGISLATED INCLUSIONS

Generally speaking, the commission or listing agreement establishes a contractual relationship between the seller on the one hand, and you as agent on the other. It sets out the precise events that entitle you to receive your commission. In theory, its contents and terms are certainly negotiable, but in practice they have largely been standardized, specifically by way of standard forms provided by the Ontario Real Estate Association, the Toronto Real Estate Board, and other Real Estate Boards. Still, these "standard" agreements can vary, so it remains important to review them carefully and to be familiar with the various legislative provisions that govern them.

The good news is that these provisions are relatively few in number: among the most straightforward is section 11 of the *Code of Ethics Regulation*[1] under the *Real Estate and Business Brokers Act, 2002*. From a strict technical standpoint, that provision states that an agent will not enter into a written listing agreement unless it:

- specifies the date on which it will expire;

---

[1]   O. Reg. 580/05.

- specifies or describes the method for determining the amount of commission payable;
- describes how commission or other remuneration will be paid; and
- sets out the services that will be provided under the agreement.

A few points are worth noting in this regard:

i. Expiry Date

As might be expected, the agreement's expiry date is the date on which the contract between you and the other party ends. If this date is absent from the contract, then the whole commission agreement is unenforceable.

Note also that pursuant to the *Code of Ethics Regulation*,[2] under the *Real Estate and Business Brokers Act, 2002*, a listing agreement must have a duration of less than six months unless the client has expressly agreed otherwise;[3] moreover the written agreement must have only one expiry date specified on its face.[4]

These requirements are relatively straightforward. However, all agents must be careful to ensure that *other* documents do not throw the precise expiry date of the listing agreement into question; this was the argument made in a case called *Re/Max Realtron Realty Inc. v. Seider*.[5] There, the agreement provided that it would expire on a certain date "specified therein", and a date was duly added to the contract. However, the agent had also provided the seller with a "Professional Marketing Plan and Warranty", that outlined all the services that he was going to provide in connection with marketing the property. This Plan contained a provision that if the seller was dissatisfied with the agent's marketing efforts, he could terminate the listing agreement on seven days' written notice to the agent. The seller argued that this Marketing Plan formed part of the listing agreement, and that the provision respecting seven days' notice conflicted with the expiry date in the listing agreement, rendering the whole contract void for lack of

[2] O. Reg. 580/05.
[3] *Ibid.*, s. 11(2).
[4] *Ibid.*, s. 11(3).
[5] [1993] O.J. No. 1283, 40 A.C.W.S. (3d) 1030 (Gen. Div.).

compliance with the *Real Estate and Business Brokers Act*[6] that was in force at the time. Fortunately, the court disagreed with the seller, finding that the Marketing Plan did not detract from the certainty of the expiry date in the listing agreement, and that the agent was entitled to his commission. However, the case serves as a warning that documentation outside the listing agreement itself might, in some circumstances, have an impact on the validity of that agreement as a whole.

ii.   Lack of Written Agreement

It is an understatement to say that, ideally, the listing agreement should be in writing. In fact, sections 14 and 15 of the *Code of Ethics Regulations* under the *Real Estate and Business Brokers Act, 2002* stipulate that where an agreement has been entered into with a client (whether buyer, or seller) but it was not made in writing, then the agent *shall* reduce that agreement to writing at the *earliest practicable opportunity*, and submit it to the customer for his or her signature.

Even if there is no written contract, it is possible to claim commission in the right circumstances; however, it is very unwise for any agent to rely on this possibility.

Section 23 of the *General Regulation*[7] under the *Real Estate and Business Brokers Act, 2002* provides that an agent cannot "charge or collect" commission unless *either* there is a written listing agreement, *or* certain other stated prerequisites have been satisfied, among them that the agent has obtained "an offer in writing that is accepted".[8] Conceivably, the entitlement to bring an action for commission will flow from these circumstances. However, it is noteworthy that the predecessor version of this Act[9] expressly stated that an agent was allowed to bring an *"action"* for commission[10] where either of these conditions was met. (Although — practically speaking — this was not without its difficulties; the agent would still have to establish: (a) that he or she "obtained" the successful offer; (b) that (if applicable) a specific commission fee or percentage was verbally agreed to.)

---

[6]   In that case, it was the *Real Estate and Business Brokers Act*, R.S.O. 1990, c. R.4, which had virtually identical provisions in this regard.
[7]   O. Reg. 567/05.
[8]   *Ibid.*, s. 23(1)(b)(i).
[9]   *Real Estate and Business Brokers Act*, R.S.O. 1990, c. R.4.
[10]   *Ibid.*, s. 23.

In any event — and no matter what the differences may be between the old and new legislation — a written listing agreement is always the safest and prudent course to take.

B.   PROVIDING A COPY OF THE AGREEMENT

Section 12 of the *Code of Ethics Regulation* under the *Real Estate and Business Brokers Act, 2002* provides that, as soon as a written agreement is reached, the agent (or brokerage) must deliver a copy of it to each of the persons who signed it.

As was made evident in the decision of *New Commerce Realty Group Inc. v. Diblasi*,[11] in this context "copy" actually means "true copy", meaning a signed original. In that case, a copy of the listing agreement was delivered by the agent to the seller's secretary. However, it was a *photocopy* of the agent's own copy, and not a true copy signed by the owner, so the question for the court was whether this complied with the relevant sections of the Act/regulations. The court decided that it did not,[12] and the agent lost out on $60,000 in commissions as a result.

It is also worth noting that, to comply with this section of the *Real Estate and Business Brokers Act, 2002* regulations, the copy of the agreement must not only be delivered "immediately", but it must very likely be *fully completed* at that time, in all respects. In *Certa Homes Ltd. v. Brown*,[13] the agent had the seller sign various blank exclusive listing agreements, with the dates to be filled in later. The court found that this did not comply with the legislation, and so the agent's claim for commission failed.

C.   CALCULATING THE COMMISSION AMOUNT

The *Real Estate and Business Broker's Act, 2002* contains detailed guidelines that deal with the *amount* or calculation of the commission that is payable to agents. The Act states:[14]

---

[11] (1990), 24 A.C.W.S. (3d) 121 (Ont. Gen. Div.).
[12] This is in keeping with the decision in *Bowes & Cocks Ltd. v. Corbeil* (1978), 20 O.R. (2d) 152 (C.A.).
[13] [1991] O.J. No. 2021 (Gen. Div.).
[14] S.O. 2002, c. 30, Sched. C., s. 36(1).

All commission or other remuneration payable to a brokerage in respect of a trade in real estate shall be either an agreed amount or percentage of the sale price or rental price, as the case may be, but not both...

Note also that under the Act, if you have not struck an agreement with your client as to the precise amount of commission to which you are entitled, then the commission rate or fee will be whatever rate prevails in the community where the real estate is located.[15]

The new Act also expressly allows for commission arrangements featuring decreasing percentages at specified increments as the sale price increases[16] (although the converse, meaning those involving increasing percentages, is prohibited by implication).

A few points to note:

- The Act prohibits a commission rate based on the difference between the closing price and the listing price;[17] and
- GST is always payable on top of the commission fee.

Effectively, these few straightforward provisions are the only legislative controls over the amount of commission payable to agents. And over the years there has been virtually no dispute about them; in a single case called *Jankowski v. 990088 Ontario Inc.*,[18] the court simply observes in passing that where an agent agrees to perform various services in exchange for certain parcels of land, this would offend the provisions of the Act which require commission to be a set price or percentage. Otherwise, however, there are really no court decisions at all that involve a claim that the commission agreement did not comply with the Act, or that deal with calculating commission under these sections.

It is important to point out that some sellers may want to insist that the commission is calculated on the *cash portion* of the sale price (which excludes the amount of any vendor take-back mortgage and any other non-cash consideration). You will accordingly want to ensure that the listing agreement uses the *sale price* as the starting point for calculations, which will include these amounts and thus maximize the commission entitlement.

---

[15]   *Ibid.*, s. 36(1).
[16]   *Ibid.*, s. 36(2).
[17]   *Ibid.*, s. 36(3).
[18]   [1998] O.J. No. 2764, 80 A.C.W.S. (3d) 1126 (Gen. Div.).

D.   THE VARIOUS KINDS OF COMMISSION
AGREEMENTS

i.   Open vs. Exclusive vs. MLS

Although the essential elements remain consistent, it is worth noting that if a seller wants to list with you as agent, he or she has three specific listing structures to choose from, each with their own pros, cons, and commission rates. Stated briefly, they are:

(1)   Open Listing. In this type of agreement, the seller gives authority to sell the property to one or several agents, but usually also retains the right to sell the property on his or her own. Commission is only payable on completion of the transaction, and the agreement terminates when the property is sold or taken off the market. In practice, this form of agreement is not frequently used, primarily because the commission rate is lower than for other types of agreements, and because there is no obligation — and thus perhaps little incentive — for the agent to show the property.

(2)   Exclusive Listing. In an exclusive listing agreement, the seller gives the agent an exclusive and irrevocable right to list the property for a specific time. The seller gives up the right to deal with other agents during the currency of the listing (except perhaps through the listing agent, *e.g.*, where provision is expressly made for him or her to use the services of other agents), and remains liable for commission even where the seller manages to sell the property him or herself. The commission payable under this type of agreement is usually greater than what is charged for an open listing agreement, and less than what is charged for a multiple listing agreement (although lately some agents have been charging similar rates for the two).

(3)   Multiple Listing. This type of agreement is the one most commonly used. The property is listed with one agent (as in an exclusive listing), but the agent uses the services of other selling agents as well. The seller is obligated only to the listing agent for the commission, and that commission is shared by the listing agent and the selling agent (if they are not one and the same person). The seller has contact only with the listing agent, who is directly responsible to the seller and co-ordinates the elements of the sale. The rate of commission for this type of arrangement has traditionally been higher than for open or exclusive listing agreements.

ii.   Who Pays the Commission?

The various listing structures demonstrate that in the contemporary real estate marketplace, it is usually the *seller* in a real estate transaction who pays your commission. However, this can certainly be changed by agreement, usually by having the buyer assume that responsibility in the Offer to Purchase.[19]

An interesting question arose in a case called *Smalley Agencies Ltd. v. Tetrault*,[20] namely whether after signing a "seller-pays" agreement, the seller could unilaterally change the commission agreement without the agent's consent, to make the buyer responsible. On the facts of that case, the seller was a corporation that entered into a listing agreement with an agent. The agent introduced the eventual buyer, and negotiations and financing arrangements between the buyer and seller ensued. As part of this financing, the buyer and seller agreed that the buyer would assume responsibility for paying the agent's commission. The issue was whether the *agent* had agreed to that change, since he was not privy to it, and as far as he was concerned, his listing contract was still with the seller. Both the seller and the buyer resisted paying his commission, so the agent sued. He was successful against the seller under his original contract; the court found that whatever financing arrangements were made between buyer and seller, they did not change the fact that:

- the original commission agreement was between the seller and agent;
- there was no evidence that the agent had accepted the change as to who would pay him; and
- the agent had fulfilled his part of the contract by introducing the buyer to the seller.

iii.   Co-operating Agents

It is currently quite common for the listing agreement to give an agent the authority to co-operate with another agent, *i.e.*, an agent for a potential buyer. If you are in this situation with a potential buyer lined up, naturally you will feel entitled to a share of the commission, and

[19] *H.W. Liebig & Co. v. Leading Investments Ltd.*, [1986] S.C.J. No. 6, [1986] 1 S.C.R. 70; and *Block Bros. Realty Ltd. v. Mason*, [1974] B.C.J. No. 791, [1974] 6 W.W.R. 36 (Co. Ct.).
[20] [1999] M.J. No. 395, 91 A.C.W.S. (3d) 514 (Q.B.).

there are essentially three possible scenarios to cover how you will get paid:

- the listing agent pays you out of his or her commission;
- you have the authority to negotiate and accept commission directly from the seller; or
- the buyer pays commission to you directly (usually under a separate buyer's agency agreement).

Despite these various permutations, in practice the typical arrangement will involve the seller's listing agent paying you out of the commission received from the seller.

(Incidentally, a seller faced with the involvement of a second agent, in addition to his or her own, may be concerned about having to pay commission to both. However, the *Real Estate and Business Brokers Act, 2002* has provisions that are designed to alleviate this precise concern.)[21]

Whenever there is more than one agent sharing commission, difficulties can arise in ascertaining entitlement. For example in a British Columbia case,[22] a real estate broker sued the listing agent for commission. The seller had entered into a multiple listing agreement giving the listing agent the right to sell the property. The broker presented an *unconditional* offer to the seller, who rejected it in favour of a *conditional* offer presented by the listing agent. (The conditions had been satisfied.) The listing agent received a commission, and the broker claimed that he was also entitled to commission as well — even though he was not a party to the listing agreement. He argued that the listing broker had made an offer in the listing agreement published by the MLS service, and that the broker had introduced a ready, willing and able buyer. However, the broker was unsuccessful in the suit. The court did not accept that there was a contract between him and the listing agent to pay a commission, and more importantly found that a person becomes a buyer (rather than just a prospective buyer), *only* after there is a sale and an exchange of money. The court concluded that simply presenting a ready, willing and able buyer was not an "acceptance" of the listing agent's offer giving rise to a completed sale.

---

[21] S.O. 2002, c. 30, Sched. C, s. 33(3).

[22] *Rosling Real Estate (Nelson) Ltd. (c.o.b. Coldwell Banker Rosling Real Estate) v. Robertson Hilliard Cattell Realty Co. (c.o.b. Re/Max RHC Realty)*, [1999] B.C.J. No. 1614 (S.C.).

In another case called *Staltari Realty Corp. v. Colliers Macaulay Nicholls (Ontario) Inc.*[23] the listing agent was sued by a second agent, who claimed that they had an agreement to split the commission on a particular sale. The listing agreement required the listing agent to co-operate with other agents in marketing the property, after a set period during which the listing was to be exclusive. The second agent contacted the listing agent, advising that he had some prospective purchasers to introduce. The listing agent wrote back to advise that any prospective purchasers needed to be registered and approved by his brokerage. The second agent got the required approval and registration, but it was given to him by the brokerage in error, since it turned out that the purchaser he had in mind had already contacted the listing agent on his own. Still, the second agent claimed he had a valid contract for commission. Ultimately, the Court of Appeal disagreed, finding that the terms involving registration and approval — which triggered the second agent's commission entitlement — had not been met and that therefore no contract had been concluded.

iv.   Commission and the Agent/Employee

Special considerations apply to situations involving agents who are employed by a real estate brokerage firm, and who are obliged under a contract of employment to share commission with that organization. First of all, a particular agent's personal right to the commission will be governed not only by the listing agreement, but also by the specific employment contract that he or she entered into with that firm. Secondly, it may be the brokerage, rather than the agent personally, that has the ultimate obligation to collect any commission from the seller.

This gives rise to an interesting question — what happens if the brokerage fails to make any effort to collect that commission owed? The case of *Crompton v. Norman Hill Realty Inc.*[24] involved this very question. There, certain real estate deals failed to close, and at issue was whether under its contract with the agents the brokerage was nonetheless obliged to pay their commission. The court held that the brokerage had a positive duty to the agents to make every effort to collect the commissions (or to negotiate a reasonable settlement), and to pay those agents their share of it. It would be unfair, the court

---

[23]   [1998] O.J. No. 5052 (C.A.).
[24]   [1995] O.J. No. 3407 (Gen. Div.).

concluded, to allow the brokerage to negotiate a settlement that was advantageous to itself, but that was reached at the agent's expense.

v.   The Seller's Capacity to Sign

As an aside, several noteworthy decisions have established as a real estate agent you are not required, prior to having a listing agreement signed, to ascertain whether the person signing that agreement is the sole owner of the property and/or has the authority to list. In *Sutton Group Bayview Realty Inc. v. Dennis*,[25] the argument was made that a listing agreement signed by only one of two co-owners was invalid and not enforceable. The court concluded that it was not the current practice in Ontario for the agent to make these types of inquiries, and moreover any such inquiries are unnecessary because a co-owner of a property has the right to list it for sale. Indeed, agents are not expected to perform title searches to determine the true nature of the property's ownership. Along these same lines, it has been held that conceptually, listing agreements are completely separate contracts, quite distinct from the agreement involving the sale of land.[26]

E.   THE ESSENTIAL PROVISIONS OF THE COMMISSION AGREEMENT

i.   What Triggers the Commission to be Payable

When it comes to disagreements arising over commission, the most frequent source of dispute centres around the question of whether any commission is owed at all. There are several important principles that are involved in this determination:

(1)   **The trigger for commission to be payable will vary according to the agreement.** In some standard listing agreements, commission is payable if the agent procures a "valid offer"; in others, the agent must procure a "sale". These seemingly-straightforward terms can still breed confusion; for example the requirement for a "sale" can mean either a binding agreement of purchase and sale, *or* the final closing and conveyance. The Supreme Court of Canada had

---

[25]   [2005] O.J. No. 583, 137 A.C.W.S. (3d) 233 (Div. Ct.).
[26]   *Val Realty Ltd. v. Athley*, [1980] A.J. No. 477 (Q.B.).

occasion to consider these subtle nuances in a case called *H.W. Liebig & Co. v. Leading Investments Ltd.*[27] where (among other things) the Court underlined two important points: (1) that in interpreting listing agreements, the words used must be read in light of the general context and the common understanding of these types of agreements; and (2) if agents want to receive or be entitled to full commission not only on sales, but also on offers, they must use "clear and unequivocal language".

This need for clarity stems from an important reality — in every listing arrangement, there are two competing interests at play. On the one hand, the seller will aim to have the commission obligation triggered only on successful completion of the sale of the property (if at all), and may ask his or her lawyer or agent to amend the listing agreement accordingly. On the other hand, the agent will ideally strive for commission to be payable on any valid offer to purchase, with commission still being due if the transaction fails to close because of the seller's default or neglect. Accordingly, you should ensure not only that the wording of the agreement reflects the proper intention, but also that consensus is reached on this important point with the seller, and that he or she understands the parties' respective obligations in this regard.

(2)   More than one document can purport to deal with commission. Sometimes it is not just the listing agreement that purports to deal with when and whether commission is payable; the agreement of purchase and sale entered into by the buyer and the seller may touch upon this as well. This can lead to serious disputes if the two documents contradict each other. This precise scenario came before the Supreme Court of Canada in *H.W. Liebig & Co. v. Leading Investments Ltd.*,[28] and the Court was asked to determine which of the two documents governed. The Court observed the basic point that the agreement of purchase and sale was not entered into between the *agent* and the seller, but rather between the *buyer* and the seller; *i.e.*, there was no privity (or contractual relationship) that affected the agent arising out of the agreement of purchase and sale *per se*. Nonetheless, and looking at the provisions of both documents, it was clear that even though the agreement of purchase and sale in that case contained a clause dealing with the agent's commission, it merely served to confirm the agreement struck between the seller and agent as reflected in the listing agreement. One of the key lessons to be learned from the *Liebig* case is that agents must ensure that the terms of any agreement of purchase and

---

[27]   [1986] S.C.J. No. 6, 25 D.L.R. (4th) 161.

[28]   *Ibid.*

sale do not serve to alter or distort the intended effect of the listing agreement reached with the seller.

Along these same lines, an interesting scenario presented itself in the case of *Canada Trust Realty Inc. (c.o.b. Canada Trust Co./Realtor) v. McKinnon.*[29] There, the agreement of purchase and sale was never concluded, and the question arose whether commission was payable nonetheless. Both the listing agreement and the agreement of purchase and sale contained commission provisions, but they contradicted each other: the former called for an agreement to be reached, while the latter required "successful completion" of a sale. The "twist" was that the listing agreement was signed *after* the agreement of purchase and sale was executed. The court found that the agreement of purchase and sale prevailed, because: (1) the listing agreement was signed later in the process, after negotiations to buy were in full swing; and (2) because the agent in these circumstances had failed to specifically point out the important change to the seller.

(3)   Entitlement to commission hinges first on the agent complying with the *Real Estate and Business Brokers Act, 2002.* As was discussed in earlier parts of this chapter, the *Real Estate and Business Brokers Act, 2002* and its regulations govern certain aspects of commission agreements; for example mandating the inclusion of certain terms, prohibiting the charging of commission in certain circumstances, and requiring the registration of agents. As a result, the evaluation of whether the agent is entitled to commission is effectively a two-stage analysis, involving first a review of whether those legislated aspects have been adhered to, followed next by a consideration of whether the agent's other contractual obligations have been fulfilled in the circumstances.[30]

(4)   The agent must also comply with, and come within the terms of, the contract. Your entitlement to commission is naturally governed by what was contemplated by the listing agreement. In this regard, it is your responsibility to establish first of all that there was such a contract, and secondly that you have complied with its terms.[31] In a case called *Bird v. Ireland,*[32] the court overturned a Small Claims Court ruling which had ordered a homeowner to pay full commission plus $2,000 in costs to a real estate agent. The agent had secured an offer to buy the home for the full asking

[29]   [1997] O.J. No. 5219, 76 A.C.W.S. (3d) 472 (Gen. Div.).
[30]   *Rooke v. Lillicroft* (1974), 4 O.R. (2d) 436 (H.C.J.).
[31]   *Ibid.*
[32]   [2005] O.J. No. 5125 (Div. Ct.).

price, but the issue was whether that offer was the same as was specified in the listing agreement, including the question of whether it was an unconditional offer. After reviewing the facts, the court found that the offer contained conditions that were not in the listing agreement, and which were not agreed to by the seller. The agent's entitlement to commission was accordingly disallowed.

This question of whether you have complied with the terms of your contract with your client can involve some less-than-obvious considerations, such as whether the seller received any benefit from your services, and whether those services were performed in a competent manner. Also, it is important to note that you have an implicit duty to exercise reasonable care and skill, including skill in offering advice, advising of risks, making inquiries, and preparing the agreement of purchase and sale and any other documents.

(5)   **Generally, the agent must be the "effective cause" of the sale.** Section 23 of the *General Regulation*[33] under the *Real Estate and Business Brokers Act, 2002* states that you cannot charge or collect commission unless:

- you have a written commission agreement; *or*
- you don't have a written agreement, but
  - you have conveyed an offer in writing that is accepted, or
  - you show the property to the buyer/introduce the buyer and seller to each other for the purpose of discussing the sale of property.

Respecting the requirements that you "introduce" the buyer and the seller to each other, essentially you must have had meaningful participation in bringing the buyer and seller together, before you can claim commission. Indeed, "introduce" has been interpreted by the courts to mean the simple dictionary meaning, which is synonymous with "first presentation".[34] In these situations there is no requirement that the agent be involved with the negotiations between the parties.[35]

On the other hand, the question of whether the agent has "obtained an offer" has been considerably more contentious, and

---

[33]   O. Reg. 567/05.

[34]   For example, see *Terry Martel Real Estate Ltd. v. Lovette Investments Ltd.* (1981), 32 O.R. (2d) 790 (C.A.).

[35]   *Capital Real Estate Services Inc. v. Evangelisto*, [2002] O.J. No. 255 (S.C.J.).

has been examined by the courts on several occasions. Quite notably, the Ontario Court of Appeal has directed that the term "obtained an offer" is to be interpreted in accordance with its plain meaning, according to contemporary understanding and practice, and in keeping with the modern context of buying and selling real estate.[36] Applying this principle, courts have held, for example, that it is insufficient for the agent claiming commission to show that the offer procured was *similar* to the one that was ultimately accepted;[37] or that it was an extension of earlier negotiations that were not facilitated by the agent in any way.[38]

Obviously, there can be many factual elements that affect the question of whether you are entitled to commission, including the circumstances surrounding interaction between the parties. However, there are two noteworthy points in this regard:

- there is no fixed standard as to when the threshold is met, but as a general rule, if through your efforts the parties are brought together, then you should be able to collect your commission;[39] and

- this does not mean that you must be the *only* cause of the sale. Instead, you need only "materially contribute" to the purchase.[40]

(6)   The deal must be struck within the time-period covered by the agreement, including any holdover period. The question of whether the deal has to have closed, or merely been struck, will normally be addressed in the listing agreement. But even the question of what constitutes "striking a deal" can be the subject of dispute. In *Epp (c.o.b. Glenview Realty) v. Shewchuk,*[41] the seller signed a listing agreement on June 3, and it had a 60-day term. The sellers negotiated directly with the potential buyers, who submitted a verbal offer. The sellers and buyer had nothing in writing, but they both believed there was a deal, with a closing date for sometime around August 1st, but that detail, and some of the financing, was still to be arranged. Although the agent had nothing to do with bringing these parties together, he successfully

---

[36] *Cash v. George Dundas Realty Ltd.* (1973), 1 O.R. (2d) 241 at 247-48 (C.A.), affd 59 D.L.R. (3d) 605 (S.C.C.).

[37] *Dani Real Estate v. Tyschtschemko* (1958), 17 D.L.R. (2d) 168 (Ont. C.A.).

[38] *William Allan Real Estate Co. v. Robichaud,* [1993] O.J. No. 75, 28 R.P.R. (2d) 262, 98 D.L.R. (4th) 285, 11 O.R. (3d) 734 (C.A.).

[39] *Robertson v. Ball,* [1996] O.J. No. 3774, 31 O.R. (3d) 30 (Gen. Div.).

[40] *Bancorp Mortgage Ltd. v. Sicon Group Inc.,* [1990] B.C.J. No. 1477, 2 B.L.R. (2d) 161 (S.C.).

[41] [1998] M.J. No. 406 (Q.B.).

sued for his commission. The commission agreement provided that commission was payable if a sale took place. The fact that there was no *written* agreement did not detract from the fact that the parties had reached an agreement within the term of the listing agreement.

(7)   **Entitlement to commission does not *necessarily* depend on whether the transaction is completed.** In cases where the purchase and sale does not close, the courts have held that the agent's entitlement to commission is governed by two factors:

- •   who caused the failure; and
- •   at what point did the transaction fail, *i.e.*, before, or after, the triggering event in the listing agreement.

Addressing this last point first: if the transaction is scuttled *after* the triggering event, then commission is usually payable; if it fails *before*, then it is likely not. (An exception can occur where the listing agreement obliges the seller in such circumstances to pay a "marketing fee", consisting of the commission or a portion of the deposit received from the purported buyer.)

But the question of who prompted the deal to abort is also relevant: a seller will usually remain liable for commission if the buyer has signed a binding agreement, but the deal does not go through due to the seller's own fault.[42] In one British case,[43] the agent was entitled to commission if he introduced the eventual buyer to the seller, which was a corporation. In fact, he did introduce a buyer who was "ready, willing and able", but the corporation for its own unrelated reasons decided not to proceed with the sale, and refused to pay commission. The agent argued that under the listing agreement there was an implicit understanding that the seller would not refuse to go ahead with the proposed sale if a willing buyer was found. The court disagreed, finding that it was not entitled to imply terms and draft the contract for the parties. Looking at the agreement before it, and as long as no binding contract had been reached between seller and buyer, the court found nothing to prevent the seller from retreating from the potential sale, thereby preventing the agent from collecting commission.

(8)   **The seller has no obligation to engage in litigation to trigger the agent's entitlement to commission.** In cases where the deal has gone sour due to the default of the potential buyer, the seller

---

[42]   *H.W. Liebig & Co. v. Leading Investments Ltd.*, [1986] S.C.J. No. 6, 25 D.L.R. (4th) 161.

[43]   *Luxor (Eastborne) Ltd. (in liquidation) v. Cooper* (1941), 1 All E.R. 33 (H.L.).

is under no obligation to sue that buyer in order to trigger the payment of the agent's commission.[44]

ii.   Holdover Clauses

The holdover clause (sometimes called the "overhold" clause) is a provision in the listing agreement that entitles the agent to earn commission for offers that are accepted during a specified period after the listing agreement expires. This justly compensates the agent for his or her efforts, by recognizing the fact that a buyer's decision-making process may be set in motion during the listing period because of the agent's marketing efforts, but may result in a formal offer being made only after that listing period expired.

The standard form listing agreement contains a holdover clause entitling the agent to commission if an offer to buy the property is accepted by the seller within 90 days after the listing period expires, provided that the buyer was introduced to or shown the property during the listing period. Other listing agreements contain a requirement that, for commission to be payable:

*   the sale is actually *completed* within the 90-day holdover period; and/or
*   the agent has given the seller written notice within 10 days of expiry of the listing agreement of all the persons to whom the agent has introduced the property.

Naturally, if one of these provisions applies to your situation, then they can impose requirements on you that are not only onerous, but may also prevent you from being entitled to commission if they are not strictly observed.

The case of *C.B. Richard Ellis Ltd. v. Swedcan Lumican Plastics Inc.*[45] is a good example. The listing agreement's holdover provision entitled the agent to commission on any sale within six months of the agreement's expiry, provided the agent notified the seller in writing of the name of the buyer that was introduced during that period. The agent technically did not comply with the written notice requirement, but claimed that the offer that was ultimately submitted satisfied that requirement. The court disagreed, observing that the notice provision

---

[44]   *Century 21 Success Inc. v. Gowland*, [2003] O.J. No. 4645 (S.C.J.).
[45]   [2002] O.J. No. 3056, 60 O.R. (3d) 551 (S.C.J.).

was more than a formality — the purpose of the notice provision in the holdover clause was to put the seller on notice that he or she had continuing potential ongoing liability for payment of commission even after the listing agreement expired.

As with the rest of the listing agreement, the holdover clause should be as clear in its wording as possible, otherwise costly disputes can arise. One example of this occurs in *Royal LePage Real Estate Services v. McArter*,[46] where the agreement of purchase and sale was *signed* during the holdover period, but the actual *closing* date was outside of it. The matter had to go to litigation before it was established that this still complied with the provisions entitling the agent to commission.

Also, generally speaking the standards of conduct that apply during the listing period proper will also apply during the holdover period. In *First City Realty v. Hermans*,[47] the seller and the eventual buyer had known each other for many years, and had previously discussed the possible sale of the seller's business, but only in vague terms. The seller signed a listing agreement with an agent, who advised the buyer that the property was for sale. Ultimately, the buyer and seller reached an agreement for a private sale during the holdover period; the seller refused to pay the agent any commission because he and his lawyers had done most of the negotiating. The agent successfully sued; the court found that the buyer became aware of the property because of the agent's efforts and because of the MLS listing, and that the sale would not have taken place without them.

Finally, just as the *General Regulation* under the *Real Estate and Business Brokers Act, 2002* requires that all listing agreements include a specified expiry date,[48] the expiry date of the holdover period should likewise be clearly set out.

iii.   The Deposit

Under the standard form listing agreement, the buyer's deposit is usually held by the agent and is applied against the commission owed to him or her. Obviously, it is in your best interests to have the buyer's

---

[46]   [2000] O.J. No. 349 (S.C.J.).
[47]   [2004] O.J. No. 1314 (S.C.J.).
[48]   O. Reg. 567/05, s. 35(2).

deposit be large enough to cover your commission plus GST. Sometimes, however, the deposit is insufficient to cover your commission, and there will be a balance owing on closing, which must be paid out of the funds received from the seller's lawyer. Payment of these funds is the seller's lawyer's responsibility; he or she will ensure that the remainder of your commission is paid from the proceeds of sale, prior to release of the balance of the funds to the seller. (However — and particularly since the commission rate is often not set out in the agreement — you should send a commission statement to the seller's lawyer, setting out the amount of the balance.) In this regard, the standard OREA and TREB listing agreement contains a provision stating that any deposit paid by the buyer is first to be applied to reduce the commission payable to the agent.

If the deposit is in fact greater than the amount of the commission and GST, you must forward the excess to the seller following completion of the transaction. In such a case, the seller's solicitor will notify you when the transaction has closed, and provide you with instructions as to where to send the balance of the deposit.

Note that if the buyer reneges, then under the terms of the standard listing agreement, half of the deposit paid by the buyer is applied to the commission owed to the agent (up to the amount that would have been payable had the deal gone through).

F.   WHEN AN AGENT HAS TO SUE FOR THE COMMISSION OWED

i.   Legislative Requirements

Firstly, you cannot bring any action for commission unless you are registered under the *Real Estate and Business Brokers Act, 2002* at the time the services were rendered.[49]

Secondly, as discussed earlier in this chapter, the requirements of section 23(1) of the *General Regulation*[50] under the Act must be met. In this regard, there are two important points to note: firstly, the three conditions in that provision are structured with an "or" between them; in other words, only *one* of the three needs to be satisfied in order for

---

[49]   *Real Estate and Business Brokers Act, 2002*, S.O. 2002, c. 30, Sched. C, s. 9.
[50]   O. Reg. 567/05.

you to be able to bring an action for commission. As such, there need not be a written contract between you and the seller before an action can be brought, but establishing the terms of an oral agreement will be an evidentiary challenge.

Thirdly, section 23(1) is subject to section 23(2) of the *General Regulation* which provides that — unless agreed to in writing by the seller — you cannot claim commission from the seller in connection with the sale of a particular property if that property is, to your knowledge, covered by an unexpired exclusive listing agreement with another agent.

It is also important to observe that these provisions merely permit you to launch an action — they do not automatically entitle you to *succeed*. Rather, the question of whether you are entitled to the commission you are asking for will depend on the terms of your contract with the seller, the proper interpretation of those terms, and the facts surrounding the transaction that gives rise to the commission sought.[51]

ii.   The Concepts of *"Quantum Meruit"* and "Unjust Enrichment" are Inapplicable

The predecessor[52] to section 23 of the *General Regulation* under the *Real Estate and Business Brokers Act, 2002* has been the subject of the courts' analysis in several cases; these decisions involve not an evaluation of the moral rights and obligations of the agent and seller, but rather the simple question of whether on the particular facts, any of the conditions in section 23 have been satisfied so that the agent is entitled to bring an action.[53] One interesting question that arose from this section's wording was whether the doctrine of *"quantum meruit"* (which, loosely translated, means "as much as he or she deserves") can apply to a situation where the agent obtained an exceptional result for the seller — *e.g.*, where additional services were rendered that were not part of the written contract, or where the offer elicited from the buyer was extraordinarily favourable to the seller. In other words,

---

[51] See *Century 21 Heritage Ltd. v. Napev Construction Ltd.* (1991), 31 A.C.W.S. (3d) 183 (Ont. Gen. Div.).
[52] The predecessor provision was found in s. 23 of the *Real Estate and Business Brokers Act*, R.S.O. 1990, c. R.4.
[53] *James Squigna Real Estate Ltd. v. Northwest Car Wash Ltd.* (1975), 9 O.R. (2d) 55 (Ont. C.A.).

the question was whether on the basis of fairness — and aside from whatever amounts were expressly agreed to in writing — an agent might be entitled to additional commissions in these cases.

Unfortunately, the courts found that *quantum meruit* does not generally[54] apply, and that an agent's commission must be limited to whatever has been agreed to in writing by the parties.[55] (The exceptions to this are very few — one might occur, for example, where the facts show that the parties intended to replace an old contract with a new one, but never did.)[56]

Likewise, where the requirements of section 23 have not been complied with, courts have found that that legislative provision overrides the legal doctrine of "unjust enrichment", which would otherwise allow the agent to sue and be fairly compensated in accordance with the benefit obtained by the seller as a result of the agent's services. Courts have expressly found that "[n]o claim can be advanced for the otherwise valuable services of an agent unless it falls within the ambit of section 23".[57]

iii. Commission Need not Relate to the Effort Expended by the Agent

Naturally, the specific responsibilities of an agent are dictated by the terms and provisions of the listing agreement. Otherwise, however, the *Real Estate and Business Brokers Act, 2002* does not impose any specific obligations on agents as a prerequisite to claiming an entitlement to commission under such an agreement.

This — along with the fact that an agent's commission is simply set as a fixed percentage of the selling price — can lead to the all-too-common perception by sellers that agents do not provide equivalent value for the money. Yet, from a legal standpoint, nothing about a

---

[54] There may be some limited exceptions, for example where the contract by its wording makes it clear that the parties intended to incorporate a *quantum meruit* amount — *i.e.*, that one party agreed to pay a reasonable, but unspecified, sum. See, for example, *Montreal Trust Co. v. Kozak*, [1983] O.J. No. 570 (H.C.J.).

[55] *Keachie v. St. John* (1958), 12 D.L.R. (2d) 21 (Ont. C.A.), and *Kanata Realty Ltd. v. Ottawa Air Cargo Centre Ltd.*, [1993] O.J. No. 1761 (Gen. Div.).

[56] *Century 21 Success Inc. v. Gowland*, [2003] O.J. No. 4645 (S.C.J.).

[57] *William Allen Real Estate Co. v. Robichaud*, [1990] O.J. No. 41, 72 O.R. (2d) 595 at 614 (H.C.J.), affd [1993] O.J. No. 75, 28 R.P.R. (2d) 262 (C.A.).

general listing agreement takes it out of the realm of enforceable contracts.

In one interesting case named *Colliers Macaulay Nicolls Inc. v. Park Georgia Properties Ltd.*,[58] the seller claimed that the agent's commission in an aborted transaction between those two parties was actually an "illegal penalty", and unenforceable in law. In that case, the seller had signed an exclusive listing agreement with the agent, but when he independently became aware of a potential buyer, he did not tell the agent. The listing agreement provided that in such a scenario, the seller would be liable for commission nonetheless. The matter went to litigation when the seller refused to pay, claiming that the commission was a form of illegal "penalty", since the amount of the commission bore no relationship to the effort expended by the agent. The court disagreed, pointing out that even in normal circumstances, the amount of commission is not dependent on the agent's effort, only on the fact of a completed sale. It held that the commission was a genuine and reasonable pre-estimate of the damages that the agent suffered due to the seller's breach of the commission agreement between them.

G.   LOSING THE RIGHT TO COMMISSION

Simply because the deal closed, it does not mean that as agent you are entitled to commission irrevocably. In fact, you can lose the right to commission for several reasons, including: failure to disclose all available offers to the seller;[59] buying the property for yourself without making adequate disclosure to the seller;[60] negligently failing to properly draft and/or review a clause in the Agreement;[61] negligently miscalculating monthly payments on the security;[62] and failing to reveal any personal benefit you have obtained in the transaction.[63]

A classic example of an agent who lost his right to commission appears in a case called *Raso v. Dionigi*.[64] There, the agent acted for both the seller and the buyers, but rather unwisely, he did not tell the

---

[58]   [2003] B.C.J. No. 2708 (S.C.).

[59]   *Krasniuk v. Gabbs*, [2002] M.J. No. 13 (Q.B.).

[60]   *Phillips v. R.D. Realty Ltd.*, [1999] O.J. No. 3269 (C.A.).

[61]   *Paul S. Starr & Co. v. Watson*, [1973] 1 O.R. 148 (C.A.).

[62]   *Academy Aluminium Products v. McInerny Realty Ltd.*, [1980] A.J. No. 660, 113 D.L.R. (3d) 289 (C.A.).

[63]   *Jankowski v. 990088 Ontario Inc.*, [1998] O.J. No. 2764 (Gen. Div.).

[64]   [1993] O.J. No. 670, 12 O.R. (3d) 580 (C.A.).

sellers that the buyers were his brother and sister-in-law. The sellers signed the agreement, but later backed out of the deal, and the agent sued for his commission. The Ontario Court of Appeal found that he was not entitled to it under the circumstances; although the agent had taken a very active part in this transaction, and was seeking to receive commission from the sellers, he had breached his duty to them by failing to disclose that he was related to the buyers. Moreover, the agent's argument that the deal would have closed even with his proper disclosure was irrelevant and speculative; instead, the proper question was whether the sellers were likely to have signed the agreement of purchase and sale, had they known the true facts. In the case, the answer was "no", and therefore the agent was not entitled to commission on the deal.

It should also be noted that section 32 of the *Real Estate and Business Brokers Act, 2002* imposes a strict requirement that you make full written disclosure any time you are personally purchasing or obtaining an interest in the seller's property, whether directly or indirectly. A failure to adhere to this requirement will scuttle your deal to buy the property — and your entitlement to commission along with it.

H.   A FEW WORDS TO THE WISE

Even in the modern age of standardized listing agreements, written buyer's agency contracts, and standardized agreements of purchase and sale, many things can and still do go wrong when it comes to agents' claims for commission.

As a means of helping you avoid unnecessary trouble in this regard, the following pointers are particularly noteworthy:

(1) **Get the agreement in writing,** *pronto.* By doing so, you will avoid a situation like the one in the case of *Claussen Walters & Associates Ltd. v. Murphy.*[65] There, the seller owned some land that could potentially be subdivided. On three separate occasions, he and the agent discussed a 10 per cent commission if the property was sold in subdivided parcels. Based on this discussion, the seller authorized the agent to commence the subdivision process, including getting planning approval, arranging for a road, and preparing to market the lots. The agent made substantial strides in this regard, but when he subsequently realized that the seller seemed to be waffling on his

---

[65]   [2001] N.S.J. No. 291 (S.C.).

commitment to pay him, the agent asked for written confirmation of their commission agreement, which the seller refused to give. Ultimately, the land was sold by another agent. The court found that (1) there had been an oral agreement between the seller and the agent; (2) that the agent had acted in good faith; (3) that his work had substantially increased the value of the property, and (4) that the seller had been significantly enriched by the agent's efforts. In the end, the court awarded the agent 4 per cent of the selling price, which was the fee the parties had agreed to for the development work (being the difference between the 10 per cent agreed on, and the 6 per cent paid to the selling agent who actually sold the properties).

(2)   Make yourself an indispensable part of the deal. In *J.J. Barnicke Vancouver Ltd. v. North-West Book Co.,*[66] the seller refused to list the property, but agreed to co-operate with and pay commission to any agent who brought the successful buyer. An agent showed the property to three members of an interested religious group, but they did not make an offer. One of the members of that group later contacted the seller's son directly, and entered into negotiations with the seller's accountant and business advisor to buy the property on behalf of the group. He did not tell the seller that he had seen the property previously, and the seller did not recognize him. He ultimately bought the property on the group's behalf, and the agent who had initially introduced the group sued for commission, albeit unsuccessfully. While the agent's introduction of the buyer was certainly a precursor to the sale, it was not the "cause"; instead, the sale resulted from the negotiations between the buyer and the seller's accountant/business agent.

(3)   Count on the fact that unscrupulous sellers may try to avoid paying your commission. In *Sekhon v. Tan,*[67] the seller was adamant that he receive a net of $3 million for certain property that he owned. The agent acted for a third party, which was interested in locating property for a mosque and school. The third party signed an agreement to buy the seller's property for $3.03 million, which included a term that the buyer was liable to pay the commission. However, to facilitate the deal and ensure that the seller attained the $3 million net that he wanted, the agent verbally agreed to take only a 1 per cent consulting fee, provided that the seller (rather than the buyer) agreed to personally pay the commission. When it came time to pay, however, the seller refused, and completely denied that any such verbal agreement

---

[66]   [2001] B.C.J. No. 2498 (S.C.).

[67]   [2002] B.C.J. No. 91 (S.C.).

with the agent was reached. The agent was then left to prove the contrary. After scrutinizing the available evidence to this effect, the court sided with the agent, finding that an oral agreement for a 1 per cent consulting fee existed, despite what the agreement of purchase and sale — and the seller — said. (In fact, the court stated that it completely disbelieved the seller — who was clearly quite content to let the agent take him to court in order to get the commission owed.)

(4) Watch out for little old ladies and other trouble-makers. In *Sutton Group Excel Realty Corp. v. Car (Guardian ad litem of)*,[68] the agent met with the 91-year-old seller, who did not speak English. The seller's granddaughter translated for her. The seller signed a MLS agreement appointing the agent as exclusive listing agent. A potential buyer made an offer, which the seller accepted, and an agreement was signed. However, on closing date for the transaction, the seller's son was appointed her committee due to her mental infirmity and dementia, a condition that had been confirmed by two doctors. The son refused to complete the sale, and eventually sold to someone else entirely. The seller resisted the agent's claim for commission on the basis that she lacked the legal capacity to enter into an agreement to sell her home. After hearing all the facts, including a lack of evidence to establish that the agent knew the seller was mentally infirm, the court awarded the agent his commission. Under these circumstances, the agent had no ability to ascertain the seller's true intentions, nor to determine that she was operating under a legal incapacity. Both the MLS agreement and the agreement of purchase and sale were fair. The court also pointed out that the facts of the case underlined the need for agents to exercise care when using a family member or friend to interpret; an agent would be wise to use a certified interpreter to ensure that all the parties understand the contract, particularly when acting for both buyer and seller.

(5) Don't be a jerk; it will eventually cost you. In *Tassy (c.o.b. Lou Tassy Realty) v. Borderless Inc.*,[69] an agent represented the sellers. He claimed that the buyer who bought the seller's property verbally agreed to pay him $15,000 in commission in addition to the 5 per cent usually payable by the seller upon a sale. During the trial, the agent made serious and slanderous comments about the buyer's ethics, and about the trustworthiness of members of the buyer's ethnic group. The court refused the agent's claim for the commission he alleged was promised orally, finding that the

---

[68] [1999] B.C.J. No. 1477 (Prov. Ct.).
[69] [2005] O.J. No. 255 (S.C.J.).

agent had great familiarity with the provisions of the *Real Estate and Business Brokers Act* of the time, and must have known that any agreement respecting commission had to be in writing. Moreover, the agent's invective against the buyer and his ethnic group warranted punitive damages against him.

CHAPTER 4

DEALING WITH SPECIAL PARTIES

A. Powers of Attorney
    i.   The Basic Types of Powers of Attorney
    ii.   The Relevant Legislation Governing Powers of Attorney
    iii. Statutory Requirements as to Form and Content
    iv.   Terminating a Power of Attorney
    v.   Legislative Considerations when Using the Power of Attorney to Sell Land
    vi.   Questions for Real Estate Agents to Ask their Clients
B. Dealing with Estate Lands
    i.   Where there is a Joint Tenancy
    ii.   Where there is a Tenancy in Common
    iii. Where there is a Will
    iv.   Where there is no Will
          1. Sales to Pay Debts
          2. Sales to Distribute Proceeds
    v.   Conveying to Beneficiaries
    vi.   Purchasing Land from a Beneficiary
          1. Proof of Death and Related Facts
          2. The Concept of "Vesting"
          3. Automatic Vesting
          4. Sales by Beneficiaries Before Vesting
          5. Sales by Beneficiaries After Vesting
    vii. What Documents are Needed for the Deal
    viii. A Note about Real Estate Deals in Progress at the Time of Death
C. Family Law Issues

It is an important — but sometimes overlooked — fact that you may have different duties, and may face unusual considerations, in cases where there is something unique about one or more of the parties to the transaction. This chapter will cover some of the more common situations.

A. POWERS OF ATTORNEY

i.   The Basic Types of Powers of Attorney

Any time you are dealing with a person acting under a power of attorney, you should be aware of several basic legal principles.

First of all, a power of attorney is given by one person (the "grantor") to another person (the "attorney"),[1] and authorizes the attorney to execute documents on the grantor's behalf. Essentially, the relationship is one of agency, with the attorney acting as the agent of the grantor.

The exact scope of the attorney's power will depend on the nature of the authority that the grantor has given to him or her, as expressed in the power of attorney document. Specifically, a power of attorney may be:

---

[1]   Although in common parlance the term "power of attorney" is often used to denote the *person* to whom the power is granted, strictly speaking, this is a misnomer. "Power of attorney" refers to the grant of the authority; the person who receives the power is simply called the "attorney".

- general;
- restricted in specified ways; or
- limited to a particular transaction or event.

Not surprisingly, a general power of attorney confers the broadest powers, while a limited power of attorney will often be situation-specific, for example where the grantor is unable to be present during the execution of certain documents, due to absence, illness or inconvenience.

A more specific type of power of attorney arrangement, called a "continuing power of attorney for property", is made by a grantor in anticipation of the possibility that he or she may become mentally incapable of managing his or her affairs.

No matter what the type, the common feature in all of these types of power of attorney is that one person is acting on behalf of — or, more precisely, pursuant to the authority granted by — another person.

ii. The Relevant Legislation Governing Powers of Attorney

Powers of attorney are governed by the mostly-repealed *Powers of Attorney Act*,[2] and in specific circumstances by the *Substitute Decisions Act, 1992*.[3] Together, these two pieces of legislation set out, among other things, the basic legal requirements for creating a valid power of attorney, and the extent of the authority that is conferred on a person under specific types of power of attorney documents.

A general power of attorney is governed by section 2 of the *Powers of Attorney Act*, which uses the term "donor" to denote the person who gives the power of attorney, and "donee" to indicate the person who receives it. That section states:

> **2.** A general power of attorney for property is sufficient authority for the donee of the power ... to do on behalf of the donor anything that the donor can lawfully do by an attorney, subject to such conditions and restrictions, if any, as are contained therein.[4]

A more specialized type of power of attorney, called the "continuing power of attorney for property", can arise in situations where the grantor becomes incapable of managing his or her affairs. Continuing powers of

---

[2] R.S.O. 1990, c. P.20.

[3] S.O. 1992, c. 30.

[4] R.S.O. 1990, c. P.20, s. 2 [as am.].

attorney for property are governed by section 7(2) of the *Substitute Decisions Act, 1992* which states:

> The continuing power of attorney may authorize the person named as attorney to do on the grantor's behalf anything in respect of property that the grantor could do if capable, except make a will.[5]

As such, and subject to any limitations imposed by the grantor, a person who is designated an attorney for another person under either a general or continuing power of attorney may have the authority to sell that person's land.

iii.   Statutory Requirements as to Form and Content

As an agent, you must also be familiar with the various elements that are a mandatory part of a valid power of attorney. Although by law there are virtually no form or content requirements for creating a regular power of attorney, a continuing power of attorney for property is subject to certain statutory prerequisites.

For example, section 7 of the *Substitute Decisions Act, 1992* sets out that a continuing power of attorney for property, in order to be valid, must:

- expressly estate that it is a continuing power of attorney; and
- indicate that the authority is to be exercised during the grantor's incapacity to manage his or her property.

Otherwise, the document need not be in any particular form, although a legislatively-prescribed format is available for use if desired.

Incidentally, in addition to the usual means (*i.e.*, whereby the grantor creates the arrangement of his or her own volition) a valid continuing power of attorney for property can also be created in one of several other ways, including by court order, and by way of a certificate issued by the Public Guardian and Trustee. All of these means are governed by specific provisions of the *Substitute Decisions Act, 1992.*

---

[5]   S.O. 1992, c. 30, s. 7(2).

iv.   Terminating a Power of Attorney

Powers of attorney can be created at will, and they can be "revoked" at will, *i.e.*, by a clear intention of the grantor to do so. In addition, a power of attorney can also be "terminated" by law under statute, based on the existence of certain circumstances. For example, the *Substitute Decisions Act, 1992* provides that a continuing power of attorney for property can be terminated in a number of ways:

- the attorney has died, has become incapable of managing property, or has resigned (except where another attorney has been appointed);
- the court has appointed a guardian of property for the grantor, under section 22 of the *Substitute Decisions Act, 1992*;
- the grantor has executed a new continuing power of attorney naming someone else (unless the grantor has expressly provided that multiple powers of attorney are intended);
- the grantor has revoked the power of attorney; or
- the grantor has died.

It should also be noted that an attorney should not be an undischarged bankrupt.

If the continuing power of attorney has been terminated or becomes invalid without the attorney knowing it, then a real estate agreement he or she enters into in good faith and after-the-fact may nonetheless be valid. Legal advice should be obtained in these circumstances.

v.   Legislative Considerations when Using the Power of Attorney to Sell Land

Whenever a purchase and sale of land involves a power of attorney, you should be aware of the various procedural and legislative requirements that will arise. This is especially important, because the purpose behind these requirements is to ensure that the real estate transaction documents have been properly executed to reflect the existence of an attorney.

First of all, you should confirm whether the signature line in the Agreement of Purchase and Sale, as signed by the attorney, indicates the attorney's status and relationship to the grantor. In particular, the signature line should look like this:

Name: Jane Smith, by her Attorney, Mary Black

Signature: "Mary Black", as Attorney for Jane Smith

Secondly, both the *Land Titles Act*,[6] and the *Registry Act*[7] (as the case may be) have certain registration requirements that need to be adhered to.

The *Land Titles Act* not only expressly recognizes the possibility of an attorney's involvement, but also goes on to provide for the manner of revocation, as well as a requirement to register the power of attorney (or a notarial or certified copy of it) on title. The relevant provision of that Act states:

> **70.** (1) A person may, under a power of attorney, authorize another person to act for that person in respect of any land or interest therein under this Act.
>
> (2) A power of attorney or a notarial or certified copy of it may be registered in the prescribed manner.
>
> (3) No registered power of attorney shall be deemed to be revoked until a revocation thereof is registered or evidence is filed with the land registrar showing that it is no longer in force.

The *Registry Act* likewise contains a number of provisions that deal with registering powers of attorney; although document registration is not a regular part of a real estate agent's duties, a prudent agent will nonetheless be aware of the relevant requirements, whether acting for a buyer or obtaining a listing on a seller's behalf.

vi.   Questions for Real Estate Agents to Ask their Clients

If you are involved in a potential transaction involving a power of attorney — whether "regular" or of the "continuing" variety — you must speak with your client and review any relevant documentation in order to determine the answer to certain important questions:

- Is the offer being submitted by, or is the listing being given, by a person who has been granted a power of attorney on behalf of someone else?
- How does the power of attorney arise? Under a formal power of attorney document? By way of a certificate issued by the Public Guardian and Trustee? Pursuant to a court order?

---

[6]   R.S.O. 1990, c. L.5.
[7]   R.S.O. 1990, c. R.20.

- Does the designated attorney have the necessary authority to execute the agreement and bind the grantor? Have all preconditions in the power of attorney been met?

- Is the power of attorney general, or else restricted and/or limited? Does it include (or expressly exclude) the power to sell the land?

- If the attorney's authority arose under a continuing power of attorney, does the document specify a means for determining whether the necessary state of "incapacity" has been met? Has the grantor reached that state of incapacity?

- If the continuing power of attorney does not specify a means for determining whether the grantor has become incapable, has the attorney applied to a court to have the grantor assessed? Has the Public Guardian and Trustee issued a certificate to the effect that the continuing power of attorney has become effective?

- Is the format and content of the power of attorney proper?

- If the power of attorney arises under a formal power of attorney document, then were the legal requirements of the *Substitute Decisions Act, 1992* and/or the *Powers of Attorney Act* (and its predecessors) met when the document was created?

- Have the real estate transaction documents been properly executed to reflect the existence of an attorney? Does the signature line signed by the indicate his or her status and the relationship to the attorney grantor?, *e.g.*:

  > Name: Jane Smith, by her Attorney, Mary Black

  > Signature: "Mary Black", as Attorney for Jane Smith

- If the deed or other document executed by the power of attorney is intended to be registered, will the power of attorney be registered on title along with it?

- Will the provisions of the *Registry Act* or the *Land Titles Act* (as the case may be) be complied with?

- Is it possible that the power of attorney has been terminated, for example, by the revocation of the grantor, or by the grantor's death?

B.   DEALING WITH ESTATE LANDS

The sale of land owned by a deceased person gives rise to a number of considerations of which you as agent should be aware.

Although these issues can be equally relevant whether you are acting for the buyer or the seller, they are most conveniently approached from the buyer's perspective, since that person will usually acquire land belonging to a deceased person from one of the following parties:

- a joint tenant;
- a personal representative; or
- a beneficiary.

In these situations you should be aware of all of the relevant issues, so that you can attempt to protect both yourself and the client from unexpected difficulties that may arise. Each of these issues will be considered in turn.

i.   Where there is a Joint Tenancy

If the deceased's property was held by him or her and another person under a joint tenancy, then once death has occurred the surviving joint tenant is *automatically* entitled to convey title to the property to someone else, without the deceased's personal representatives intervening. In other words, the property does not pass to the deceased's personal representatives at all, but rather the right to deal with it remains with the surviving joint tenant.

A purchase from a surviving joint tenant is reasonably straightforward, but it would be wise for the buyer to have a Proof of Death Certificate registered on title to the property.

ii.   Where there is a Tenancy in Common

If a deceased holds property with another person as tenants in common, the deceased's death operates to sever the relationship. With tenancy in common, there is no "right of survivorship" as there is with joint tenancy. As a result, in a tenancy in common situation, each party receives title to their respective share of the property, which share must be dealt with by each owner.

In these cases, the deceased should deal with his or her share by way of Will; however, if there is no Will, then the rules involving intestacy situations will apply.

iii.   Where there is a Will

Except where there is a joint tenancy, as described above, the right to dispose of a deceased's property is usually governed by the terms of his or her Will. Specifically, if there is an express or implied power of sale in the Will (or if it arises under statute), then the deceased's personal representative(s) will have the capacity to enter into an agreement to purchase or sell land.

The official title for the personal representative is Estate Trustee with a Will (formerly called "Executors"). The personal representatives are expressly named in the Will and are confirmed by a certificate of appointment from the Ontario Superior Court of Justice in the jurisdiction where the property is located.

In this situation, the first steps that a prudent real estate agent should take are the following:

- confirm that probate has been obtained;
- determine the personal representative's identity under the Will; and
- make sure that the representative has either expressly or impliedly been granted the power to sell the property.

Note that even if the Will does not expressly provide for the right to sell the property, such power can be implied if:

- the land has been devised to the personal representative; and
- the land has been charged with some payment.

(This is set out in section 44(1) of the *Trustees Act*.)[8]

Provided that this power to sell exists in the Will, the buyer may safely accept title, and need not requisition additional proof of authority: *Caldwell v. Lamothe*.[9] With this authority in hand, the personal representative has the right to sell the land *at any time*, unless the Will provides for a certain time-period before it can be sold. Generally speaking, the personal representative need not obtain the approval of the beneficiaries (although the spouse of the deceased must give written consent, under section 6(13) of the *Family Law Act*).[10]

---

[8]   R.S.O. 1990, c. T.23.

[9]   (1996), 62 A.C.W.S. (3d) 617 (Ont. Gen. Div.).

[10]   R.S.O. 1990, c. F.3.

In such cases, the personal representative effectively becomes the "transferor" of the property, and signs both the Agreement of Purchase and Sale and the deed or transfer. The seller is described in the Agreement of Purchase and Sale as "Estate of John Doe by his Estate Trustee with a Will Mary Smith".

The transfer itself will contain certain recitals as to the following:

- the registered owner's date of death, and the specific interest he or she had in the property;
- the date of the Certificate of Appointment of the Estate Trustee with a Will (formerly "Letters Probate"), and the registration information;
- the purpose behind the personal representative's exercise of the power of sale; and
- if applicable, the specifics of the surviving spouse's election under section 6 of the *Family Law Act.*

In this regard, an interesting factual circumstance arose in a case named *Peters v. Vallier.*[11] The owner of the land died without a Will, and his wife was appointed the Estate Trustee without a Will. She was under the misapprehension that any money realized on the sale would belong to her personally, and that the children of the marriage were not entitled to anything. She therefore executed the sale documentation in her own name only, without indicating that she was the Estate Trustee. Upon realizing that this was estate property that the wife did not personally own, the purchaser sued for breach of the agreement. After realizing her mistake, the wife refused to complete the transaction in her capacity of Estate Trustee. The court took no issue with this approach, finding that the original agreement was void, and that the wife had no obligation to go through with the agreement a second time.

iv.   Where there is no Will

If the landowner has died without a Will (*i.e.*, intestate) then an interested party can apply to the court to appoint a specific type of personal representative for the estate called an Estate Trustee without a Will (formerly called an "Administrator"). The appointment is then confirmed by obtaining a Certificate of Appointment of Estate Trustees without a

---

[11]   (1982), 18 A.C.W.S. (2d) 128 (Ont. H.C.J.).

Will, and the personal representatives can then proceed to deal with the estate as provided for by the *Estates Administration Act*[12] (the "*EAA*").

If there are no heirs at all, title to the land transfers to the Crown. In *Whitelaw v. Georges*[13] the landowner died intestate and (as is usual in these circumstances) the property was appropriated by or "escheated" to the government. However, Letters of Administration were mistakenly granted to the deceased's niece, who purported to sell the property to a buyer. The buyer refused to close, so the sellers sued for damages. The court held that although certain legislation was available to cure the fact that Letters of Administration were issued in error, there was nothing to alter the inescapable fact that title was held by the Crown, and was not for the niece to give.

As before, where there is a sale of land arising from an intestacy situation, the personal representative becomes the "transferor" of the property, and signs both the Agreement of Purchase and Sale and the deed or transfer. Moreover, the seller is described in the Agreement of Purchase and Sale as "Estate of John Doe by his Estate Trustee without a Will Mary Smith".

Once the appointment is made, the personal representative has the power under section 16 of the Act to deal with the property for the purposes of paying debts, and distributing or dividing the estate among the beneficiaries as provided for under section 17 of the *EAA*. Different considerations apply, depending on the reason behind the personal representative's sale of the intestate's land.

1.   *Sales to Pay Debts*

If the property is being sold within three years of the deceased's death in order to pay debts, then the beneficiaries are not required to approve the sale, in accordance with section 17(5) of the *EAA*.

2.   *Sales to Distribute Proceeds*

If the personal representative is selling the deceased's land within three years of the death in order to distribute the proceeds to the beneficiaries,

---

[12]   R.S.O. 1990, c. E.22.

[13]   [1991] O.J. No. 1791, 30 A.C.W.S. (3d) 282 (Div. Ct.).

then under section 17(1) of the *EAA*, the beneficiaries must concur in the transaction.

However, it is not necessary to obtain *unanimous* concurrence: rather the majority of the beneficiaries, representing not less than one-half of the interests in the property, must approve. This is set out in section 17(2) of the *EAA*.

As before, in these situations the personal representative becomes the "transferor" of the property, and signs both the Agreement of Purchase and Sale and the deed or transfer. Moreover, the seller is described in the Agreement of Purchase and Sale as "Estate of John Doe by his Estate Trustee without a Will Mary Smith".

The transfer itself will contain certain recitals as to the following:

- the registered owner's date of death, and the specific interest he or she had in the property;
- the date of the Certificate of Appointment of the Estate Trustee without a Will (formerly "Letters of Administration"), and the registration information;
- the purpose behind the Estate Trustee without a Will's exercise of the power of sale; and
- the names of the heirs at law and the next-of-kin who survive the registered owner;
- whether any children of the deceased have predeceased him or her, such that there are surviving children;
- that the personal representative has made reasonable efforts to identify anyone who might be entitled, and the results of those inquiries;
- that the personal representative has had no notice of any application to establish the parentage of anyone who might be entitled; and/or
- if applicable:
  - that the Children's Lawyer has consented to the transaction on behalf of any minors;
  - that all debts have been paid; and
  - the specifics of the surviving spouse's election under section 6 of the *Family Law Act*.

It should be noted that if all the beneficiaries are minors, then the *Children's Law Reform Act*[14] applies, and the specific provisions of that legislation should be consulted.

Certain other written statements must be completed by the relevant parties as part of this type of sale. For example, the personal representative must make a statement in keeping with section 5(1) clause 3 of the *Land Registration Reform Act*.[15] Moreover, each adult beneficiary must complete a statement as to spousal status and comply with section 21 of the *Family Law Act*,[16] if relevant. As an agent, you should be generally aware of these requirements.

v.   Conveying to Beneficiaries

Although most agents are not likely to be involved in this sort of transaction, you should nonetheless be aware that special considerations apply to the situation involving a personal representative who is conveying the property to a beneficiary (rather than to a third-party buyer).

In particular, the *Estates Administration Act* sets out that the personal representative need not obtain a court order to make this type of transfer, although the personal representative or any beneficiary *may* apply to a court to direct such a conveyance (under section 17(5) of the Act). Before granting such an order, the court must be satisfied that there are sufficient assets left in the estate to pay any creditors, or that all known creditors have been paid.

In a transfer from the personal representative to a particular beneficiary, the other beneficiaries must concur, and usually join as parties to the transaction. The recitals will largely be the same as those discussed above.

---

[14]   R.S.O. 1990, c. C.12.
[15]   R.S.O. 1990, c. L.4.
[16]   R.S.O. 1990, c. F.3.

vi.   Purchasing Land from a Beneficiary

1.   Proof of Death and Related Facts

Whenever you are representing a buyer who wants to buy land from someone who has inherited the property, you should consider confirming a few key pieces of information as a routine part of the transaction.

The first step is to establish that the registered owner has indeed died. This can be accomplished by ensuring that some or all of the following have been registered:

- the Will;
- a death certificate; or
- certificates of appointment of Estate Trustees with a Will, or without a Will (formerly called "letters probate" and "letters of administration", respectively), as the case may be.

Secondly, you should also make inquiries as to whether:

- the person conveying the property has authority to do so;
- there are any taxes owed by the estate that remain outstanding; and
- there is any outstanding right to possession of the property, or an order made under the *Family Law Act* or its predecessor legislation.

In connection with the actual transfer of the property, you might also want to ensure that the proper beneficiary is attempting to convey the property, and that he or she has the power to sell it — either expressly or impliedly — pursuant to the Will.

(Note that different considerations apply where the deceased did not give his property in trust to Estate Trustees with a Will (formerly "executors"), but rather left the property to the beneficiaries *directly* by Will. The latter situation is now quite uncommon, and will therefore not be dealt with here.)

2.   The Concept of "Vesting"

Any discussion of the sale of land from a beneficiary must involve consideration of the concept of "vesting". "Vesting" is the legal term used to describe the point at which the full possession of land is delivered to the person entitled to it; it is the moment at which the right to the land accrues.

Broadly speaking, the property must first vest in the beneficiary before the land can be sold by him or her, although there are some exceptions which are discussed below.

3.   Automatic Vesting

Vesting can occur automatically, pursuant to section 9 of the *Estates Administration Act*,[17] if the deceased's personal representatives have not disposed of or conveyed the property within three years after death.

In these cases, the property vests automatically in the beneficiaries, without the need for a deed to be registered from the personal representative. The beneficiaries then become the appropriate parties to enter into the Agreement of Purchase and Sale with a subsequent buyer.

Note, however, that section 9 of the *Estates Administration Act* also provides that vesting can be prevented where a "caution" has been registered by someone else against the property. To register a caution, certain procedures must be followed; generally the caution will prevent vesting for three years, though that can be extended in certain situations.

Also, under the provisions of the *Registry Act*[18] and the *Land Titles Act*,[19] the property will not vest in certain circumstances unless the consent of the provincial Minister of Finance has been obtained. It is therefore wise to ensure that this consent has also been secured.

4.   Sales by Beneficiaries Before Vesting

A beneficiary can also sell the land within the three-year period *before* it vests, but a court order is required, unless the personal representative has actually conveyed the property to the beneficiary.

It should be noted that special legislative provision is made for a *bona fide* buyer's liability for debts during that three-year period; section 17(8) of the *Estates Administration Act* sets out both the extent

---

[17]   R.S.O. 1990, c. E.22.

[18]   R.S.O. 1990, c. R.20, s. 53(3).

[19]   R.S.O. 1990, c. L.5, s. 126.

of those liabilities and the buyer's rights to relief in those circumstances.

5.   *Sales by Beneficiaries After Vesting*

The beneficiary has full, unqualified entitlement to sell the property after it has vested. The transfer will contain the usual recitals listed above, and will also contain a statement as to spousal status.

As with sales prior to vesting, the subsequent buyer's liability for debts is governed by sections 21(2) and 23(1) of the *Estates Administration Act.*[20] Those sections state:

Extent to which real property remains liable to debts and personal liability of beneficiary

21. (2) Real property that becomes vested in a person beneficially entitled thereto under section 9 continues to be liable to answer the debts of the deceased owner so long as it remains vested in such person, or in any person claiming under that person, not being a purchaser in good faith and for valuable consideration, as it would have been if it had remained vested in the personal representative, and in the event of a sale thereof in good faith and for value by such person beneficially entitled that person is personally liable for such debts to the extent of the proceeds of such real property.

.....

Rights of purchaser in good faith against claims of creditors

23. (1) A purchaser in good faith and for value of real property of a deceased owner that has become vested under section 9 in a person beneficially entitled thereto is entitled to hold it freed and discharged from the claims of creditors of the deceased owner except such of them of which the purchaser had notice at the time of the purchase.

vii.   What Documents are Needed for the Deal

Different documents are needed depending on whether or not the property was held by way of a joint tenancy.

Where title is passing to the buyer by way of a surviving joint tenant, the registration of the death certificate on title will be required to provide evidence of the death of the deceased joint tenant.

---

[20]   R.S.O. 1990, c. E.22.

Where title is passing to the buyer other than as a surviving joint tenant, a conveyance of a deceased person's land will require a number of documents. As agent, you should ensure that the following are available:

- proof of the death of the registered owner;
- proof that the Will, or a grant of certificate of appointment of the Estate Trustee with/without a Will (formerly called "letters probate" and "letters of administration") has been registered;
- evidence of claims for taxes owed by the estate, if any;
- proof that the deceased's interest in the property has passed, and evidence that the personal representative has power to deal with the property (note: this may be satisfied by the *Estates Administration Act*);[21]
- proof that there are no creditor's claims; and
- evidence as to whether there are any spousal claims under the *Family Law Act* or other legislation.

viii. A Note about Real Estate Deals in Progress at the Time of Death

Note that where a person has entered into an Agreement of Purchase and Sale but has died prior to the transaction being completed, the contract is still valid, and the deceased person's personal representatives have the capacity and the obligation to complete the transaction on the deceased's behalf.

C.   FAMILY LAW ISSUES

i.   The "Matrimonial Home" and the Definition of "Spouse"

As a real estate agent, you must first of all be aware of an important distinction between a "matrimonial home" and other property. A "matrimonial home" is defined by the *Family Law Act* as being a home *ordinarily occupied by a person and his or her spouse as a family residence.*

---

[21]   R.S.O. 1990, c. E.22.

A second important definition is the term "spouse" as it pertains to deals involving matrimonial homes. "Spouse" for these purposes includes only *married* couples; *common-law* couples are not subject to the same legislative provisions (although rights in property may be obtained by way of the legal concept known as a constructive trust).

Note however that as of June 10, 2003, same-sex couples have been granted the right to marry in Ontario, effective immediately. For these purposes, therefore, such married same-sex couples would be subject to essentially the same provisions of the *Family Law Act* as are married opposite-sex couples. As such, in this discussion the term "spouse" is used to refer to both opposite-sex and same-sex married couples.

ii.   *Family Law Act* Provisions

Part II of the *Family Law Act*,[22] governs a spouse's rights in connection with the matrimonial home. Particularly when acting for a buyer, you must be aware of certain provisions of that Act that may have to be complied with.

1.   Consent of Spouse to Dispose of Matrimonial Home

Section 19 of the *Family Law Act* provides that spouses have "equal right" to possess the matrimonial home. More importantly, section 21 of the Act prohibits one spouse from disposing or encumbering the home without the consent of the other (although consent can be dispensed with by the court in certain circumstances). If one spouse breaches this provision, and attempts to dispose of or encumber the property without the other's consent, section 21(2) of the Act allows for the transaction to be set aside in the right circumstances.

2.   Lack of Notice of Home's Status

Even where the required spousal consent is absent, the transaction will not *automatically* be set aside, provided certain factors are present. In particular, if the buyer acquired the home for value, in good faith and

---

[22]   R.S.O. 1990, c. F.3.

without notice that the home was a matrimonial home, then the transaction may be upheld.

When acting for a buyer, it is therefore important for you to establish that neither the buyer nor his or her lawyer have any information that can constitute "notice" for the purposes of section 21(2) of the Act. The required level of notice can be "actual" or "constructive", meaning notice that a court will deem to have been sufficient for the purposes of the Act.

For example, information obtained by the buyer's lawyer as part of the title search, which might indicate the existence of a spouse, could be construed as notice of spousal status, and may jeopardize the validity of the deal.

In such cases, if you are acting as the agent of a potential buyer, you should ensure that both co-owners (*i.e.*, the sellers) execute the Agreement of Purchase and Sale.

3. *Statements as to Status*

As a means of ensuring that the home's status has been communicated to the potential buyer, sellers of property can verify their status and the status of the property by making certain statements as part of the real estate transaction. Pursuant to section 21(3) of the Act, these are statements made by the seller:

- verifying that he or she is not, or was not, a spouse at the time of the disposition or encumbrance;
- verifying that the person is a spouse who is not separated from his or her spouse and that the property is not ordinarily occupied by the spouses as their family residence;
- verifying that the person is a spouse who is separated from his or her spouse and that the property was not ordinarily occupied by the spouses, at the time of their separation, as their family residence;
- where the property is not designated by both spouses as a matrimonial home, verifying that a designation of another property as a matrimonial home, made by both spouses, is registered and not cancelled; or
- verifying that the other spouse has released all of his or her rights under this Part by a separation agreement.

Under most circumstances, these statements are considered to be sufficient proof that the property is not a matrimonial home. As discussed above, the exception occurs when the buyer has "notice" to the contrary, the threshold being knowledge of facts that would prompt a person to make further inquiries.

4.   *Independent Legal Advice*

Even where one spouse has apparently given consent to sell the matrimonial home, that spouse may benefit from independent legal advice in connection with the proposed transaction.

From the standpoint of the buyer's real estate agent, independent legal advice is necessary where it is clear that the potential buyer knows (or ought to have known in the circumstances) that one spouse is exerting undue influence over the other.

iii.   **Property and Parties to which Family Law Issues Do Not Usually Apply**

1.   *Properties Other Than the Matrimonial Home*

As discussed above, only the sale of property that constitutes a "matrimonial home" will be governed by the provisions of the *Family Law Act*; this means that not every piece of land that happens to be sold by two spouses will give rise to family law-related issues.

Even for couples who own multiple properties, the matrimonial home is usually easy to identify, since it must be "ordinarily occupied" as a "family residence". However, the distinction may be more blurred for sellers who own several properties and spend relatively equal portions of a year in different locales.

Nonetheless, as long as a given property is *not* a matrimonial home, spouses are free to sell land which is owned by them separately or under a joint tenancy; the consent of the other spouse is not required.

Additionally, a property that is owned in joint tenancy may or may not require a spousal consent, depending on whether or not the registered owners are spouses of each other; alternatively, if they are not spouses of each other but the property is not a matrimonial home of either of the registered owners, then spousal consent will not be required.

2. *Common-law or Unmarried Same-sex Couples*

At present, while common-law or unmarried same-sex partners may own property together, the home shared by them will not amount to a "matrimonial home" for the purposes of the *Family Law Act*. As a result, the matrimonial home provisions of that Act will not apply, and in fact only Part III of the Act (dealing with support in specific circumstances) has any relevance to such couples.

Nonetheless, common-law or unmarried same-sex partners may have claims as against each other by way of a claim for what is known as "unjust enrichment". Property that one partner is trying to sell can therefore be subject to a claim by the other partner, and real estate agents should be aware that there are various procedural means of securing the other partner's claim to the property.

iv. Spousal Disputes

Where a relationship between married spouses has deteriorated, disputes inevitably arise as to property ownership, including entitlement to land. Often parties move quickly to try to preserve their rights as against the other party.

In such circumstances, one spouse who has commenced separation or divorce-related proceedings can file a certificate of pending litigation (also known as a certificate of *lis pendens*) against land owned with or by the other spouse, pursuant to the provisions of the *Family Law Act*. The Act prohibits any dealing with the registered title to the land unless those dealings are made subject to the claim of the spouse who has filed the certificate of pending litigation.

Another avenue of recourse for separated or divorcing spouses is an application for partition and sale. While usually few issues arise in connection with purchases from parties acting under an order for partition and sale, the real estate agent should nonetheless be aware of the concept.

v.   Advice for the Real Estate Agent who Acts for a Buyer

Any real estate agent who acts for a buyer should ask the following questions in connection with a potential purchase from sellers who are spouses:

- Are the sellers legally married to each other?
- If the parties are married, does the Agreement of Purchase and Sale refer to any type of housing unit that might constitute a matrimonial home?
- Has the consent of both married spouses been obtained, if applicable?
- Even if the spouse's consent has not been obtained, is this a situation where the issue of the buyer's notice of the status of the property as matrimonial home might be in issue?
- If the parties are not married, is one partner is attempting to sell the property, and is it possible that the land might be subject to a constructive trust claim?
- Is the property possibly the subject of a claim by a common-law partner, or otherwise subject to a certificate of pending litigation?

vi.   Advice for the Real Estate Agent Acting for a Seller

Comparatively speaking, a real estate agent who represents a seller has few family-law related concerns to worry about; most of the issues revolve around the protection of the potential buyer.

Nonetheless, whenever you are in a situation where you represent a seller, you must ensure that if the property is a matrimonial property, and if the property is registered in only one of the spouse's name, the consent of the other spouse has been obtained for purposes of the Agreement of Purchase of Sale. If the spouse who is not registered on title does not execute the Agreement of Purchase and Sale, problems could arise with respect to the closing of the transaction, as the non-registered spouse may take the position that they did not agree to the sale.

Notwithstanding this, in situations where there is concern that the real estate transaction might fall through, you should consider having the buyer's spouse execute the Agreement of Purchase and Sale. This would help protect the seller by making both buyer spouses' assets available in the event the transaction does not close or as a result of the buyers' default where the seller has to launch a subsequent lawsuit against the buyers, arising out of their failure to complete the real estate transaction.

D. BUYING FROM A NEW HOME BUILDER

i. How the Transaction Differs

Although the actual *mechanics* of the transaction are not out of the ordinary, any time the seller is a new home builder, there are a number of significant points that must be kept in mind.

The first is that several aspects of the lead-up to the signing of the agreement are a little unusual: buyers enter into the contract of sale based on the builder's plans and — if they are lucky — a walk-through of a model home. The Agreement of Purchase and Sale form might be a customized document provided by the builder, and any changes to it will be hard-won. This Agreement may also contain some unexpected provisions, for example clauses allowing the builder to make reasonable modifications to the home, or to substitute materials, at its sole discretion and without the buyer's approval. The buyer's deposit will be payable directly to the builder, rather than to the real estate agent or seller's lawyer; and additional deposits may be payable prior to closing, after a specified period of time. Extras and upgrades that the buyer may want installed will be paid for when ordered, rather than on closing. Finally, the number and type of adjustments for which the buyer will be responsible on closing is extensive. They may include:

- the Law Society of Upper Canada transaction levy;
- the cost to obtain a bond to protect up to $40,000 of the purchaser's deposit;
- the cost of excess deposit insurance for deposits of over $40,000;
- sewer impost charges;
- realty taxes;
- provincial sales tax on the value of appliances included in the deal;
- any charges paid to a public utility (water and hydro) for connection of services and/or the installation of a meter;
- the enrolment fee required by the Ontario New Home Warranty Program;
- costs to prepare a foundation survey;

- deposits for damage to the subdivision (refundable after the subdivision is assumed by the municipality);
- tree planting and landscaping fees;
- the costs of the partial discharge of the builder's construction financing;
- "bookkeeping fees" for each in a series of deposit cheques tendered by the buyer pursuant to the agreement of purchase and sale;
- costs to install fencing; and
- grading and paving fees.

Perhaps the most important distinction between purchases from a builder and other types of transactions is the protection provided by the Ontario New Home Warranties Program. Under the Program, the buyer's deposit is protected to a maximum of $40,000. There is also a warranty by the builder that the home is:

- constructed in a workmanlike manner;
- free from defects in material;
- fit for habitation;
- constructed in accordance with the Ontario Building Code; and
- free of major structural defects.

(Certain exclusions and exceptions apply.)

The Agreement itself will also contain an Addendum which ensures Program-related disclosure of certain information to the buyer, such as the builder's address, its registration number under the Program, the individual registration number for the house or unit, and various provisions dealing with the consequences of delay in construction. The buyer also has certain legislated remedies in the event of undue delay by the builder, and is entitled to conduct a pre-delivery inspection.

If the builder has breached any of the relevant warranties, the Program provides the buyer with certain remedies, and provides monetary compensation to a maximum of $100,000, exclusive of deposits (which are covered to a maximum of $40,000). Different aspects of the home's construction are covered by differing warranty periods; these periods range from one year (for certain smaller defects); to two years (for basement water seepage and problems with the building envelope); to seven years (for major structural defects). Warranty claims to the Program must be made in writing.

ii.   Background on GST

Before discussing its application to new homes sales, it is worthwhile to consider the basics as to how GST applies to real estate sales generally.

GST of 7 per cent must be added to the sale price of all real property, subject to certain legislative exceptions, including sales of "used" residential housing, buildings or condominiums, and sales of owner-built-and-occupied homes. Essentially, the sale of a used residential complex is exempt, and the sale of a new or substantially renovated residential complex is taxable, so it is important to determine when a residential complex is "used".

(Incidentally, "residential complex" is expressly defined to mean all or part of any building defined as a "residential unit", together with related land and common areas associated with such buildings. It includes a detached or semi-detached house, a condominium unit, and even a mobile home.)

Unfortunately, the legislation does not provide a definition for "used" residential housing; it is unclear how many days, weeks or months of occupancy it takes for a residential complex to become "used". As a general rule, though, a residential complex will be considered to have been used from the time it is substantially complete and has been sold and occupied as a place of residence.

If the transaction is indeed subject to GST, then the buyer of the property has the obligation to take steps to pay the tax; this is set out in the Agreement of Purchase and Sale. The seller is required to collect the tax from the buyer and pay it to the government, and generally it is payable on the date ownership is transferred.

It is important for agents to draw buyers' attention to whether GST is included in the purchase price, or is in addition to the purchase price; this should be clearly set out in the offer.

iii.   GST and Newly-built Homes

Returning to sales of newly-built homes, GST is generally payable on these types of transactions. However, a GST New Housing Rebate applies to both newly-built and substantially renovated homes and condominiums which sell for under $450,000 exclusive of taxes, provided certain conditions are met. Specifically, for homes priced at or below $350,000, a GST rebate of 36 per cent of the GST paid or $8,750, whichever is less, is available. This amounts to approximately 2.5 per cent of the purchase price. For homes priced between $350,000 and $450,000, the amount of the rebate is gradually reduced on a sliding scale. Purchasers of new homes priced over $450,000 receive no rebate.

The GST rebate is available to eligible individual buyers who:

- buy a new or substantially renovated home (including the land) from a builder;
- buy a new mobile home (including a modular home) or a new floating home from a builder or vendor;
- buy a share of the capital stock of a co-operative housing corporation;
- construct or substantially renovate their own homes, or carry out a major addition (or hire another person to do so); or
- own a home that was destroyed in a fire and was subsequently rebuilt.

There are certain other stipulations, namely:

- the unit purchased from the builder must be a new or substantially renovated single unit residential complex, or a residential condominium unit;
- the builder must sell to the buyer both the building and land on which the home is located;
- the home must be intended as the primary place of residence for the buyer or a "family member" (which term now includes a common-law spouse or former common-law spouse);
- ownership of the home must be transferred to the buyer after the construction or renovation is substantially completed;
- the buyer, or a relative of the buyer, must be the first occupant of the property being bought from the builder.

Eligible buyers have up to two years from the final closing date (or for condominiums, from the unit transfer date) to claim the rebate.

There is also a rebate available in situations where the buyer purchases, or constructs/substantially renovates, a new residential complex, and then leases out the unit or units in that complex for at least one year. In those cases, the rebate application must be filed within two years after the end of the month in which the buyer first rents out the unit(s).

In order to make the rebate available more quickly to buyers, builders are permitted to credit them with the amount of the GST rebate at the time of purchase; the builder then offsets its GST remittance or refund by the amount of the credit, and asks the buyer for an assignment and indemnity in respect of the rebate.

E.   CHARITABLE, RELIGIOUS AND EDUCATIONAL ORGANIZATIONS

Most real estate professionals will seldom act on a purchase made on behalf of a charitable, religious or educational organization. The *sale* of land owned by one of these institutions to an individual may be a little more common.

Nonetheless, it is important that real estate agents have a general awareness of the considerations that may apply to either situation. Note also that many sales of real property by charities and non-profit organizations are exempt from GST.

i.   Charities and Non-profit Organizations

First of all, it is important to note the difference between charities and non-profit organizations.

A charitable organization carries on charitable activities, and may be either an incorporated or an unincorporated body. On the other hand, a non-profit organization may or may not be incorporated, but it need not *necessarily* carry on charitable activities (although some do). This is the key distinction between these two types of organizations.

Special provisions apply to real estate transactions involving charitable or non-profit organizations. First of all, a sale to a charity is governed by the *Charities Accounting Act,*[23] particularly sections 7 to 10. Purchases of land from a charity may also be governed by general or special legislation that applies specifically to that particular organization, and which may limit or otherwise affect its ability to deal with the land.

---

[23]   R.S.O. 1990, c. C.10.

Non-profit organizations are usually subject to fewer constraints, but note that the *Conservation Land Act*[24] may apply to land owned by a non-profit organization if the property is part of a conservation area.

Finally, if the charity or non-profit organization that is selling land is unincorporated, the by-laws or constitution of the organization must provide for the authority to dispose of the property, which will be held by trustees on behalf of the organization. Therefore, in order to conclude the deal, proof will be required to show that the proper authority has been obtained.

ii.   Religious Organizations

Real estate agents should be aware that the sale of land by religious organizations is expressly covered by statute. In particular, the *Religious Organizations' Lands Act*[25] governs the purchase and sale of land by religious organizations, and dictates that land must be acquired or held *for religious purposes*. The Act further defines the power of the religious organization to deal with the land, and the use of that power must first be approved by resolution made by the organization.

Note that in addition to these restrictions, individual religions or religious groups may also be governed by special statutes which may proscribe the organization's ability to deal with land. The relevant legislation must be ascertained, and its text reviewed thoroughly to ensure that any requirements have been met.

A good example of this occurs in the Quebec case of *Corporation de la Paroisse de St.-Telesphore v. La Societe D'Habitation du Quebec.*[26] The land had been gifted in 1875 to a religious organization, with the condition that a church or parsonage be built on it. Part of the land was later sold to the municipality, who wanted to use it for the construction of low-rise housing. The municipality applied to the court for a declaration that the condition as to the use of the land was no longer valid. The court refused, confirming that housing was not one of the religious or educational uses stipulated in the original gift of the land. That condition remained attached to the property, and was binding upon all future buyers.

---

[24]   R.S.O. 1990, c. C.28.

[25]   R.S.O. 1990, c. R.23.

[26]   (1984), 31 R.P.R. 288 (Que. S.C.).

iii. Educational Institutions

As with religious and charitable organizations, most universities and many other similar educational institutions are incorporated by special legislation, which will set out the nature and extent of the authority of the board of directors to deal with land on behalf of the institution. This means that a sale by a university, for example, will require evidence (in the form of a resolution) that the board of directors has approved the sale.

You should therefore be aware of these approval requirements, and should take steps to ascertain that the relevant stipulations have been met.

F. NON-RESIDENTS

i. Income Tax Obligations

Special tax rules can apply to buyers involved in a purchase from a "non-resident" of Canada. (Although the *Income Tax Act*[27] does not define either "resident" or "non-resident" for these purposes, it does prescribe certain factors that are relevant to the determination, and courts have further defined them to include elements such as length of time, intention, and continuity with respect to a physical presence in Canada and elsewhere.)

The rules do not apply in two circumstances:

- where, prior to the sale, the buyer obtains a clearance certificate from the Canada Customs and Revenue Agency ("CCRA"), specifically exempting him or her from the Act's obligations; or
- where, after making a reasonable inquiry, the buyer has no reason to believe that the seller is not a Canadian resident. From a practical standpoint, the "reasonable inquiry" is generally satisfied once the seller provides an affidavit attesting to a lack of non-residency status for the Act's purposes.

Unless either of these exceptions apply, a buyer who intends to purchase property from a non-resident is required by the *Income Tax Act* to:

---

[27] R.S.C. 1985, c. 1 (5th Supp.).

- notify the Canada Customs and Revenue Agency about the transaction either before closing, or within ten days after; and

- withhold a portion of the purchase price, in an amount sufficient to satisfy the non-resident seller's tax liability that arises from the gain he or she may realize on the sale.

This withholding will take place even if it has not been specifically agreed to in the contract of purchase and sale, and amounts to either 25 or 50 per cent of the purchase price, depending on whether the seller holds the property as capital property, or as inventory. The buyer then remits this amount to CCRA within 30 days after the end of the month in which the property was acquired.

If the reporting and withholding requirements are not complied with, the seller is subject to a penalty of $25 a day (with a minimum of $100 and a maximum of $2,500). Although the CCRA has been somewhat lax in enforcing this penalty in the past, as of January 1, 2004 it has expressed a firm commitment to do so in connection with sales occurring after that date.

ii.   GST

A non-resident seller of real estate is not required — and indeed *should not* — collect GST on the transaction. Instead, it becomes the buyer's obligation to report the tax directly to the CCRA (and he or she may be able to claim an input tax credit to offset the tax).

Courts have held that a seller who nonetheless collects GST from the buyer will still leave that buyer liable for the tax; in such cases the seller should refund the tax to the buyer and allow CCRA to assess him or her directly.

G.   TRANSACTIONS INVOLVING BANKRUPT PERSONS

For a debtor who is either considering or has already declared bankruptcy, his or her right to deal with land and property is strictly proscribed by legislation. Real estate agents should therefore be aware of the restrictions placed on such debtors to sell or deal with their land.

i.   Terminology

First of all, it may be useful to outline the general legal terminology that applies to such situations:

- The "debtor" is the person who owes money, goods or services to a creditor.
- The "creditor" is a person or entity that has a claim against the debtor provable under the *Bankruptcy and Insolvency Act*.[28]
- A "secured creditor" is a creditor who has a security or a right in some property belonging to the debtor, so that he or she can sell or realize on it.
- An "insolvent person" is a debtor who is not yet bankrupt, but who owes at least $1,000 and whose liabilities exceed either his or her assets, or his or her ability to pay.
- A "proposal" is the insolvent person's plan for repaying creditors, as a means of avoiding bankruptcy altogether. ("Consumer proposals" are a specific type of proposal, available to individuals whose debts do not exceed $75,000.)
- A "bankrupt" is an insolvent person who has declared bankruptcy (technically called making an "assignment in bankruptcy"), or who has had a receiving order made against him or her.
- A "trustee in bankruptcy" is a person appointed (either by assignment in bankruptcy or pursuant to a receiving order) to administer the bankrupt's estate.

ii.   Bankruptcy Legislation as it Applies to Sales of Land

First of all, the land that is owned by a debtor who has become insolvent, but who has not yet declared bankruptcy, is protected for a certain period, under the provisions of the *Bankruptcy and Insolvency Act*.[29] That Act provides that until the debtor files a proposal or actually declares bankruptcy, the creditors (including mortgagees) are prevented from trying to realize on their security.

Generally speaking, this means that creditors cannot take any steps toward realizing their security during this protection period (including starting foreclosure proceedings, or accelerating mortgage payments).

---

[28]   R.S.C. 1985, c. B-3.
[29]   *Ibid.*

There are certain exceptions, however: for example where the creditor took possession of the land before the protection period started.

Once the debtor has actually made an assignment in bankruptcy, he or she no longer has the capacity to deal with his or her land; rather, the property vests in the trustee, who takes control of it and can distribute it in accordance with the priorities set out in the Act.

In this capacity, the trustee can sell the bankrupt's land, but in doing so, the trustee assumes no greater rights in the land than the bankrupt had, and gives no guarantee as to the state of the title. Valid liens, mortgages and securities on the property remain effective, but executions are no longer enforceable and those who have registered executions simply become unsecured creditors.

iii.   The Mechanics of a Sale from a Trustee

First of all, if the debtor entered into a contract for the sale of land prior to declaring bankruptcy, then the trustee is obliged to complete that sale as if no bankruptcy had occurred. Otherwise, after an assignment in bankruptcy, the trustee is able to deal with the land largely unfettered, although he or she is subject to a general requirement as to reasonableness.

The trustee's appointment must have been confirmed by the creditors at their first meeting. Also, certain inspectors that are appointed at the first meeting of creditors must give their approval of the sale of the property. The trustee's ability to transfer the appropriate title to the property is contingent on obtaining this approval. Therefore, when buying from a trustee, it is important to ascertain that these two steps have been completed.

The trustee will register a certified copy of the assignment or receiving order on title, along with certain other documents. Once the sale is complete, the buyer receives a deed, which contains various declarations attesting to the authority of the trustee.

Note however that if the bankrupt's land contains a matrimonial home, then under family law legislation each spouse has equal right to it; this means that the trustee may have difficulty delivering vacant possession upon closing.

H. BUYING FROM A RECEIVER

Security documents may entitle the secured party to appoint a receiver upon the debtor's default in the underlying loan. (Alternatively, a receiver may be appointed by the court in certain circumstances, which will not be covered here.)

A receiver's role is to act as an agent for the lender, for the specific purpose of realizing on the lender's security. His or her powers and duties are set out in the security document that governs the relationship between the lender and the debtor.

Whenever someone is buying land from a receiver, it is important to ensure that the receiver was properly appointed, that the security document covers all of the property being purchased, and that the receiver has authority to sell the property in the manner it is being sold. The transfer documentation will contain information confirming the receiver's proper appointment, attesting to the particulars of the debtor's default, and confirming that the relevant notice-of-sale requirements were adhered to.

The existence of these factors were in issue in a case called *Warsh v. International Freehold Financial Services Ltd.*[30] The buyer refused to close because of several alleged minor deficiencies in the closing documentation provided by the receiver; a motion judge had found that these deficiencies went to the heart of the receiver's ability to give the buyer good title. The Ontario Court of Appeal disagreed, finding that the motions judge had erred on this point. It noted that an earlier court had approved the sale, which suggested that it had been satisfied as to the receiver's authority. It also concluded that, other than the deed to the property, the receiver was not required to deliver the appropriate documents in registerable form, and that the receiver was entitled to keep the buyer's deposit in connection with the aborted sale.

I. SHERIFF'S SALES

In cases where a debtor has defaulted on a loan from a creditor, the creditor may pursue collection of the outstanding amount through various

---

[30] [2000] O.J. No. 1100 (C.A.).

mechanisms. One such means is through the Sheriff's sale, which is prompted by the issuing of a writ of seizure and sale.

The process is as follows: the creditor first obtains a court judgment against the debtor for the amount of the outstanding debt. If the debtor owns land, the creditor then applies to the court for a writ of seizure and sale, which is a legal document authorizing the Sheriff to seize the debtor's land and ultimately sell it to a third party.

The writ must set out in detail the name of the debtor, the amount of the judgment, and various other specific information. It is filed with the Sheriff of the judicial district in which the judgment was obtained, and covers the land that the debtor owns in that jurisdiction.

However, no steps toward selling the land may be taken until four months after the writ is filed, and the actual sale itself cannot take place until two months after that.

The Sheriff will advertise the sale of the debtor's land in accordance with certain prescribed regulations. The Sheriff must also give notice to both the creditor and the debtor, and must follow certain timelines in connection with the conduct of the sale. The successful buyer of the land from the Sheriff will receive what is known as a "deed poll".

Buyers of land from a Sheriff's sale should be aware of two things:

(1) The Sheriff is able to convey only the right, title and interest in the lands that the debtor had. In other words, the Sheriff does not provide any warranty or representation of the title that was held by the debtor, and so a buyer who purchases land at a Sheriff's sale and finds that the title is defective has no remedy against the creditor, the debtor or the Sheriff.

(2) Any encumbrances on the land, except executions, remain on title. This means that a buyer of land from a Sheriff's sale will still be liable to the creditor for the original debt owed by the debtor. Executions, however, are extinguished through the sale.

Note also that for property subject to a Sheriff's sale that is held jointly, the debtor's interest is severable, and can be sold. However, a buyer who decides to purchase such an undivided half-interest in the land may have to negotiate with the co-owner (*i.e.*, the other joint tenant) before the land can be further dealt with.

J.   LAND OBTAINED THROUGH A TAX SALE

As with sales by the Sheriff, land that is made available for sale through the mechanism of a Tax Sale is subject to specific rules and procedures. Currently, all aspects of the procedure governing Tax Sales are set out in the *Municipal Act, 2001*.[31]

Essentially, a Tax Sale is a method by which the municipality can recover tax arrears owed by the land owner. For these purposes, tax arrears cover mainly real property taxes, but can also include certain other taxes or payments that are deemed to be recoverable under the legislation.

If tax arrears remain unpaid by the land owner for a specified period of time, the municipal treasurer may prepare a tax arrears certificate which is registered against the title to the land. It will specify a "cancellation price" (essentially the amount of the arrears); once that price is paid, the tax arrears certificate is cancelled. If the cancellation price is not paid within one year of the certificate being registered, however, then the land can be sold at a public sale.

One very recent Ontario Court of Appeal decision called *Cunningham v. Front of Yonge (Township)*[32] sheds light on the discretion that the municipal treasurer may exercise in this regard. There, husband-and-wife owners of a family farm had failed to pay their taxes for four years, and so the land was targeted for a Tax Sale. Although the wife had received all of the required notices of the sale from the municipality, she hid them from her husband out of concern for his health, and to conceal her own personal overspending. The husband found out from a neighbour that his home was already being advertised in the newspapers for sale. The husband arranged for funds to pay the cancellation price, but by then several (low) offers to buy had been made, the tenders had been made public, and a successful buyer had been chosen. The court found that the municipal treasurer still had the discretion to cancel a Tax Sale in these circumstances, and that the existence of such discretion did not adversely affect the integrity of the tender process.

All Tax Sales are subject to certain regulations respecting notice and advertising. In some cases the land owner can agree with the municipality to extend the time within which the cancellation price can be paid.

---

[31]   S.O. 2001, c. 25.
[32]   [2004] O.J. No. 4104 (C.A.).

Once the sale is completed, the successful buyer receives what is known as a tax deed. The buyer takes the land subject to any easements, restrictive covenants, Crown interests, or the interests of abutting land owners which were obtained by adverse possession before the tax deed is registered. The buyer also cannot take a greater interest in the land than the seller had at the time of the Tax Sale.

Note that by providing the tax deed to the buyer, the municipality is not obliged to provide vacant possession. Also, the municipality still has the right to collect certain taxes that were imposed *before* the tax deed was registered, but which became due *after* registration.

For the most part, once a tax deed has been registered, it is final and is generally not subject to challenge except on certain narrow grounds prescribed by statute. An interesting Ontario case named *Bay Colony Ltd. v. Wasaga Beach (Town)*[33] went all the way to the Supreme Court of Canada on the question of what notice an owner of the property must receive before a Tax Sale is valid. In that decision, the *Municipal Tax Sales Act* dictated that the owner was to receive two notices of the impending sale. In fact, the Town sent him only one notice, but he never received it. (It was sent to the firm of lawyers whose name appeared on the ten-year-old deed, and moreover the firm had moved twice in that time.) A Tax Sale was held, and the owner sued to have it set aside. The Ontario Court of Appeal found that, given the drastic result of a Tax Sale, it is important that the statutory notice provisions are strictly complied with. There was nothing to prove that the owner actually received notice of the sale in any manner, and therefore he was entitled to damages against the Town.

K.   TENANTS

Several unique considerations apply in situations where the property being purchased or sold contains rental units that are inhabited by tenants. This section will accordingly touch upon the legislative scheme and concepts relevant to these situations.

---

[33]   [1997] O.J. No. 1686 (C.A.), leave to appeal to the S.C.C. refused with costs [1997] S.C.C.A. No. 361.

i. The Scope of the *Tenant Protection Act, 1997* (the "Act")[34]

1. *Who is Covered by the Act?*

Most of the provisions of the Act are applicable to all landlords, and to all tenants. In fact, landlords and tenants are not permitted to enter into agreements to avoid the provisions of the Act, or waive their rights or obligations under it.

2. *What is Considered a "Rental Unit"?*

First of all, real estate professionals should be alert to the very broad nature of what is considered to be a "rental unit" under the Act. The Act specifically provides that a rental unit can be:

- an apartment;
- a house;
- a site in a mobile home park or land lease community;
- a room in a rooming house, lodging house or boarding house; or
- a room in a care home or retirement home.

3. *Types of Rental Accommodation Not Covered by the Act*

Notwithstanding this broad definition of "rental unit", the Act does contain some exemptions. Specifically, it does not apply *at all* to certain specific types of rental units or accommodation, including:

- units provided for the vacationing or travelling public in a hotel or motel, resort, lodge, inn, campground, trailer park, *etc.*;
- living accommodation whose occupancy is conditional upon the occupant being employed on a farm;
- units in a non-profit housing co-operative;
- living accommodation in a correctional facility;
- living accommodation that is subject to certain health-care related legislation;
- accommodation in an emergency shelter;

---

[34] S.O. 1997, c. 24.

- certain accommodation provided by education institutions to its students and staff;
- premises used for business purposes where there is living space attached, and where a single lease covers both;
- living accommodation occupied for the purpose of receiving rehabilitative or therapeutic services;
- living accommodation located in a building or project, where the occupancy is conditional upon the occupant performing services related to the business carried out in that building or project; and
- living accommodation whose occupant is required to share a bathroom or kitchen with the owner or owner's immediate family (*i.e.*, a spouse (which includes a same-sex partner), a child or parent, or the spouse's or same-sex partner's child or parent), and where the owner, spouse, same-sex partner, child or parent lives in the building in which the living accommodation is located.

Also, as will be discussed later, landlords and tenants are subject to certain rules about assignment and subletting, and about rent and rent increases. However, certain rental units are wholly exempt from these particular provisions, specifically:

- certain specified non-profit and public housing;
- rental units owned or operated by a religious institution for charitable use on a non-profit basis;
- rental units provided by a non-profit housing co-operative to tenants in non-member units;
- certain accommodation subject to the *Developmental Services Act*;[35] and
- residences at schools, colleges, and universities.

(Note that despite this exemption, these types of units are still covered by most other rules in the Act dealing with things such as repair, maintenance, and eviction.)

ii.   Tenancy Agreements

Tenancy agreements (*i.e.*, leases) must contain the legal name and address of the landlord. All written tenancy agreements entered into after the Act came into force must be signed by both the landlord and

---

[35] R.S.O. 1990, c. D.11.

the tenant, and a copy must be given to the tenant within 21 days after it is signed by the tenant and given back to the landlord.

For tenancy agreements that are not in writing, the landlord must give the tenant written notice of the landlord's legal name and address within 21 days after the tenancy begins.

Until the landlord has complied with these provisions, the landlord may not demand rent from the tenants and in fact the tenant's obligation to pay rent is suspended. Prudent real estate agents who act for buyers of rental properties will therefore want to ensure that these provisions have been complied with by the seller prior to closing.

iii.   Acceleration Clauses

The Act prohibits any provision in a tenancy agreement that calls for an acceleration clause; *i.e.*, that upon default by the tenant in paying rent, all or part of the remaining rent for the term becomes due.

iv.   Pets

Under the Act, any clause in a tenancy agreement that prohibits the presence of animals in or around the residential complex is void.

Essentially, this means that a "no pets" clause in a lease, or a clause that requires a tenant to vacate the rental unit or pay damages to the landlord because of the mere presence of a pet, is completely unenforceable even if the tenant has signed it.

(Keep in mind, however, that the Act does not apply at all to certain rental unit situations, such as living accommodation that involves the tenant sharing a kitchen or bathroom with the owner or the owner's immediate family, for example. In those circumstances a "no pets" clause would still be enforceable by the landlord.)

Notwithstanding the Act's prohibition against "no pets" clauses, a landlord may still evict a tenant for keeping an animal if it:

- caused undue damage;
- caused a serious allergic reaction in another person or in the landlord;
- interfered with the normal enjoyment of the property by another tenant or the landlord (for example, by causing undue noise or

acting aggressively toward others, such that their safety is affected); or

- is a species or breed of animal that is inherently dangerous.

v.   Non-Smoking Clauses

The Act does not restrict a landlord's right to choose his or her tenants, nor does it prohibit landlords from inserting "no smoking" clauses in their tenancy agreements.

As a result, landlords can refuse outright to rent to smokers, and can enforce a "no smoking" clause in a lease.

vi.   Privacy Issues

1.   Changing Locks

Under the prior version of this legislation, locks could not be changed on a rental unit except by mutual consent of the tenant and landlord. Under the current Act, this is no longer the case: — the landlord no longer requires the tenant to consent to a change of locks, provided the tenant is furnished with a replacement key. In fact, a landlord who fails to provide the tenant with a replacement key may, on application by the tenant, be fined up to $10,000 by the Ontario Rental Housing Tribunal, or may face an order to abate the tenant's rent.

Also, if the Tribunal determines that the unit is vacant, it may order that the landlord allow the tenant to recover possession of the rental unit, and order the landlord not to rent the unit to anyone else. Such an order has the same effect, (and can be enforced in the same manner) as a writ of possession in favour of the tenant. The order expires 45 days after it was issued if it has been filed with the sheriff of the jurisdiction where the rental unit is located; otherwise, if it has not been filed with the sheriff, then it expires 15 days after it was issued.

Tenants are not allowed to change the locks without the consent of the landlord. If the tenant does change the locks, on application by the landlord, the Tribunal may order that the tenant provide the landlord with the replacement keys, or pay the landlord's reasonable expenses in replacing the tenant's unauthorized lock.

2.   *Landlord's Right to Enter a Tenant's Unit*

The rules concerning tenants' rights to privacy are clearly set out in the Act, which provides that a landlord has no right to enter a rental unit, except under very specific circumstances.

(I) ENTRY WITHOUT NOTICE

A landlord may enter a rental unit at any time *without written notice* in only the following circumstances:

- in cases of emergency;
- if the tenant consents to the entry at the time of entry (note that an advanced written note which consents to the landlord's entry is not sufficient);
- to clean the rental unit where the tenancy agreement requires regular cleaning, and the landlord enters the unit at the times specified in the agreement; or between 8 a.m. and 8 p.m. if no times are specified in the agreement;
- to show the unit to prospective tenants where:
  - the landlord and tenant have agreed that the tenancy will be terminated or one of them has given notice to the other;
  - the landlord enters the unit between the hours of 8 a.m. and 8 p.m.; and
  - prior to entering, the landlord informs or makes a reasonable effort to inform the tenant of their intention to do so.

(II) ENTRY WITH NOTICE

A landlord may enter a rental unit in accordance *with written notice* given to the tenant *at least 24 hours* before the time of entry under the following circumstances:

- To carry out a repair or do work in the rental unit;
- To allow a potential mortgagee or insurer of the residential complex to view the rental unit;
- To allow a potential purchaser to view the rental unit;
- To allow a certified engineer or architect to physically inspect the rental unit for the purposes of the *Condominium Act, 1998*;[36] or

---

[36] S.O. 1998, c. 19.

- For any other reasonable reason for entry specified in the tenancy agreement.

Incidentally, the written notice must specify the reason for the entry, the day of entry, and the time of entry, which must be between the hours of 8 a.m. and 8 p.m.

3.   *Disputes About Privacy*

Disputes about privacy matters are settled by the Ontario Rental Housing Tribunal. If a tenant feels that a landlord is interfering with their rights by entering their apartment, the tenant can make application to the Tribunal within one year of the incident.

If the Tribunal determines that the landlord has illegally entered the rental unit, the Tribunal may order an abatement of rent or require the landlord to pay an administrative fine of up to $10,000.

If the Tribunal determines that the tenant was induced by the conduct of the landlord to vacate the rental unit, the Tribunal may order that the landlord pay compensation for any increased rent which the tenant has incurred or will incur for the one-year period after the tenant has left the rental unit; and any other reasonable moving or storage expenses incurred by the tenant.

vii.   Tenant's Additional Responsibilities to Landlord

The tenant has an obligation not to harass, obstruct, coerce, threaten, or interfere with the landlord. Moreover, the tenant has positive obligation to be responsible for the ordinary cleanliness of the rental unit (except where the tenancy agreement requires the landlord to clean it). The tenant is also responsible for the repair of damage to the rental unit or residential complex caused by the willful or negligent conduct of the tenant or their guests.

viii. Landlord's Additional Responsibilities to Tenants

1.   Generally

The Act expressly defines several general obligations of the landlord that real estate agents who act for buyers and sellers of rental properties should be aware of.

In particular, the landlord is prohibited by the Act from substantially interfering with the tenant's reasonable enjoyment of the rental unit or the residential complex in which it is located. This applies to the tenant's use (or use by the members of the tenant's household) of the property for all usual purposes.

The landlord is also prohibited from harassing, obstructing, coercing, threatening or interfering with a tenant.

2.   Maintenance and Repairs

The Act contains rules to ensure that rental units are safe and well maintained. A landlord is responsible for maintaining both the entire residential complex and its individual rental units in a good state of repair, and for complying with all health, safety, housing, and maintenance standards. The landlord's responsibility exists even if the tenant was aware, prior to entering into the tenancy agreement, that the complex or the unit was in a state of non-repair or was in contravention of any of these standards.

Most municipalities in Ontario have property standards by-laws, and building inspectors who enforce these by-laws. Where these by-laws are absent, however, the Act provides that the prescribed standards set out in the regulations will apply, and will be subject to enforcement by an inspector who can issue a work order requiring the landlord to comply with the prescribed standards. If the landlord is not satisfied with the terms of the work order, within 20 days after the order is issued, the landlord may apply to the Ontario Rental Housing Tribunal for a review of the order.

A tenant also has the right to apply to the Tribunal for an order determining that the landlord has breached its maintenance obligations. If the Tribunal makes such a determination, the Tribunal can:

* terminate the tenancy;

- order an abatement of rent;
- authorize a repair that has been or is to be made, and order the landlord to pay the tenant for damage caused to the tenant's property due to the maintenance and repair problems, or to pay the tenant his or her out-of-pocket expenses that resulted; and
- order the landlord to do the specified work or repairs within a specified time; and/or make any other order that it considers appropriate.

Note that the Act also prohibits a landlord from disrupting the reasonable supply of vital services to a tenant, such as heat, hydro, natural gas, or water. The nature of these vital services are prescribed by municipal by-law.

3.   *Recovering Possession of a Rental Unit and Dealing With Tenant's Property*

(I) RECOVERING POSSESSION AFTER TENANT VACATES, ABANDONS, OR IS EVICTED

A landlord is not entitled to recover possession of a rental unit that is subject to a tenancy unless:

- the tenant has vacated or abandoned the unit; or
- the eviction order obtained from the Ontario Rental Housing Tribunal by the landlord authorizes the possession.

As for the contents of a rental unit, the Act is specific. A landlord may sell, use or dispose of property left in a rental unit if it has been vacated:

- in accordance with a notice of termination of the landlord or tenant;
- in accordance with an agreement between the landlord and tenant to terminate the tenancy;
- in accordance with an Order of the Tribunal terminating the tenancy or evicting the tenant; or
- by a superintendent, in which case the landlord may deal with the superintendent's property after one week.

Where an eviction order is made, the landlord must wait until 48 hours have elapsed before disposing of the tenant's property, and must make the property available to the tenant at a location proximate to the rental unit for those 48 hours. After these time periods, the landlord is free to dispose of the property and is not liable to anyone for selling, retaining or disposing of the tenant's property in compliance with the Act. Also, the Act says that no landlord shall, *without legal process*, seize a tenant's property for default in the payment of rent or for the breach of any other obligation.

(II) POSSESSION AFTER TENANT ABANDONMENT

If the landlord believes that the tenant has abandoned the unit, the landlord can apply to the Ontario Rental Housing Tribunal for an order terminating a tenancy. The landlord also gains the right to deal with the tenant's abandoned property (including making arrangements to dispose of it) if: (1) the landlord has obtained an order to terminate the tenancy as described above, or (2) if the landlord has given to the tenant and to the Tribunal notice of their intention to dispose of the property. Notice to the tenant can be given by mail to the last known address of the tenant, which will usually be the abandoned unit.

However, the landlord must wait until 30 days after the order has been obtained or the notice has been given, at which point the landlord may sell, use, or otherwise dispose of any items of abandoned property.

Within the 30 days, a tenant may notify the landlord of the tenant's intention to remove the property, and the landlord must make the property available to the tenant at a reasonable time and within a reasonable proximity to the rental unit.

The landlord may require the tenant to pay the landlord any arrears of rent and any reasonable expenses incurred in moving, storing, or securing the tenant's property before allowing the tenant to remove the property.

Note that where the tenant has abandoned any unsafe or unhygienic items, the landlord may dispose of those items immediately, and need not wait for the expiry of the 30 days.

Note also that a rental unit is not considered abandoned if the tenant is still paying rent.

ix.   Assignment and Subletting

A landlord is permitted to charge whatever the market will bear upon vacancy, so the question of when a true "vacancy" arises is critical.

Again, these issues will be relevant to real estate agents who deal with the buying and selling of rental properties, particularly in the context of potential rental income.

1.   *Assignment of a Tenancy Agreement*

Every tenant has the right to assign their lease, subject to the landlord's consent, regardless of whether the tenancy is periodic, fixed, contractual, or statutory. Moreover, the landlord has an express right under the Act to absolutely refuse to consent to an assignment of the lease as proposed by a tenant.

However, where a landlord refuses to consent to an assignment, the tenant has the right to terminate the tenancy on 30 days' notice regardless of the terms of the existing tenancy. Similarly, if the landlord fails to respond to an assignment request made by a tenant within seven days after the request is made, the tenant may terminate the tenancy on 30 days' notice.

If a landlord does consent to an assignment, the landlord has a further right to refuse to consent to the prospective assignee, provided such consent is not unreasonably withheld. If the landlord does refuse to consent to a particular assignee, the tenant also has the right to terminate the tenancy on 30 days' notice.

If a tenant has assigned a rental unit to another person, the tenancy agreement continues to apply to the new tenant on all the same terms and conditions. The new tenant has a right to insist that the landlord's obligations under the lease are met (including, in some cases, obligations arising before the assignment of the lease took place), and conversely the landlord can ensure that the new tenant complies with all the provisions of the lease from the date of the assignment forward. The former tenant is still liable to the landlord for any breach of the tenant's obligations occurring before the assignment, however.

2.   *"Deemed Assignment"*

Where a tenant transfers possession of the rental unit to an occupant *without* the consent of the landlord, the landlord must act quickly so as to avoid a "deemed assignment". If a deemed assignment occurs, the landlord may be stuck with an assignee whom they do not want, or find themselves in a situation where they have lost the opportunity to increase the rent to market rent.

Once an unauthorized assignment is discovered by the landlord, the landlord has a period of 60 days in which to negotiate a new tenancy agreement with the assignee, or file an application for an eviction order. If the landlord takes no action within 60 days of the discovery, the landlord is deemed to have consented to the assignment of the rental unit under the same terms and conditions as existed with the vacating tenant.

3. Sublets

Subletting occurs when a tenant provides another person with the right to occupy the rental unit for a term ending on a specified date before the end of the tenant's term. In a sublet situation, the original tenant remains the tenant for legal purposes during the tenure of the new subtenant. The landlord still looks to the original tenant to ultimately fulfill their obligations under the lease, such as payment of rent, and it is the original tenant alone who can enforce their rights against the landlord.

A tenant may only sublet a rental unit to another person with the consent of the landlord; however, the landlord may not arbitrarily or unreasonably withhold consent.

In a sublet situation, upon expiration of the original lease, and unless the original tenant returns to the unit, a vacancy arises. Even if the subtenant has not moved out, a new tenancy is created between the landlord and subtenant, and the landlord can charge the "new tenant" whatever the market will bear. The use of the sublet provisions could give rise to a "handing down" of the rental unit from one tenant to another (*i.e.*, an unauthorized assignment) unless the landlord implements administrative processes to protect its interests. Landlords should therefore insist that a tenant specify the term of the sublet, and the appropriate documentation should make it clear to the original tenant of their liability for all obligations under the lease during the period of the sub-tenancy.

If it appears that the original tenant is simply handing off their unit to another tenant, the landlord should insist that the original tenant provide a written notice of termination of their tenancy, failing which consent to the sublet should be denied.

It should be noted that the Act stipulates that the original tenant may not sublet a rental unit for more than the lawful rent amount, and may not charge the sublessor a fee, premium, commission, bonus, penalty, key money or the like, in exchange for subletting the rental unit.

4.   *Overholding Subtenant*

The Act provides the landlord with the opportunity to make application to the Ontario Rental Housing Tribunal for an order evicting a subtenant that overholds at the end of the sub-tenancy. If the landlord fails to apply for an eviction order, or negotiate a new tenancy agreement, within 60 days of the landlord discovering an unauthorized occupancy, the subtenant's occupation of the unit is deemed to be an assignment of the rental unit with the consent of the landlord as of the date the unauthorized occupancy began.

x.   **Rent**

1.   *Rent for a New Tenant*

Although many of the rules concerning rent have remained the same under the *Tenant Protection Act, 1997*,[37] there are some important changes as compared to the previous legislation.

The most significant change relates to vacancy de-control and the elimination of maximum rent upon the turnover of a rental unit. Under the Act, for any new tenancy created after June 17, 1998, there is no limit on the amount of rent that can be charged — a landlord can charge whatever the market will bear. Once the new tenant moves in, however, the unit is again subject to rent control, using the new rent as the base upon which annual Guideline increases are calculated.

2.   *Rent Deposits*

The Act stipulates that the only type of security deposit that may be collected by a landlord from a tenant is a "rent deposit" as defined by the

---

[37]   S.O. 1997, c. 24.

Act. The rent deposit can only be collected before entering into the tenancy agreement, and cannot be more than one month's rent or the rent amount for one rent period, whichever is less. Certain exceptions apply, involving new and deemed landlords as described by the Act.

The tenant's rent deposit is to be applied by the landlord to the last rent period before the tenancy terminates. Also, the landlord is obliged to pay the tenant interest on the rent deposit at the rate of 6 per cent per year, failing which, the tenant may deduct the amount of the interest payment from a subsequent rent payment. In a decision called *626114 Ontario Ltd. v. Tirado*,[38] the Ontario Divisional Court overturned a previous decision by the Ontario Rental Housing Tribunal that had limited a tenant's rights to claim multiple years' interest on a rental deposit. Instead, a tenant is entitled to interest on the deposit for the full period of the tenancy.

Under the Act, the landlord is not allowed to collect — whether directly or indirectly — a fee, premium, commission, bonus, penalty, key deposit or similar payments even if they are refundable.

3.   *Post-dated Cheques*

A landlord cannot demand that a tenant provide post-dated cheques or other negotiable instruments for the payment of rent.

4.   *Rent Receipts*

A landlord shall provide free of charge to a tenant, upon the tenant's request, a receipt for the payment of any rent, rent deposit, arrears of rent or any other amount paid to the landlord.

5.   *Rent Reductions*

The Act contains provisions dealing with reductions in rent. Specifically, the lawful rent will be reduced in the following circumstances:

- Where the municipal property tax for a residential complex is reduced by 2.5 per cent or more; or

---

[38]   [2005] O.J. No. 4350 (Div. Ct.).

- Where there has been a reduction or discontinuance in services or facilities provided in respect of either the specific rental unit or the residential complex.

In all these cases, the tenant of the affected rental unit can apply to the Tribunal for an order reducing the rent charged.

6. Increasing a Current Tenant's Rent

A landlord cannot charge more than lawful rent. Increases to rent can only be brought about in accordance with the provisions of the Act.

As under the *Rent Control Act, 1992* (the "*RCA*"),[39] the "one-increase-per-twelve-months" rule still applies. Thus, where a tenant is living in a rental unit, the rent can only be increased if a minimum of 12 months have elapsed since the day of the last rent increase for that tenant in that unit, if there has been a previous increase; or since the day that the unit was first rented to that tenant.

Under the Act the landlord must give the tenant at least 90 days' written notice of a rent increase. The notice must be in the proper form, and must set out the landlord's intention to increase the rent as well as the amount of the new rent. An increase in rent is void if proper notice is not given as required by the Act.

A tenant who does not give the landlord notice of termination of the tenancy after receiving the notice of intended rent increase is deemed to have accepted that increase (subject to the parties exercising their rights under the Act).

7. The Rent Increase Guideline

The increase cannot exceed the Guideline amount set each year by the Minister of Municipal Affairs and Housing, except in accordance with certain exceptions which are discussed below. For 2006, the Guideline has been set at 2.1 per cent.

If a landlord charges less than the maximum Guideline allowed in a given year, the landlord cannot make up the difference in subsequent years. (This is a change from the previous legislation.)

---

[39] S.O. 1992, c. 11 [repealed by S.O. 1997, c. 24, s. 218].

8. *Increases Above Guideline Amounts*

A landlord is permitted to increase the rent above the annual statutory Guideline, in the circumstances specified in the Act. This is accomplished through the use of a negotiated agreement with the tenant.

There are two types of these agreements: the first occurs where the landlord and tenant have agreed to a rent increase because the landlord has carried out (or has undertaken to carry out) a specified capital expenditure, or has provided a new or additional service. Some points to note:

- The Agreement must be on the approved form available from the Tribunal office. The Agreement must set out the new rent, and the date that the Agreement is to take effect (which cannot be earlier than six days after it is signed).
- The increase is limited to the Guideline amount plus 4 per cent, but there is no requirement to base the amount of the increase on the actual cost to the landlord.
- There is no requirement to provide the tenant with a notice of rent increase.
- The increase must be taken at the same time as the annual statutory Guideline increase (to satisfy the one-increase-per-12-months rule).
- A tenant may cancel the Agreement by giving written notice to the landlord within five days after signing it.
- A tenant may apply to the Tribunal for relief if the landlord fails to carry out the undertaking, or provide the service, agreed upon. But the application must be made within two years after the rent increase becomes effective.

The second type of agreement is used where the landlord and tenant have agreed for the landlord to add any of the following additional services: a parking space; cable or satellite television; an air conditioner or extra hydro for an air conditioner; extra hydro for a washer or dryer in the rental unit; block heater plug-ins; lockers or other storage space; heat; hydro; water or sewage services; or floor space. Note the following:

- This type of increase is not treated as a rent increase *per se*. Thus the increase can take effect at any time during the year, and is not subject to the one-increase-per-twelve-months rule.
- The 4 per cent cap does not apply, but the increase must be based on the actual cost to the landlord.

- There is no requirement to provide the tenant with a Notice of Rent Increase.

9. *Applications to the Tribunal Respecting Rent Increases Above Guideline — Security Services or Capital Expenditure*

If attempts to negotiate a rent increase above the Guideline are not successful, a landlord may apply to the Tribunal for an order to increase the rent above the Guideline in two circumstances. The first is where the landlord applies to the Tribunal to increase the rent charged by more than the Guideline for operating costs related to security services provided in respect of the complex, or for capital expenditures incurred respecting the whole complex or one or more of the rental units in it. Note the following:

- The landlord must make application to the Tribunal at least 90 days before the effective date of the first intended rent increase.
- Capital expenditures must have been completed within 18 months preceding the date that application is made.
- The application may include all, some, or one of the rental units in the complex.
- The increase is limited to 4 per cent above the Guideline per year; but if the Tribunal determines that an increase of more than 4 per cent is justified, the Tribunal will order increases in rent for the following year(s), until the expenditures are fully recovered. The annual Guideline amount is not reduced by this carry forward.
- With respect to increased operating costs for security services, the landlord may only apply for rent increase where the services are provided by persons not employed by the landlord.

The Tribunal may disallow capital expenditures where it finds the expenditure to be unreasonable. However, the Tribunal cannot make a finding that an expenditure is unreasonable if:

- it is necessary to protect or restore the physical integrity of the complex;
- it is necessary to maintain health, safety, or other housing related standards required by law;
- it is necessary to maintain the provision of a plumbing, heating, mechanical, electrical, ventilation, or air conditioning system;
- it provides access for persons with disabilities;

- it promotes energy or water conservation; or
- it maintains or improves the security of the residence.

Note that this does not mean that a capital expenditure which fails to meet any of the above criteria will be denied recognition. The Tribunal must first find that an expenditure is unreasonable before it may consider disallowing the landlord's application. However, a capital expenditure which does meet the above criteria cannot be found to be unreasonable and thus can never be disallowed.

10. *Applications to the Tribunal Respecting Rent Increases Above Guideline — Municipal Taxes and Utilities*

The second instance in which the landlord may apply for an above-Guideline rent increase is where there has been an extraordinary increase in the cost of municipal taxes and charges and/or utilities. The following considerations apply:

- Landlords are not required to report tax and utility costs in every above Guideline application, but may choose when to do so.
- An increase is 'extraordinary' if it is greater than the percentage increase set out for the corresponding category in the table used for calculating the annual statutory Guideline.
- There is no limit on the amount of the rent increase which results from an extraordinary increase in taxes and charges and/or utilities.

xi. Terminating a Tenancy

1. *Certain Agreements as to Terminating a Tenancy are Void*

An agreement between a landlord and tenant to terminate a tenancy is void if it is entered into:

- at the time the tenancy agreement is entered into; or
- as a condition of entering into a tenancy agreement.

Moreover, a tenant's notice to terminate a tenancy is void if given to the landlord under either of these conditions.

2. *Notice of Termination Generally*

Generally speaking, notice of termination is subject to certain formal requirements. It must be in a form approved by the Tribunal, must identify the rental unit for which the notice is given, must state the date on which the tenancy is to terminate, and must be signed by the person giving notice.

If the notice is being given by the landlord, it must also set out the reasons and details regarding the termination, as well as the fact that recourse may be had to the Tribunal for an order either terminating the tenancy or otherwise resolving the dispute.

Also, except where the termination is based on a tenant's failure to pay rent, notice of termination becomes void 30 days after the date specified in the notice, unless the tenant vacates before that time, or the landlord applies for an order terminating the tenancy and evicting the tenant before that time.

3. *Deemed Renewals*

The expiration of the term of a lease does not mean that the tenant must move out of the rental unit, unless they wish to do so. A lease can be renewed, or if the landlord and tenant agree, a new lease can be made.

If the landlord and tenant do not renew or terminate a *fixed-term* lease (meaning a lease whereby the landlord and tenant have agreed that the tenancy would last for a specific period of time, with defined start and end dates) or enter into a new tenancy agreement, the Act stipulates that the tenant can stay as a month-to-month tenant. All of the rules of the former lease will still apply, however the landlord can increase the rent by the amount allowed under the Act if 12 months have passed since the last increase. In this case, the landlord must give the tenant 90 days' written notice of the rent increase in the proper form.

If the landlord and tenant do not renew or terminate a *periodic* tenancy, then the landlord and tenant are deemed under the Act to have renewed it for another week, month, year or other period (as the case may be), with the same terms and conditions as existed under the expired lease, subject to any increases in rent under the Act.

4. *Termination at End of Term*

(I) TERMINATION BY LANDLORD — GROUNDS FOR TERMINATION

The grounds for termination at the end of the term of a tenancy which relate to the conduct of the tenant are as follows:

- persistent late payment of rent;
- ceasing to meet the income qualifications required for occupancy of public housing;
- rental unit provided by employer to employee, and employment has ceased; and
- tenancy arose by virtue of agreement to buy proposed condominium unit, and agreement has been terminated.

(II) TERMINATION BY LANDLORD — NOTICE PERIODS

The notice periods in respect of the above grounds for termination are as follows:

- Daily or weekly tenancies — at least 28 days' notice. The termination date given must be on the last day of a rental period.
- Monthly tenancies — at least 60 days' notice. The termination date must be on the last day of a rental period.
- Yearly tenancies — at least 60 days' notice. The termination date must be on the last day of a rental period.
- Fixed term tenancies — at least 60 days before the expiry date of the agreement, to be effective on that expiry date.

In all cases, the date must be a day a period of the tenancy ends or, where the tenancy is for a fixed term, the end of the term.

If the tenant does not move out by the termination date specified in the notice, the landlord can apply to the Tribunal for an eviction order.

(III) TERMINATION BY TENANT — NOTICE PERIODS

If the tenant wishes to terminate a tenancy at the end of the lease, the tenant may do so by giving the landlord proper notice. The length of the notice period is governed by the nature and term of the tenancy, as follows:

- Daily or weekly tenancies — at least 28 days' notice. The termination date given must be on the last day of a rental period.

- Monthly tenancies — at least 60 days' notice. The termination date must be on the last day of a rental period.
- Yearly tenancies — at least 60 days' notice. The termination date given must be on the last day of a yearly period on which the tenancy is based.
- Fixed-term tenancies — at least 60 days before the expiry date of the agreement, to be effective on that expiry date.

Note that there are special provisions in the Act dealing with notices that are to take effect at the end of February, it being a 28-day month.

A tenant may move out *at any time before the end of a lease* where the landlord and tenant agree to end the tenancy. Where such an agreement is entered into, notice of termination is not required, but the agreement should be in writing.

Security of tenure is preserved under the Act. A tenant can only be evicted by a landlord for reasons specified in the Act.

5.   *Termination by Landlord on Specific Grounds Allowed by the Act*

(1) WHERE LANDLORD REQUIRES POSSESSION FOR USE BY THE
      LANDLORD OR A SPECIFIED MEMBER OF THE LANDLORD'S
      FAMILY

Generally. The landlord has the right to obtain vacant possession from a tenant where the landlord requires possession of the premises for residential occupation by the landlord, the landlord's spouse or same-sex partner, or a child or parent of one of them. At least 60 days' notice must be given to the tenant, with the last day falling on the day a period of the tenancy ends. Where the tenant has a lease for a fixed term (*i.e.*, with a start and end date agreed to between the landlord and tenant), the termination date cannot be earlier than the end of the term of the lease.

If the tenant does not move out by the termination date specified in the notice, the landlord can apply to the Tribunal for an eviction order. Also, the tenant may move out earlier than the termination date, provided that they give at least ten days' notice in writing to the landlord.

Where there is a Prospective Purchaser of the Residential Complex. The Act expressly limits the circumstances in which a landlord may give notice of termination to a tenant on behalf of a prospective purchaser.

If the residential complex contains three or fewer residential units, the landlord may give notice to the tenant on behalf of the purchaser of the residential complex, subject to the following stipulations:

- the landlord must have entered into an agreement of purchase and sale; and
- the purchaser in good faith requires possession of the complex or a unit in it for their own use (or for the use of the purchaser's spouse or same-sex partner, or a child or parent of one of them).

Also, if a landlord owns a rental unit and has entered into an agreement of purchase and sale of that particular unit, the landlord may give the tenant notice terminating the tenancy on behalf of the purchaser, again provided that the purchaser in good faith requires possession of the complex or a unit in it for their own use (or for the use of the purchaser's spouse or same-sex partner, or a child or parent of one of them).

The date for termination specified in a notice given under either of these circumstances must be at least 60 days after the notice is given, and must be the day a period of the tenancy ends or, where the tenancy is for a fixed term, the end of the term.

A tenant who receives notice of termination under these provisions may, at any time before the date specified in the notice, terminate the tenancy, effective on a specified date earlier than the date set out in the landlord's notice. The date for termination specified in the tenant's notice shall be at least 10 days after the date the tenant's notice is given.

(II) WHERE LANDLORD REQUIRES VACANT POSSESSION TO PERMIT EXTENSIVE RENOVATIONS OR EEPAIRS

The landlord may give notice of termination of a tenancy if possession of a rental unit is required in order to:

- demolish it;
- convert it for a purpose other than residential premises; or
- do repairs or renovations to it that are so extensive that they require a building permit and vacant possession of the rental unit.

In these cases, the following considerations apply:

- the landlord must give the tenant at least 120 days' notice and the notice must be in the proper form;

- where the lease is for a fixed term, the termination date cannot be earlier than the end of the term of the lease;
- the tenant may move out earlier than the termination date, provided that they give at least ten days' notice in writing to the landlord; and
- if the tenant does not move out by the termination date specified in the notice, the landlord can apply to the Tribunal for an eviction order.

Note that a renovation or repair which requires the issuance of a building permit is *not* sufficient to trigger the landlord's right to terminate the tenancy, as it must also be demonstrated that vacant possession is required in order to permit the renovation/repair to proceed.

In addition, the notice of termination must inform the tenant that they have the right to re-occupy the rental unit after the repairs or renovations are complete. Where the tenant wishes to exercise this right, the tenant must notify the landlord in writing prior to vacating the unit. Where the tenant does elect to return to the unit, the tenant is entitled to be charged a rent that is no more than the rent which the landlord could have lawfully charged if there had been no interruption in the tenancy.

To summarize, if a landlord intends to demolish residential rental property, the landlord should:

- ensure that there are no written tenancy agreements with terms extending beyond the time lines established for vacant possession to permit intended demolition;
- serve Notices of Termination at least 120 days prior to the date of termination;
- obtain all regulatory approvals prior to the termination dates; and
- have the necessary funds available to compensate tenants, or make the arrangements for alternative acceptable accommodation.

(III) WHERE RENTAL UNIT IS PART OF A RESIDENTIAL COMPLEX OF FIVE OR MORE UNITS

There are specific provisions in the Act dealing with compensation to tenants in the event that the rental unit is to be demolished; however, these compensation provisions do not apply to residential complexes which contain four units or less.

For residential complexes containing five or more residential units, if a tenant elects not to return to the unit (or fails to give the landlord written notice of their intention), the landlord must pay the tenant compensation equal to three months rent or offer them another unit that is acceptable to the tenant. Compensation is not required, however, where the landlord has been ordered to carry out the renovations or repairs under the authority of the Act or any other Act.

Note that tenants who fail to give written notice of their intention to re-occupy the unit, and who receive their three months compensation, are not later able to assert their right to re-occupy the unit at their old rent. Also, where a tenant gives the landlord notice of their intention to re-occupy the unit, and where the complex contains five or more residential units, the tenant is entitled to compensation in an amount equal to the rent the tenant would have paid while the repairs were being done or three months rent, whichever is lower.

(IV)   WHERE LANDLORD REQUIRES POSSESSION FOR CONVERSION OF PROPERTY TO NON-RESIDENTIAL USE

A landlord has the right to terminate a tenancy where the landlord requires possession of the rental unit in order to convert it to use for a purpose other than rental residential premises (*i.e.*, commercial use). Points to note:

- the landlord must give the tenant at least 120 days' notice and the notice must be in the proper form.
- where the lease is for a fixed term, the termination date cannot be earlier than the end of the term of the lease.
- the tenant may move out earlier than the termination date, provided that they give at least ten days' notice in writing to the landlord.
- if the tenant does not move out by the termination date specified in the notice, the landlord can apply to the Tribunal for an eviction order.
- if the complex in which the unit is located contains five or more residential units, the landlord must compensate the tenant in an amount equivalent to three months rent, or provide alternative accommodation which is acceptable to the tenant. Where the complex contains four units or less, no ompensation is required.

It is important to note that it is only where the conversion is to a use for a purpose *other than residential premises* that the Act allows vacant possession to be obtained. Thus termination of tenancies to facilitate conversions for use as owner-occupied co-op housing or short-term emergency residential shelters would not be possible under the Act.

(V)   CONVERSION OF RESIDENTIAL PROPERTY TO CONDOMINIUM STATUS

Upon its enactment in 1998, the Act introduced new rules to be followed whenever a condominium conversion occurs. These rules protect the rights of existing tenants by prohibiting landlords from evicting tenants in order to convert a rental building to a condominium.

The principal way in which this protection is accomplished is by extending lifetime security of tenure to such tenants. Lifetime security of tenure means that a tenant can continue to live in their rental unit for their entire life even after the building becomes a condominium. Each tenant continues to be protected by the rent control provisions contained in the Act, and can only be evicted for the reasons set out in the Act.

If registration of the declaration and description under the *Condominium Act, 1998*[40] has occurred, or will occur, the tenant has the right of first refusal to purchase the condominium unit. Thus if a prospective buyer offers to purchase the unit, the tenant must be given at least 72 hours to match the offer on the same terms and conditions. If the tenant does not match the offer, they cannot be evicted as they continue to retain their lifetime security of tenure.

Note that this right to purchase *does not* apply when the offer to purchase is for more than one unit; or where the unit has previously been purchased since registration. Thus, where a tenant is in the unit at the time of conversion and someone purchases the unit, that tenant has the right of first refusal. If the tenant does not exercise their right at that time, and the unit is sold, and then subsequently resold to another purchaser, the tenant no longer has the right of first refusal. Regardless of who owns the unit, however, the tenant always retains their lifetime tenure status.

These lifetime security-of-tenure provisions extend to abrogate some of the normal termination rights of landlords. For example, provided the tenant was the tenant in the unit on the date the residential complex (or part of it) becomes subject to a registered declaration and

---

[40] S.O. 1998, c. 19.

description, the landlord may not terminate a tenancy on the grounds that he or she requires personal possession of the unit. (Note: this only applies to condominiums registered after June 17, 1998.)

Also, where a landlord has entered into an agreement of purchase and sale of a rental unit that is a proposed unit (as defined in the *Condominium Act, 1998*) the landlord may not terminate the tenancy on the grounds that the purchaser requires personal possession of the unit, as long as the tenant was the tenant on the date that the agreement of purchase and sale was entered into. However, these restrictions do not apply in certain narrow circumstances.

Thus, with a newly-created condominium complex a landlord is able to require vacant possession for purchasers over existing tenants during the first two years of its existence. This allows flexibility to a landlord who wishes to rent some or all of the units for a period of time prior to registration under the *Condominium Act, 1998*.

It should be noted that the existence of a large number of lifetime tenants in a particular development would constitute a significant barrier to a landlord's plans to convert a condominium complex and then sell the units to owner-occupiers, as the prospective owner-occupier is prevented from obtaining vacant possession of the condominium unit until such time as the residential tenant voluntarily vacates the premises.

6.   *Termination upon Death of a Tenant*

If a tenant of a rental unit dies, and there are no other tenants living in the unit, the tenancy is deemed to be terminated 30 days after the death of the tenant. The landlord may dispose of any property of the tenant which is unsafe or unhygienic immediately following the death of the tenant. However, the landlord must preserve any other property of the tenant for the 30 days until the tenancy is terminated.

The landlord is also required to afford access to the executor or administrator of the deceased's estate for the purpose of removing the tenant's property. If there is no executor or administrator, the landlord must afford access to a member of the deceased tenant's family for that purpose.

After the 30 days, the landlord may sell, use, or otherwise dispose of the deceased tenant's property. Within six months of the tenant's death, if the executor or administrator (or family member) claims property of the tenant that the landlord is using, the landlord must return it to the tenant's estate. Within six months after the tenant's death, if the administrator or executor (or family member) claims property of the tenant that the landlord has sold, the landlord must pay the proceeds of sale to the tenant's estate less any arrears of rent and reasonable expenses of moving, storing, securing, or selling the tenant's property.

Note that the landlord and the executor/administrator of a deceased tenant's estate may agree to terms other than those set out in the Act, with regard to termination of the tenancy and disposal of the tenant's property.

7.   *Early Termination*

(I)   GROUNDS FOR EARLY TERMINATION

The grounds for early termination of a tenancy which relate to the conduct of the tenant, are listed in the Act. They are as follows:

- Non-payment of rent;
- Committing an illegal act or carrying on an illegal business;
- Causing undue damage;
- Interfering with the reasonable enjoyment of the complex by the landlord or other tenants;
- Impairing the safety of other tenants; or
- Permitting overcrowding in contravention of health, safety, or housing standards required by law.

(II)   NOTICE PERIODS AND RIGHTS TO REMEDY

The Act sets out various notice periods relating to early termination. However, the Act allows a tenant to remedy most of the breaches, upon which the notice of termination is void. If the tenant commits a second breach within six months after the first notice became void, there is a different notice period.

Where the tenant has the opportunity to remedy the breach, the landlord must wait for the expiration of the period of time given to the tenant to remedy the breach.

If the breach is not remedied within the period allowed, and the tenant does not move out by the termination date specified in the notice, the landlord can apply to the Tribunal for an eviction order.

If the tenant has no opportunity to remedy the breach, the landlord can apply to the Tribunal to evict the tenant immediately after giving the notice of termination (or can wait to see if the tenant moves out by the termination date specified in the notice).

The following chart outlines the relevant notice periods and remedies available after various breaches:

Reason for Termination	First Breach: Notice Required and Tenant Remedy	Second Breach: (within six months after first Notice void): Notice Required
Non-payment of Rent (s. 61)	seven days for daily or weekly tenants 14 days for all other tenants **Remedy:** Tenant can pay arrears before notice of termination is effective.	Does Not Apply
Illegal act or business (s. 62)	20 days, except where illegal business involves production, trafficking or possession of illegal drugs (as defined by the Act), in which case notice is ten days. **No Remedy**	Does Not Apply
Misrepresentation of income, where rental unit is part of social housing (s. 62(2))	20 days for all tenants **No Remedy**	Does Not Apply
Undue damage to property (s. 63)	20 days for all tenants **Remedy:** Tenant has seven days to pay landlord reasonable costs of repair or make repairs.	14 days
Interfering with the reasonable enjoyment of other tenants or landlord (s. 64)	20 days for all tenants **Remedy:** Tenant has seven days to stop the conduct.	14 days
Impairing the safety of others (s. 65)	ten days for all tenants **No Remedy**	Does Not Apply
Permitting overcrowding contrary to law (s. 66)	20 days for all tenants **Remedy:** Tenant has seven days to reduce the number of persons occupying the unit.	14 days

The Ontario Court of Appeal decision in *Canada (Attorney General) v. Chomcy*[41] illustrates the interplay between a tenant's breach and the

---

[41]   [2002] O.J. No. 355, 48 R.P.R. (3d) 1 (C.A.).

landlord's remedies. In that case the lease — which had been prepared solely by the landlord — contained a provision stating that in the event of the destruction or partial destruction of the premises, the tenants' requirement to pay rent would cease until the premises were rebuilt. When the barn and an old house on the property began to collapse, the landlord demolished them; the tenants stopped paying rent soon after.

The landlord applied to the Ontario Rental Housing Tribunal for termination of the tenancy, and for arrears of rent. Because of the dollar-value of those arrears, the matter was transferred from the Tribunal to the Ontario courts, which had jurisdiction. In that court, the judge — who was clearly unimpressed with the landlord's lease-drafting skills and his unreasonable conduct in the dispute — found that the tenants had no obligation to pay rent.

On appeal, the landlord claimed this ruling put him in a "catch-22": the tenants owed no rent and could effectively live on the property rent-free. But under the *Tenant Protection Act, 1997*,[42] failure to pay rent was the sole basis on which the landlord could terminate the lease. In other words, according to the landlord, the sole basis for his removing the tenants had been removed by the trial judge's ruling.

Fortunately for the landlord, the Ontario Court of Appeal acknowledged that this would result in a "commercial absurdity", *i.e.*, that the destruction of an old barn, and the demolition of a frame house that was in disrepair, would allow the tenants to remain on the property rent-free forever. Accordingly the court restricted the scope of the trial judge's determination, observing that the ruling was on a narrow point and that the judge had never considered the lease as a whole.

8.   *Procedure upon Termination and Eviction*

(1)   APPLICATION TO TRIBUNAL BY LANDLORD FOR TERMINATION AND EVICTION — WHERE LANDLORD HAS GIVEN NOTICE

The eviction process commences with the landlord giving notice to the tenant of the landlord's intention to terminate the tenancy:

- Landlords must use the proper notice forms which can be obtained from any Tribunal office. (Note that for each ground of termination a different form is used.)

---

[42]   S.O. 1997, c. 24.

- Landlords must adhere to the notice periods set out in the Act.
- The application to the Tribunal must be made within 30 days of the date specified in the notice to the tenant, except in the case where the application is based on a tenant's failure to pay rent.

(II) SERVICE OF NOTICE

The landlord must serve the Notice of Termination on the tenant. The acceptable means of service are as follows:

- by handing it to tenant;
- by handing it to an apparently adult person in the rental unit;
- by faxing it to the tenant;
- by leaving it in the mailbox where mail is ordinarily delivered to the tenant;
- if there is no mailbox by leaving it where mail is ordinarily delivered to the tenant; or
- by sending it by mail to the last known address where the tenant resides or carries on business. (Note: Notice sent by mail is deemed to have been given on the *fifth* day after mailing.)

It is no longer acceptable to post the notice on the tenant's door.

(III)   APPLICATION BY LANDLORD FOR TERMINATION AND EVICTION — WHERE NO NOTICE HAS BEEN GIVEN

Even if no notice has been given to the tenant, a landlord can apply to the Tribunal for an order terminating and evicting the tenant if:

- the landlord and tenant have entered into an agreement to terminate the tenancy; or
- the tenant has given the landlord notice of termination of the tenancy.

The application cannot be made more than 30 days after the termination date specified in the agreement or notice.

A landlord can also apply to the Tribunal without notice to the tenant where he or she made a previous application to the Tribunal that resulted in an order that imposed conditions on the tenant, that stipulated that the tenancy would be terminated upon further breach, and where those conditions were not met by the tenant.

9. *The Ontario Rental Housing Tribunal*

(1) THE TRIBUNAL'S ROLE

One of the most significant features of the Act is the creation of the Ontario Rental Housing Tribunal (the "Tribunal") as the mechanism for the resolution of all disputes between landlords and tenants. The creation of this Tribunal is in keeping with the overriding purpose of the Act, which is to encourage speedy, fair and efficient justice in residential tenancy matters. Indeed, in a case called *Metropolitan Toronto Housing Authority v. Godwin*,[43] the Ontario Court of Appeal confirmed that the Act was to be interpreted liberally and in a manner that was consistent with its tenant protection focus; in this spirit the court found that the Tribunal was entitled to hear a single application on behalf of multiple parties, as a means of facilitating an expeditious resolution of several landlord/tenant disputes.

The Tribunal's jurisdiction is accordingly quite broad. Under the Act, it has jurisdiction over all landlord and tenant matters including:

- whether or not a certain unit is governed by the Act;
- rent increases;
- rent arrears;
- compensation arising from overholding tenants or subtenants;
- claims arising from misrepresentation of income by tenant, compensation for damage to the unit;
- evictions;
- maintenance of rental premises; and
- privacy issues.

Also, if the Tribunal determines that the tenant was induced by the conduct of the landlord to vacate the rental unit, the Tribunal may also order that the landlord pay compensation for any increased rent which the tenant has incurred or will incur for the one-year period after the tenant has left the rental unit; and any other reasonable moving or storage expenses incurred by the tenant.

Decisions of the Tribunal may be appealed to the Ontario Divisional Court, provided that they are questions of law alone. On such appeals, the

---

[43] [2002] O.J. No. 2514, 115 A.C.W.S. (3d) 706 (C.A.).

standard of review is one of correctness. (See the judgments in *Dollimore v. Azuria Group Inc.*[44] and *626114 Ontario Ltd. v. Tirado.*)[45]

(II) APPLICATION TO THE TRIBUNAL

- To file an application, the landlord must obtain the correct form from the Tribunal Office.
- The application may be filed in person, by mail, or by fax; and the proper application fee (if applicable) must be paid at the time of filing. Currently, the fees for all types of applications are as follows:

Items	Application Fee
Landlord applications (except as shown below)	$150
Application to Terminate a Tenancy where Tenant Failed to Meet Conditions of Settlement or Order	No charge
Application for Rent Increase Above the Guideline	$500 for first unit + $5 each other unit to a maximum of $1,000
Tenant applications (except as shown below)	$45 for first unit + $5 each other unit to a maximum of $450
Application about Tenant Rights	No charge
Tenant Application — Landlord Gave a Notice of Termination in Bad Faith	No charge
Application to Determine if the Act Applies	$45
Application about a Sublet or Assignment	$45 if filed by tenant $150 if filed by landlord
Application to Vary the Amount of a Rent Reduction	$45
Review of an Order of the Tribunal	$75
Set Aside Motions	No charge

- The landlord must file a copy of the notice of termination and certificate of service of the notice with the application.
- Upon filing the application, the landlord is given a notice of hearing.

---

[44] [2001] O.J. No. 4408 (Div. Ct.).
[45] [2005] O.J. No. 4350 (Div. Ct.).

- The landlord is responsible for serving the tenant with copies of the application and notice of hearing, at least five days before the hearing, by one of the means of service described above.

- If the tenant wishes to dispute the application, the tenant must file a dispute in writing with the Tribunal within five days of receiving the application and notice of hearing.

- The landlord must also file a certificate of service of the application and notice of hearing as soon as possible.

- If the tenant has filed a dispute the landlord must attend the hearing date ready to proceed with the case.

(III)   HEARINGS

- The hearing is a formal process where both parties are given the opportunity to tell their story, present evidence, and call witnesses to give testimony.

- It is not necessary for the landlord or tenant to have a lawyer present at the hearing as the parties can represent themselves.

- The hearing is conducted by an adjudicator who makes a decision and issues an eviction order.

- Once an order is issued it has the same effect as a writ of possession, and may be enforced in the same manner.

- The Sheriff will serve a notice to vacate and the tenant has seven days to do so.

(IV)   DEFAULT ORDERS

- For applications to terminate a tenancy or evict a person, if the tenant does not file a dispute within five days of receiving the application and notice of hearing, on the sixth day, the Tribunal will issue a default order for termination and eviction.

- For other applications that may result in a default order, the dispute must be filed by the fifth day after the day on which the notice of hearing was received.

- The default order takes effect on the later of the date of termination set out in the notice of termination, or else 11 days after the date of the default order, whichever is later.

- The Tribunal will serve the default order on the landlord and tenant.

- Exception: Where the application for eviction is based on an allegation that a tenant has impaired safety, the Tribunal must hold a hearing.

(V)   DISPUTE RESOLUTION

One of the more important powers of the Tribunal is the ability to attempt to resolve disputes between landlords and tenants by mediation, rather than by the use of the more formal hearing process.

Mediation can only be undertaken if all parties agree, in which case the Tribunal will assign a neutral mediator to attempt to settle the dispute in a manner that is acceptable to all. In fact, the mediated settlement agreed to by the parties may actually override provisions or contravene provisions of the Act, except that negotiated rent increases cannot exceed 4 per cent above the annual Guideline.

Even if the dispute cannot be settled definitively, the mediator can work with the parties to clarify the issues and discuss alternative resolutions.

If mediation is unsuccessful, the Tribunal is obliged to hold a hearing to resolve the dispute.

For certain specific disputes (such as those arising from the transfer and eviction of a tenant out of care homes), the Act provides for mandatory mediation; otherwise, participation in mediation is optional.

CHAPTER 5

DEALING WITH SPECIAL TRANSACTIONS

A. Condominiums
- i. The Basics
  1. Ownership Structure — Units and Common Elements
  2. Condominium Types
  3. Governance Structure
- ii. Creation of the Condominium as an Entity
  1. Creation By Way of Registration of Declaration and Description
  2. The Condominium Corporation
- iii. Easements and Mutual Use Agreements
  1. Easements
  2. Mutual Use Agreements
- iv. The Board and Its Obligations
  1. First Board
  2. Turn-over Meeting
  3. Developer Retaining Control
- v. Rights and Obligations of Unit-Owners
  1. Repairs and Maintenance
  2. Use of Common Elements
  3. Owner Adherence to Rules
  4. Pets
  5. Owner's Right to Sell or Assign Unit
  6. Leasing
  7. Financing

A.   CONDOMINIUMS

i.   The Basics

1.   *Ownership Structure — Units and Common Elements*

The concept of condominiums is already familiar to most people, but it is nonetheless surprising how much confusion remains over this particular model of home ownership. As such, it is worthwhile to start with the basics.

First of all, "condominium" does not refer to a style of building construction, but rather to a form of legal ownership. Essentially, it represents a system of what is known as "fee simple" ownership of individual units, together with an "undivided interest" in all the elements that are owned in common.

For these purposes, a "unit" is defined in section 1 of the *Condominium Act, 1998*[1] (the "Act") as follows:

> "unit" means a part of the property designated as a unit by the description and includes the space enclosed by its boundaries and all of the land, structures and fixtures within this space in accordance with the declaration and description.

Each owner is entitled to exclusive ownership and use of his or her unit, with that interest being registered on title. The boundaries of a unit are described in the various documents that are registered in connection with the condominium project, but practically speaking, in a typical high-rise condominium a unit will usually extend as far as the unfinished surfaces of floors, drywall and ceiling slabs, and the mid-point of a wall that separates one unit from another.

Common elements, on the other hand, are described by the Act as consisting of all the property *except* the units. In other words, anything that is not part of the units are common elements. In a typical high-rise condominium, the common elements may include the hallways between units, windows and entrance doors, the lobby, party and meeting rooms, exercise rooms, swimming pools, the parking garage and any landscaped areas.

---

[1]   S.O. 1998, c. 19, s. 1.

(It should be noted that balconies that are adjacent to units are usually common elements, rather than part of the unit itself. Unit owners are generally granted *exclusive use* of the balcony in the declaration, however.)

Common elements are not owned by the condominium corporation; rather, they are essentially owned by the unit owners *collectively*. From a legal standpoint, the unit owners have what is considered an "undivided interest" in the common elements of their condominium, and are considered "tenants in common" of the common elements. In other words, the buyer obtains a shared interest in the common areas such as the hallways between units, entrance doors, elevators, yards, the lobby, parking facilities, recreational or meeting facilities, swimming pools, and any landscaped areas. He or she — along with other owners — is free to use and enjoy these areas; they are not owned by the condominium corporation, but rather are owned by the owners collectively.

Moreover, the right to use the common elements is connected to the ownership of the unit; it cannot be separated from the ownership. For example, an owner cannot claim a reduction in his or her common expense contribution by waiving the right to use all or part of the common elements.

The owner is assessed his or her pro-rated share of common expenses; these can include the costs of maintenance, insurance, security, management fees, recreational facilities, and some of the utilities.

Note also that the nature and extent of common elements will vary widely from project to project. In some condominium developments, parking spaces are automatically assigned to owners, while in others, owners may purchase a designated space which can be sold to another owner along with the residential unit itself. (For security purposes, parking spaces usually cannot be separately sold to someone who is not an owner of a unit.) In self-contained condominium units such as townhouses, there may be few common elements.

The registered declaration will contain a schedule that sets out the proportionate share of the common elements that attach to each unit.

2. Condominium Types

(I) TYPICAL CONDOMINIUMS (RESIDENTIAL, MIXED-USE, TOWNHOUSES, DUPLEX/TRIPLEXES, ETC.)

As many real estate agents will be aware, while most people associate condominiums with high-rise buildings, the concept of the condominium can be applied to virtually any residential, commercial, industrial or mixed-use building.

For example, in residential developments, a condominium may be a low-rise structure, a townhouse, a duplex, a collection of single-family homes, or another configuration of residential accommodation.

Moreover, unit ownership may not be confined to just the structure built upon the land — the concept of the "lot-line" condominium encompasses ownership of a free-standing home including the surrounding land right up to the lot line, including parking areas, landscaping and trees. Using a single-family condominium home as an example, the lot-line condominium concept is distinct from the more common configuration, where the condominium unit consists only of the home that is constructed on the land, and not the land itself.

(II) CONDOMINIUM TITLE

Title to condominiums can be held on a freehold basis, or on a leasehold basis. A condominium declaration or description cannot be registered unless

- it states whether the condominium corporation is of the freehold or leasehold variety; and
- it creates one of these two types of condominium.

(III) FREEHOLD CONDOMINIUMS

Freehold condominiums can further be divided into the following types. It should be noted that if the condominium corporation is of the freehold variety, then the declaration that is to be registered must also state which of these four types of condominium is being created.

(a) Common elements condominium corporations

With this type of condominium, common elements are created, but the land is not divided into units. Since there are no units, each owner instead has a common interest in the corporation, and that interest attaches to the owner's parcel of land and cannot be severed from it.

Practically speaking, common elements condominium corporations are used by developers of new properties. A developer will create (1) a common elements condominium corporation that includes all the buildings, facilities, roads, services, and (2) separate parcels of tied land that are not part of the common elements condominium corporation. The developer sells buyers a freehold interest in the separate parcels of tied land together with a percentage interest in the common elements condominium corporation. The owners of the separate parcels of the tied land share the ownership, use and enjoyment of the facilities on the common elements condominium corporation, and have shared responsibility for the cost of maintaining and repairing those facilities.

In effect, in a common elements condominium, it is the individual owners rather than a local government that own the plan of subdivision, including roadways, services and facilities that are created as a condominium.

(b) Phased condominium corporations

A phased unit condominium arises where a condominium development is being built in "phases". To complete a phase, the builder must create both blocks of units and common elements, and must register an amendment to the declaration and description.

The amendment can only be registered, however, if all necessary facilities and services have been installed to allow the condominium corporation to operate independently, in the event that no subsequent phases are created.

A builder who creates a phased condominium may have additional obligations to provide certain documents at the turn-over meeting with the Board of the condominium corporation. Moreover, the Act provides special provisions in connection with the election of directors, the preparation of a reserve fund study and financial statements, and other requirements pertaining to those phased condominiums that contain residential units. See section 153 of the Act.

(c) Vacant land condominium corporations

A vacant land condominium corporation can be created where, at the time of registration, the units are not part of a building or structure, and none of the units are located above or below any other unit. In other words, as the name implies, the units consist of vacant land. (This does not mean that the land is wholly vacant — rather, the common elements can house buildings or structures.) A vacant land condominium must be a freehold condominium corporation, but cannot be a common elements corporation.

If a building or structure is planned for a unit of the vacant land condominium after the declaration and description are registered, then the declaration may contain restrictions as to the size, location, constructions and architectural standards of the building. Units in a vacant land condominium corporation cannot be sold until draft approval for the project has been obtained under the *Planning Act*.

Any building erected on either a unit or the common elements becomes part of that unit or the common elements (as the case may be). The cost of maintaining roads, facilities and services will be common expenses to be shared by the unit-owners.

In practice, the concept of vacant land condominium allows developers to sell lots as units in a condominium corporation, rather than on a plan of subdivision, meaning the buyer can buy a condominium unit that consists only of vacant land at the time of purchase. This also allows buyers and developers to reach their own agreements respecting whether it will be the developer or the buyer who builds on the land. Buildings constructed by the buyer may be subject to restrictions imposed by the developer, to ensure a consistency in the types of buildings that can be constructed on the land.

It should be noted that the *Ontario New Home Warranty Plan Act* does not apply to the common elements, buildings, structures, facilities and services in a vacant land condominium corporation.

(d) Standard condominium corporations that are not any of the above

(IV)   LEASEHOLD CONDOMINIUM CORPORATIONS

Leasehold condominiums are distinct from freehold condominiums, and as compared to other types of condominiums, are not particularly common. They may be most often seen where an institution wants to deal with property that they are not permitted to sell, or do not want to sell because they may have need for the property in the distant future.

Leasehold condominium corporations feature property that is divided into leasehold units and common elements. The owner of the property will be the landlord, and the persons leasing the units are the condominium owners.

It should be noted that the owner of a unit of a leasehold condominium can only transfer the whole leasehold interest to someone else; they cannot transfer something less than the whole.

The condominium corporation exercises all the rights and performs all the duties of the owners in connection with their leasehold interests; the owners themselves do not exercise those rights. For example, the corporation remits to the landlord, from the contributions collected from the owners, the amounts to which the landlord is entitled. The landlord can apply to a court for an order terminating all the leasehold interests if the corporation fails to remit the required amounts.

The declaration to be registered in connection with the leasehold condominium must contain, among other things, a statement setting out the term of the leasehold interests of the owners, a schedule setting out the amount of rent payable by the corporation to the landlord, and the time when the rent amounts are due.

3. *Governance Structure*

All Ontario condominium corporations are governed by the *Condominium Act, 1998.*[2] This legislation contains detailed requirements as to the structure, formation, and amalgamation of condominium corporations, as well as provisions dealing with financial requirements, maintenance responsibilities, and obligations to owners.

The management of the condominium is the responsibility of the condominium corporation, which is a separate legal entity that owns neither units (except, perhaps, for a superintendent suite or a guest suite), nor common elements itself. Rather, its sole purpose is to manage the property on behalf of the owners. In this role, the condominium corporation also administers the declaration and by-laws.

The Board of Directors, elected by the owners, is the entity responsible for decision-making in connection with the management of the property on behalf of the condominium corporation. Except

---

[2] S.O. 1998, c. 19.

perhaps for very small condominium projects, the physical property on which the units are housed is usually serviced by a property management firm, which is responsible for the day-to-day management of the building, including the provision of security, and the maintenance of the physical grounds and the common areas.

ii.   Creation of the Condominium as an Entity

1.   *Creation By Way of Registration of Declaration and Description*

A condominium comes into existence only once a "declaration" and a "description" are registered in the relevant Registry Office (either the land titles division, or the registry division, as the case may be).

Once, this registration has been completed and a condominium unit is created, it becomes a distinct piece of property that can be sold, mortgaged or leased by the owner.

(1)   THE CONTENTS OF THE DECLARATION

The declaration must contain, among other things:

- the address of the condominium corporation;
- a statement that the *Condominium Act, 1998* applies to the land;
- consent of all mortgagees who hold mortgages registered against those lands that are the subject-matter of the condominium corporation's registration application;
- a description of those common elements which are for the exclusive use of the owners of particular units; and
- a statement of the respective percentage interest proportions that the common interests and units will comprise.

The declaration may also contain other information concerning common expenses, allocation of responsibility for repair and maintenance, and any restrictions that apply to dealing with the land.

In the event that the declaration requires an amendment, the expanded requirements of the *Condominium Act, 1998* with respect to approval of the unit-owners, must be adhered to.

(II) THE CONTENTS OF THE DESCRIPTION

The description must include, among other things:

- a plan of survey showing the land and its perimeter;
- architectural and structural plans of the buildings;
- boundaries and size/shape descriptions for each unit;
- an architect's certificate, attesting that the buildings have been constructed accordingly to regulation; and
- a surveyor's certificate, confirming that the unit diagrams are substantially accurate.

Once a condominium comes into existence, the land described in the description is divided into:

- units, and
- common elements

in accord with the divisions set out in the description, and is governed by the provisions of the *Condominium Act, 1998*. A description can be amended in the same way as a declaration.

2. *The Condominium Corporation*

Most people are familiar with the concept of the corporation, being a legally-created entity or body that has certain rights and duties. However, it is less widely understood that not all corporations have shareholders; some corporations, of the non-profit variety, have "members" instead. A condominium corporation falls into this latter class of corporation, with its membership being constituted of the owners of the units.

The condominium corporation is a concept designed to facilitate property ownership. It is a legal entity whose primary purpose is to manage the condominium property and the affairs of the corporation itself, subject to the provisions of the *Condominium Act, 1998*, the condominium declaration, by-laws and rules.

Among other things, the *Condominium Act, 1998* sets out the various standards that the condominium corporation must adhere to in connection with procedures, record-keeping and conduct of the owners' and Board of Directors' meetings.

(I) SOURCE OF CORPORATION'S OBLIGATIONS

The condominium corporation finds its guidance, responsibilities and direction in various documents. In particular, the declaration, described above, is the guiding document of the condominium corporation, outlining how the ownership is divided within the corporation. The by-laws enacted by the corporation deal with how the corporation will be organized, matters affecting the Board of Directors, conduct of meetings, collection of common expenses, occupancy standards, and so on. The rules, on the other hand, deal with the day-to-day living conditions and obligations of the owners.

(II) MANAGING AFFAIRS AND RECORD-KEEPING

Pursuant to the Act's provisions, the corporation has certain defined functions and goals, mainly the general duty to control, manage and administer the property and assets of the corporation on behalf of the owners.

More particularly, it has certain responsibilities in connection with the managing of its affairs and related record-keeping. For example, the corporation is required to keep adequate records, including financial records, minute books, and copies of the declaration, required reports, and agreements. Financial records in particular must be kept for at least six years from the end of the last fiscal period to which they relate.

Upon written request and with reasonable notice, an owner can ask to examine certain records of the corporation such as financial statements, banking information, *etc.* The exceptions to this rule include any records relating to: (1) actual or pending litigation involving the corporation, (2) specific units or owners, or (3) employees of the corporation — except for contracts of employment between any employees and the corporation. Moreover, the owner's request to see the records must be made for a purpose reasonably related to the purposes of the Act.

If the corporation refuses to allow such an examination, it may be liable to a $500 penalty payable to that owner. The corporation may also be required to provide copies of those records, provided the person requesting them pays a reasonable copying fee for them.

(III)   MANAGEMENT OF THE BUILDING

The condominium corporation's fundamental role is to represent the interests of owners, and — through the Board of Directors — to manage the corporation's affairs.

This includes the management of the physical condominium building and the surrounding grounds. In some cases, the condominium corporation may self-manage the operations of the condominium, directly hiring various contractors to undertake needed maintenance and repairs. More commonly, however, the condominium corporation will hire a property management firm to oversee day-to-day management. These types of firms are usually hired to collect monthly common expense fees, clean common areas, maintain hot water heating and air conditioning systems, and to remove snow and garbage.

As was alluded to earlier, the *Condominium Act, 1998* divides repair and maintenance responsibilities between the condominium corporation and the owners. Note, however, that the Act distinguishes between *repair* obligations and *maintenance* obligations — maintenance covers work required because of normal wear and tear; repairs are of a more fundamental nature. Accordingly, the Act dictates that the corporation is responsible for both repair and maintenance of common elements, but only responsible for repair of units. The responsibility for maintenance of units falls to the individual owners. The corporation also has a legislated responsibility to repair both the units and the common elements after certain types of damage have occurred.

(To a limited extent, this allocation of responsibilities between condominium corporation and owner can be changed by declaration. Also, there are different obligations respecting (1) common elements for which the owner has exclusive use; and (2) responsibility for repair of improvements made to a unit.)

(IV)   FINANCIAL MANAGEMENT

The financial management of the condominium corporation is governed by strict rules that are embodied in the *Condominium Act, 1998*.

In particular, the Act requires the condominium corporation to establish and maintain one or more "reserve funds", designed to cover the cost of major repairs and/or replacement of the common elements and assets. The reserve fund represents the amount reasonably expected to provide sufficient funding for these purposes, taking into consideration the expected repair and replacement costs, as well as the life expectancy of the common elements and assets. The fund must be held in an account in the corporation's name, with a chartered bank, trust or loan company, or with an authorized credit union.

In order to determine the reserve fund amount, the Act and its regulations require the condominium corporation to commission a "reserve fund study" within a specific period of time and on a regular basis. The Board may charge the costs of conducting the study to the reserve fund.

The study must be "comprehensive", meaning that it must contain both a physical and financial analysis. The physical analysis may include an inventory and assessment of common element components, the date they were acquired, their age, life expectancy, and the anticipated cost to replace them. The financial aspect of analysis includes the status of the reserve fund at the date of the study, estimated interest, future replacement and repair costs, and any recommended increases in the previous year's contribution to the fund.

Once the reserve fund study is complete, the Act also imposes obligations in connection with the time by which the reserve fund itself must be adequately funded. The corporation collects contributions to the reserve fund from the owners, as part of their contributions to the common expenses; any interest or other income earned from the investment of money in the reserve fund (which is also governed by the Act) remains part of the fund.

Until the study is completed, however, the contributions to the reserve fund will be either 10 per cent of the total for common expense contributions, or 10 per cent of the amount needed to fund major repair and replacement of common elements and assets, whichever is greater.

The financial aspect of analysis includes the status of the reserve fund at the date of the study, estimated interest to be earned and future replacement and repair costs based on the predicted inflation rate, and any recommended increases in the previous year's contribution to the fund. Within 120 days of receiving the study, the corporation must propose a plan, which sets out the expected budgeted amount that needs to be contributed to the reserve fund. Within 15 days of proposing the plan, the corporation must deliver a summary of the study and the proposed plan to the unit-owners, and must implement the funding plan within 30 days after that.

The corporation must also conduct periodic studies to determine whether the reserve fund will be adequate to cover the anticipated costs of major repair and replacement.

The reserve fund account must be held with a chartered bank, trust or loan company, authorized credit union. The accounts must be held in the name of the corporation.

The Board may invest all or part of the money in the reserve fund in "eligible securities" (specifically bonds, debentures, guaranteed investment certificates, deposit receipts, deposit notes, certificates of deposit, term deposits or similar) provided they are:

- registered in the name of the corporation, or
- held in a segregated account, in the corporation's name, by a member of the Canadian Investment Dealer's Association and insured by the Canadian Investor Protection Fund.

However, before investing any of the reserve funds, the Board must first develop an investment plan based on the anticipated cash requirements of the reserve fund, based on the most recent reserve fund study.

In addition to setting up and administering the reserve fund, condominium corporations must also prepare Audited Financial Statements on a yearly basis, and must issue copies of them to all owners. Reserve fund studies must be updated at least every three years, alternating those update portions that require site inspections (*i.e.*, a visual inspection) and those that do not. It should be noted that the Act prohibits certain specified people — namely those who have an interest in the corporation or are related to directors — from conducting the reserve fund study. Also, no auditors need be appointed if the corporation consists of fewer than 25 units, and as of the date of the turn-over meeting, all the owners consent in writing to dispense with the audit until the next annual general meeting.

Note that the financial affairs of a condominium corporation are usually managed by a professional management company, dedicated to dealing with day-to-day financial arrangements.

iii.   Easements and Mutual Use Agreements

1.   Easements

"Easements" are the right to use or enjoy land owned by someone else, for a specific purpose.

The *Condominium Act, 1998* expressly provides that each unit (and unit owner) must tolerate a number of easements that are for the benefit of the condominium as a whole and the unit owners collectively. These easements are in addition to those common-law easements and rights of way that may arise legally over time.

The easements that are specifically provided for in the *Condominium Act, 1998* include:

- easements to provide service through the common elements or any unit;
- an easement for support by all buildings and structures necessary for providing support to the unit (*e.g.*, a particular unit will have an easement in connection with those walls, ceiling and floors of adjacent units that provide it support); and
- if one corporation is entitled to use the service or facility in common with another corporation, an easement for access to/maintenance of a service or facility that exists on the land of that other corporation.

Likewise, the common elements are also subject to certain easements:

- an easement for the provision of a service through a unit or through a part of the common elements of which an owner has exclusive use; and
- an easement for support by all units necessary for providing support.

(Note that the *Condominium Act, 1998*[3] provides for special provisions dealing with easements that are deemed to be created in the case of phased condominiums. See section 151 of the Act.)

---

[3]   S.O. 1998, c. 19.

2.   *Mutual Use Agreements*

A condominium corporation may also enter what are called "mutual-use agreements", usually with one or more other corporations as a means of managing shared facilities. A ready example is found in condominiums with underground parking, where there is a common ramp or driveway into the parking area, or in condominiums with shared recreation facilities.

These mutual-use agreements usually provide for the creation of a management committee that consists of a certain number of board members from each corporation, and usually deal with the provision of easements, sharing of costs, management and assorted other matters related to facilities, buildings and services.

Finally, a condominium corporation may enter into agreements covering the provision or upgrade of services respecting telecommunications (by wire, cable, radio or other technical system). These agreements create a necessary easement, lease or licence through the condominium corporation property to allow for the installation and updating of these services.

iv.   **The Board and Its Obligations**

The Board of Directors of a corporation is responsible for managing the corporation's affairs. An essential mechanism for fulfilling this obligation involves the passing of by-laws, which may deal with corporate administration, management of the property, assessment and collection of common expense contributions, occupancy standards, and maintenance and repair of units and common elements.

Under the Act, there must be a minimum of three Board members, but the corporation's by-laws may authorize a greater number. The term of any one Board member cannot exceed three years.

Board members must be at least 18 years old, and cannot be either an undischarged bankrupt or a mentally incompetent person. They are elected to the Board by a vote of the owners. Generally speaking, there is no requirement that a director must be a unit-owner or otherwise live in the condominium. An exception occurs where at least 15 per cent of the units of the corporation are owner-occupied on or after the time the turn-over meeting (described below) must be called; in this case, at least one position on the Board must be held by an owner of one of the owner-occupied units.

The Act contains specific provisions dealing with the conduct of Board meetings, what constitutes quorum, how to fill vacancies and conduct elections, and how the president and secretary are elected.

1. First Board

Pursuant to the provisions of the Act, within ten days after registration of the declaration and description, the condominium developer must appoint the first Board of a condominium corporation. The members of the first Board are entitled to hold office until a new Board is elected at the turn-over meeting.

The first Board must consist of at least three members, or more if the declaration provides accordingly.

The first Board must call and hold a meeting of the owners (called the "first owners' meeting") on either of the following two dates, *whichever is later*:

- the 30th day after the developer has transferred 20 per cent of the condominium units; and
- the 90th day after the developer transfers the first unit in the corporation.

(It should be noted that there is no requirement to call and hold a first owners' meeting if the developer no longer owns a majority of the units on the day set for the meeting. This is discussed further, below.)

At the first owners' meeting, the owners other than the developer are entitled to elect *two* directors to the first Board.

2. Turn-over Meeting

The first Board must call a meeting to elect a new Board within 21 days after the developer ceases to be a registered owner of a majority of the units. The meeting itself must be held within 21 days of being called.

At this meeting, the developer turns over various records to the Board, including:

- the condominium corporation's seal and minute book;
- a copy of the registered declaration;
- a copy of the registered by-laws, current rules, and minutes of owners' and Board meetings;
- copies of all agreements entered into by the corporation (*e.g.*, management contracts, deeds, leases, licences and easements), plus copies of insurance polices.

Moreover, within 30 days of the turn-over meeting, the developer must also deliver certain other documents, including:

- any existing warranties for equipment, fixtures and chattels that are part of the units;
- the as-built architectural and structural plans, drawings and specifications;
- existing plans for underground site services, landscaping, and telecommunication services;
- proof of enrolment in the *Ontario New Home Warranties Plan Act* (if applicable);
- copies of any final reports or inspections pertaining to the common elements;
- a table setting out whether the owners or the corporation are responsible for certain repairs and maintenance;
- a schedule describing what constitutes "standard units";
- financial records and banking documentation of the corporation from the date of registration;
- a copy of the reserve fund study (if available); and
- a copy of the most recent disclosure statement.

Finally, within 60 days after the turn-over meeting, the developer must deliver audited financial statements to the Board, current to the last day of the month in which the meeting is held.

If the developer fails to do any of these things, the Board may apply to the court to compel the developer to do so.

3.   *Developer Retaining Control*

It is not uncommon for developers to retain ownership of at least some of the units in a condominium, while selling the majority to unit buyers. It is important to note that the extent to which the developer retains unit ownership may constrain the powers of the subsequent Board of Directors.

For example, if a developer has retained title to *any* of the units, the condominium corporation is not permitted to amend the declaration for a period of three years following registration, unless the developer consents in writing.

Further, if the turn-over meeting is held at a time when the developer still owns a *majority* of the units, then the elected Board might not, in fact, consist largely of members chosen by the new unit-owners but rather of members chosen by the developer. While this happens only infrequently since most developers refrain from voting in such cases (thereby relinquishing control of the Board after the turn-over meeting), in some cases it may be prudent for a developer to retain control for the time being. For example:

- By retaining Board control, the developer can stall the corporation's right to terminate or enter into certain management agreements, as provided for in the Act.
- The developer may manipulate unit-owners' perceptions as to anticipated common expenses. By staying in control of the Board and delaying necessary repairs and maintenance, the developer can minimize the corporation's expenses during the first year after registration. This becomes relevant in light of the developer's obligation to provide unit buyers with "disclosure statements", which include a budget statement covering that same one-year period.

It should be noted that if a Board was elected at a time when the developer owned a majority of the units, the Act provides for the creation of at least one owner-occupied Board position in certain circumstances. In particular, an owner-occupied Board position is created if, at the time the Board is required to call a turn-over meeting, at least 15 per cent of the the condominium corporation's units are owner-occupied. At the first and any subsequent elections, only the owners of these owner-occupied units have the right to elect the Director for this owner-occupied Board position.

v.   Rights and Obligations of Unit-Owners

1.   *Repairs and Maintenance*

The *Condominium Act, 1998* expressly delegates certain maintenance and repair responsibilities to the owner in general terms, but the condominium's governing documentation will set out the owner's obligations in detail. Generally speaking, the unit-owner has an obligation to *maintain* his or her unit in order to remedy the result of normal wear and tear; and the condominium corporation has the obligation to *repair* the units.

Maintenance encompasses work that is required as a result of normal wear and tear, while repairs are usually of a more fundamental nature. Generally speaking, the breakdown of responsibilities is set out in the Act as follows:

- the condominium corporation is responsible for repairing both the units and the common elements;
- the condominium corporation is responsible for maintaining the common elements; and
- the unit-owners are responsible for maintaining the units.

However, the responsibility for these repair/maintenance obligations can be changed by way of the declaration, with one exception: The corporation's responsibility for repairing common elements (except those that are exclusive use common elements) cannot be divested to the unit-owner.

It should also be noted that notwithstanding the unit-owner's obligation to maintain his or her unit, the condominium corporation is obliged to repair both the units and common elements after certain damage, again except for common elements of which the owner has exclusive use. (Unit-owners are generally obliged to maintain these exclusive use areas.)

The condominium corporation's obligation to repair after damage does not extend, however, to repair of *improvements* made to a unit. In this regard, the Act allows for a "standard unit" to be defined by the condominium corporation (normally through the enactment of a by-law). This designation of a standard unit will facilitate in determining which repair obligations fall to the unit-owners and which ones fall to the condominium corporation, since enhancement or addition to the standard unit will be considered an improvement.

If an owner does not carry out maintenance or repair within a reasonable time, then the condominium corporation becomes entitled to do so. (However, note the use of the word *entitled*; the condominium is under no *obligation*, unless the situation presents a potential risk of damages to the property, or else injury to a person.)

Moreover, after giving reasonable notice to the owner, the condominium corporation can authorize a maintenance or repair person to enter a unit or exclusive-use portion of the common elements in order to perform the needed work. The cost of doing the work will be added to the individual owner's common expenses.

Also, and subject to certain conditions detailed in the Act, the unit-owner may also make additions, alterations or improvements to the common elements, provided that they have been approved by the Board.

2.   *Use of Common Elements*

An owner is entitled to make reasonable use of the common elements, subject to the by-law and rules of the corporation, plus its declaration. However, this is subject to a prohibition against activities that are likely to damage the property or cause injury to someone.

The Act also allows unit-owners to make a change to common elements, subject to certain specified prerequisites that include:

- obtaining the approval of the Board;
- entering into an agreement with the corporation with respect to the cost; and
- the condominium corporation giving adequate notice to the unit-owners.

If the proposed change by the owner involves only his or her exclusive use common elements, then these steps need not be followed, provided the Board is satisfied that the proposed change will not (among other things):

- contravene the by-laws, declaration, rules or regulations of the corporation;
- adversely affect other units;
- give rise to expense on the corporation's behalf; and
- detract from the building's appearance.

3.   *Owner Adherence to Rules*

Notwithstanding this relative freedom to deal with the property, in other respects the owner of a condominium unit remains subject to the declaration, by-laws and rules of the condominium corporation, which may cover such things as making improvements to the unit, restrictions on pet ownership, leasing of the unit, and other similar matters.

In particular, the *Condominium Act, 1998* specifically authorizes the Board of Directors to make rules that:

- promote the safety, security or welfare of the owners and of the property and assets of the corporation; or
- prevent unreasonable interference with the use and enjoyment of the common elements, the units, or the assets of the corporation.

In practice, this may translate into many different things. For example, a condominium corporation may have restrictions on how many occupants may live in each unit, restrictions on pets or noise, or rules relating to parking or to when amenities may be used.

But no matter what their scope, the rules must be reasonable, consistent with the *Condominium Act, 1998*, and consistent with the declaration and the by-laws. Any rules promulgated by the condominium corporation will be enforced in the same manner as by-laws.

(Note that there are a few procedural requirements in connection with the implementation of rules; there is no need for them to be registered, but they become effective once the unit-owners have had 30 days' notice of their implementation. Also, if the unit-owners request a meeting to challenge them, then the rules only become effective once the owners approve them at that meeting. Finally, once rules become effective, the owners may amend or repeal them, at a meeting that has been called for that specific purpose.)

4.   *Pets*

Condominium corporations are entitled to insert a "no pets" clause into the declaration, and to enforce a reasonable "no pets" rule among unit-owners. However, according to a recent Ontario court decision,[4] these

---

[4]   *215 Glenridge Ave. Ltd. Partnership v. Waddington*, [2005] O.J. No. 665, 137 A.C.W.S. (3d) 643 (S.C.J.).

types of clauses and rules must relate to protecting the safety, security or welfare of unit-owners and the property/assets of the corporation; otherwise, they could be unenforceable.

Moreover, a "no pets" clause in the declaration may be changed if the owners of at least 80 per cent of the units have consented in writing, and provided certain other stipulations respecting changes to the declaration have also been met.

Incidentally, the Act also specifies that when marketing to prospective buyers, the developer must provide a disclosure statement with a table of contents indicating whether it contains any restrictions on pets.

5.   *Owner's Right to Sell or Assign Unit*

Because an owner of a condominium unit obtains true ownership of that unit, he or she is free to sell or assign that interest at will, and without restriction.

(However, as a practical matter, any subsequent buyer will naturally be obliged to conform with and be bound by any rules or by-laws of the condominium corporation. These types of obligations are discussed further, below.)

6.   *Leasing*

An owner can freely lease his or her unit to tenants, subject to: (1) the usual law governing tenancies, which in Ontario is the *Tenant Protection Act, 1997*;[5] (2) the relevant rules and provisions set out in the *Condominium Act, 1998*;[6] and (3) the declarations and rules of the condominium corporation.

If there are conditions or restrictions on a unit-owner's right to lease his or her unit, they must appear in the declaration that is registered for the condominium, and not in the by-laws or the rules. A declaration cannot, however, prohibit a unit-owner from leasing his or her unit entirely, since the right to lease is considered to be a fundamental right of ownership.

---

[5]   S.O. 1997, c. 24.
[6]   S.O. 1998, c. 19.

(In this regard, there is some support for the right of condominium corporations to prohibit very *short-term* leases, which form the basis of executive or hotel-style rental arrangements. Although most condominium declarations contain provisions prohibiting use for "commercial purposes" and insisting on use as "private single-family residences" only, some Ontario courts have found this wording to be inadequate. Instead, the condominium declaration should contain a clearly-worded prohibition against this type of short-term lease, or at the very least, there should be an expressly-worded rule to that effect.)

In any event, a unit-owner who wishes to lease out his or her unit must, within 30 days of entering into the lease with a tenant:

- give the tenant a copy of the declaration, by-law and rules;
- notify the condominium corporation that the unit is leased;
- give the condominium corporation a copy of the lease; and
- provide the corporation with the tenant's name.

The corporation is obliged to keep a record of such lease notices; for this reason it must also be advised in writing when the tenancy is terminated. Also, most declarations will also require the unit-owner to provide the corporation with a copy of the lease itself.

Under the Act, tenants are subject to the same duties as the owners from whom they are leasing. In fact, unit-owners must take all reasonable steps to ensure that their tenants comply with the relevant rules and duties. Tenants who fail to comply may be ordered to do so by a court, and may have their lease terminated. While there is no provision in the Act requiring tenants to sign an acknowledgment agreeing to be bound by the declaration and by the rules of the condominium corporation, such a requirement is usually contained in the condominium's declaration and/or by-laws. Likewise, the condominium rules may require that certain information be collected from the prospective tenant, that there be an inspection of the unit prior to the tenant's occupancy, and that non-residential uses, partitioning of units, and structural alterations by the tenant are all prohibited.

In addition to these constraints, a tenant who leases a condominium unit is also subject to the provisions of the *Tenant Protection Act, 1997* (the "*TPA*"), which governs all residential tenancies in Ontario. The *TPA* sets out the rights, remedies and obligations of both the unit-owner/landlord and the tenant, including the right to have any disputes heard by the Ontario Rental Housing Tribunal. It is worth noting that for most purposes, the unit-owner is considered the "landlord" under the

TPA, and it is this individual, not the condominium corporation, that has the right to bring the tenant before that Tribunal in the event of a dispute.

It is worth noting that such rental arrangements effectively forge a three-way relationship between the unit-owner/landlord, the tenant, and the condominium corporation: for example, if the tenant looks to the landlord for certain repairs or maintenance, for example, the landlord/unit-owner must pursue the condominium corporation to have those repairs effected. On the other hand, if an owner of a leased unit is in arrears in paying common expenses, the condominium corporation can require the *tenant* to pay his or her rental fees to the corporation directly, and those amounts will be credited against the unit-owner's common expense arrears.

This being the case, a unit-owner should not enter into lease agreements with a tenant lightly; he or she must first fully understand the various ramifications of introducing a third party tenant into the mix.

7.   *Financing*

The owner of a condominium is at significant liberty to deal with his or her unit. For example, the owner can arrange for financing without needing to obtain the consent of the condominium corporation, and therefore can negotiate his or her terms individually. As an added advantage, such financing for buyers is generally readily available, since lenders can register their mortgage security directly against the title to the unit that is being purchased.

8.   *Owners' Meetings*

The Act contains extensive provisions dealing with the timing, conduct, and procedure of owners' meetings. For example, there are requirements in connection with the holding of Annual General Meetings, as well as meetings that have been requisitioned by at least 15 per cent of the owners.

There are also detailed requirements in the Act respecting the giving of notice of meetings, what constitutes a quorum, and voting, proxies and advance polling.

9.   *How Owner's Share of Common Expenses is Calculated*

Common expenses are apportioned according to the size of the owner's unit, as a percentage of the total size of the units in the condominium corporation. In other words, owners with larger units will be responsible for a proportionately larger share of the common expenses.

The fees collected from all owners in connection with common expenses are then used by the Board of Directors to provide for the operation, care, upkeep, maintenance, replacement, and improvement of the common elements.

10.   *Owner's Status and Participation in Management*

The condominium corporation does not issue shares; instead, the owner becomes a "member" of the condominium corporation and is entitled to vote at the Annual General Meeting of the corporation. Generally speaking, the owner of each unit will be accorded one vote.

The owner can also participate in management decisions by becoming a member of the Board of Directors, and/or by being involved in one or more committees.

11.   *Other Responsibilities of the Owners*

- Land transfer tax is payable on the purchase of a condominium unit just as it would be payable on any freehold conveyance: on registration, the buyer must pay the Land Transfer Tax ("LTT") on the sale price.
- The buyer receives a separate realty tax assessment for his or her condominium unit.

vi.   **Lien Rights**

The Act features significant enhancements to the lien rights that may be imposed by the condominium corporation against defaulting unit-owners. The legislation allows for a properly-registered certificate of lien to take priority over every other prior registered and unregistered encumbrance over the property.

The lien can cover arrears of common fees, interest, reasonable legal costs and reasonable expenses incurred by the corporation for the collection (or attempted collection) of the outstanding amount. Such a lien will take priority over any prior encumbrance, which is defined by the Act as a claim that secures payment of money or the performance of any other obligation. It includes a mortgage or a lien, as well as a charge under the *Land Titles Act.*[7]

However, the lien's priority over other encumbrances will not arise unless certain requirements are met. First of all, the certificate of lien must have been registered within three months of the date of the owner's first default. Also, written notice of the intended lien must be given to those persons who have prior encumbrances registered on the property on or before the date that certificate of lien is registered. This notice must be delivered by personal service or sent by registered, pre-paid mail to the encumbrancer's last known address. The Act contains special provisions to deal with reviving the priority of liens that have been registered without giving proper notice to the registered encumbrancers.

Note that there are a few exceptions to the priority status — the priority enjoyed by these certificates of lien will not arise:

- Against claims for taxes, charges, rates or assessments levied under the *Municipal Act, 2001,*[8] *Local Improvement Act,*[9] *Education Act*[10] and specific other legislation;

- Against other claims of the Crown, except those arising under a mortgage; or

- Against any other prescribed claims or lien. (Note: no additional types have been legislatively enacted yet.)

It should also be noted that, because the condominium corporation's lien has priority over the mortgage, the mortgagee of the defaulting unit-owner's property usually has an interest in paying the outstanding amount on the defaulting owner's behalf. In fact, the Act has special provisions to deal with this situation, and provides that the mortgagee can request from the condominium corporation, free of charge, a written statement setting out the common fees allocated to the unit and any outstanding amount in connection with common fees and collection costs. Further, the Act deems the defaulting unit-owner to be in default under the mortgage for failure to

---

[7] R.S.O. 1990, c. L.5.

[8] S.O. 2001, c. 25.

[9] R.S.O. 1990, c. L.26 [repealed by S.O. 2001, c. 25, s. 484(2)].

[10] R.S.O. 1990, c. E.2.

pay common fees, thus triggering the mortgagee's right to add the amount paid to cover arrears to the mortgage amount, at the interest rate specified in the mortgage.

The defaulting unit-owner must be given at least ten days' notice that the certificate of lien is about to be registered. If the owner or registered encumbrancer do not discharge the lien, the corporation has the right to enforce it in the same manner as a mortgage would be enforced — *i.e.*, foreclosure, or power of sale.

If the lien amount has been paid, then the condominium corporation must register a discharge of lien, and provide full particulars of the discharge to the owner.

vii.   Mediation and Arbitration

The Act provides that disagreements between unit-owners and the condominium corporation in connection with the declaration, by-laws or rules are to be subject to first mediation, and then arbitration. It does not, however, specify a procedure for mediation; it allows the condominium corporation itself to establish its own process. This is usually accomplished by enacting a by-law.

Arbitrations, on the other hand, are mandated by the Act to be governed by the provisions of the *Arbitrations Act, 1991.*[11]

viii.   Buying a Condominium from a Developer

1.   Practical Considerations

Potential buyers who are interested in purchasing a condominium unit should inform themselves in advance as to the key concepts involved in condominiums. Real estate agents representing such potential buyers should recommend that the buyer consider making the necessary inquiries in order to determine the following:

- the contents of the declaration, by-laws and rules, and the corporation's budget;

---

[11]   S.O. 1991, c. 17.

- whether parking spaces are exclusive-use common elements, or whether they are themselves units subject to separate ownership;
- the amount of common expenses and what those expenses cover, in terms of services (*e.g.*, legal fees, landscaping/snow removal services, *etc.*); and
- whether there are any restrictions on pet ownership, leasing, or obligations in connection with lawn maintenance or snow clearance.

In addition to these items, real estate agents should also recommend that the potential buyer speak to a lawyer within the ten-day cooling-off period allowed for by the Act (which is discussed below).

2. *Buying a Yet-To-Be-Constructed Unit*

If a builder has entered into an agreement of purchase and sale of a proposed unit, the builder must take all reasonable steps to complete the building as required by the agreement and to register the required documents. A developer cannot rely on his or her failure to register a declaration or description as a means of avoiding or terminating a purchase agreement, unless the buyers or a court agree.

A developer may want to construct two or more condominium buildings on a site in successive phases, *i.e.*, by completing construction and selling units in that building first, before constructing and selling units in the second or subsequent phases.

In contrast to the previous version of the Act, which required each of the buildings to be registered as separate condominium corporations, the Act allows for the construction of "phased" condominiums which are all part of the same condominium corporation. Subsequent phases can be registered under the umbrella of a single condominium corporation by way of the amalgamation provisions in the Act, which are described below.

3. *Cooling-off Period*

A potential unit buyer may terminate a purchase agreement by giving the developer written notice of rescission within the following dates, *whichever is later*:

- Within ten days of the buyer receiving the disclosure statement from the developer; or
- Within ten days of the buyer receiving a copy of the agreement of purchase and sale that has been executed by both the developer and the buyer.

The buyer need not provide any reason for terminating the agreement within those ten days.

If the agreement has been validly terminated, the developer must refund all deposit moneys promptly, and may not deduct any interest or penalty from the deposit amount.

4.   *Deposits, Interest and Interim Occupancy*

Deposits — All money received by the developer from potential buyers (and all interest earned on that money) must be held in trust. The trustee can be the developer's lawyer or certain other agents, and the money must be deposited in a separate bank account at a chartered bank, trust company or similar institution. The funds will be subject to security measures, usually insurance or a deposit receipt.

The buyer's money that is held in trust will be credited against the purchase price of the unit if a purchase agreement is accepted or completed. The developer will be entitled to receive the money when title to the unit is transferred to the buyer.

Interest — The buyer is entitled to interest on all amounts paid to the developer from the date of payment until the date that the unit is available for occupancy. Pursuant to the regulations under the Act, the interest rate is set at 2 per cent per annum below the Bank of Canada's bank rate at the end of March and September of each year.

Interim occupancy — An Agreement of Purchase and Sale may allow for interim occupancy of a proposed unit, which means occupancy of a proposed unit before the buyer receives a deed to the unit that is in registerable form.

On assuming interim occupancy of the proposed unit, a buyer may elect to pay the balance of the purchase price in full. However, the builder is entitled to charge the buyer a *monthly occupancy fee*, which takes into account:

- interest on any unpaid amounts (the prescribed rate of interest being defined by the regulations as the rate of interest that the

Bank of Canada has most recently reported as the chartered bank administered rate for a conventional one-year mortgage as of the first of the month in which the buyer assumes interim occupancy of a proposed unit or is required to do so under the agreement of purchase and sale),

- an amount reasonably estimated to cover monthly municipal taxes for the unit, and
- the projected monthly common expenses for the unit.

If the builder charges the unit-owner an interim occupancy fee, then the builder has a corresponding obligation to maintain the property and unit in the same manner as immediately after the registration.

The Act expressly gives unit-owners special rights during the interim occupancy of their units, and provides that these rights supersede the provisions of the *Tenant Protection Act, 1997*.[12] In particular, if a buyer assumes interim occupancy of a proposed unit, the developer:

- must provide those services that the corporation will have a duty to provide to owners after the registration of the declaration and description that creates the unit;
- must repair and maintain the proposed property and the proposed unit in the same manner as the corporation will have a duty to repair after damage and maintain after the registration of the declaration and description that creates the unit;
- has the same right of entry that the corporation will have after the registration of the declaration and description that creates the unit;
- may withhold consent to the buyer's assignment to a third party of the right to occupy the proposed unit, and/or may withhold consent to the buyer listing the property for resale prior to the final transfer of the unit (*i.e.*, the deed registration date);
- may charge a reasonable fee for consenting to an assignment of the right to occupy the proposed unit; and
- shall, within 30 days of the registration of the declaration and description that creates the unit, notify the buyer in writing of the date and instrument numbers of the registration, unless within that time the buyer receives a deed to the unit that is in registerable form.

---

[12]   S.O. 1997, c. 24.

5.   *Disclosure Statement*

Contents of disclosure statement — As most real estate agents who deal in condominiums are aware, an agreement to purchase a condominium unit from a developer is not binding on the buyer until he or she receives a current "disclosure statement" from the developer.

Under the Act, this disclosure statement must contain statements indicating (among other things):

- whether the condominium is leasehold or freehold (and if freehold, what type);
- the address of the developer and the address of the condominium;
- a general description of the property;
- if the property is subject to the *Ontario New Home Warranties Plan Act*,[13] whether the units and common elements have already been enrolled in the Plan as of the date the buyer receives the disclosure statement, or are to be enrolled at a later date;
- whether the building has been converted from a previous use; and
- the portion of the units that the developer intends to lease.

Additional disclosure statement requirements are provided for in the Act regulations, and include:

- Copies of sections 73 and 74 of the Act (the provisions allowing for a ten-day cooling-off period);
- Whether there is visitor parking on the property or elsewhere, plus whether visitors must pay for parking and the anticipated cost;
- Whether a part of the common elements can be used for commercial or other non-residential purposes, and whether any adjoining land is intended to be used for this purpose (to the developer's knowledge);
- A specification of major assets that the developer has indicated that it *may* provide (*i.e.*, recreational facility, meeting rooms, *etc.*), even though the developer is not required to do so; and
- Whether there are restrictions relating to pets or to the occupancy or use of units or common elements.

Insufficient disclosure statement or material change — As has been discussed above, a purchase agreement is not binding on a potential

---

[13]   R.S.O. 1990, c. O.31.

buyer until the developer delivers a disclosure statement. Because the Act does not specify what degree of inaccuracy or incompleteness will render a disclosure statement invalid, in the event of a dispute it may be up to the buyer to establish that the deficiency in the disclosure statement would have prompted a reasonable buyer to rescind within the ten-day period.

If there is a significant or "material" change in the disclosure statement, then the developer must deliver a revised disclosure statement to each buyer within a reasonable time after the material change occurs, or at the latest must take place within ten days before a deed for the unit — in registerable form — is delivered to the buyer.

A proposed buyer may choose to rescind the purchase agreement based on the material change, but must do so within ten days of the following dates, *whichever is later*:

- The date the potential buyer receives the revised disclosure statement;
- The date the buyer becomes aware of the material change (if no revised disclosure statement has been received); or
- If one of the parties has applied to a court, the date on which the court makes a determination whether a material change has taken place.

Upon a valid rescission by the buyer, the developer must refund all money received from the buyer within ten days, and may not deduct any interest or penalty from that amount.

For phased condominiums, the developer can add additional units and common elements in subsequent phases, but must deliver an amended declaration and description to the condominium for registration. At least 60 days before that registration, the developer must also deliver a copy of the disclosure statement from the previous phase, along with a statement of the difference between the proposed amendments and the previous disclosure statement. A proposed buyer who buys a unit in a phased condominium may be entitled to damages from the builder if there is a material change between the previous phase, provided the change affects the use and enjoyment of the property by that owner.

6.   *Status Certificate*

Upon request from the buyer or his or her lawyer, the condominium corporation must provide a "status certificate" — formerly called an "estoppel certificate" under the old Act — within ten days of receiving the request and the fee charged by the corporation (which the regulations under the Act provide may be up to $100 including taxes).

The status certificate must be in a prescribed format, must bear the date on which it was made, and must contain a great deal of information, including:

- a statement of the common expenses for the unit and any default in payment of the common expenses;
- a statement of any increase in the common expenses for the unit that the board has declared since the date of the corporation's budget for the current fiscal year, and the reason for the increase;
- a statement covering any assessments that the board has levied against the unit to increase the contribution to the reserve fund since the date of the corporation's budget for the current fiscal year, and the reason for the assessments;
- a statement of the address for service of the corporation;
- the names and addresses for service of the directors and officers of the corporation;
- a copy of the current declaration, by-laws and rules;
- a statement of all outstanding judgments against the corporation and the status of all legal actions to which the corporation is a party;
- a copy of the budget of the corporation for the current fiscal year, the last annual audited financial statements and the auditor's report on the statements;
- a list of all current management agreements, agreements for the provision of goods, services and facilities, and certain other agreements, plus a list of all current agreements between the corporation and another corporation or between the corporation and the owner of the unit;
- a statement whether the parties have complied with all of the listed current agreements with respect to the unit;
- a statement with respect to:
  - the most recent reserve fund study and updates to it;

- the amount in the reserve fund no earlier than at the end of a month within 90 days of the date of the status certificate; and

- current plans, if any, to increase the reserve fund under subsection 94(8) of the Act;

- a statement of those additions, alterations or improvements to the common elements, those changes in the assets of the corporation and those changes in a service of the corporation that are substantial and that the board has proposed but has not implemented, together with a statement of the purpose of them;

- a statement of the number of units for which the corporation has received notice under section 83 of the Act that the unit was leased during the fiscal year preceding the date of the status certificate;

- a certificate or memorandum of insurance for each of the current insurance policies;

- a statement of the amounts, if any, that the Act requires be added to the common expenses payable for the unit;

- all other material that the regulations made under this Act require.

In addition to the items listed above, a status certificate that covers either a leasehold condominium or a phased condominium must contain certain other items, as prescribed by special provisions of the Act.

Moreover, if a corporation fails to give a status certificate within the required time, the Act provides that it will be deemed to have given a status certificate on the day immediately after the required time has expired, stating that:

- there has been no default in the payment of common expenses for the unit;

- the board has not declared any increase in the common expenses for the unit since the date of the budget of the corporation for the current fiscal year; and

- the board has not levied any assessments against the unit since the date of the budget of the corporation for the current fiscal year to increase the contribution to the reserve fund.

Aside from these deemed statements, the Act does not set out the effect of a corporation failing to give all of the other status certificate information listed above.

The regulations under the Act provide that a condominium corporation must keep copies of the status certificates for ten years.

7.   *Amalgamation Provisions in the Act*

Condominium corporations must be of the same type in order to qualify for amalgamation; *i.e.*, two or more leasehold condominium corporations, or two or more freehold condominium corporations of the same type, may amalgamate. Common element and vacant land condominiums cannot be amalgamated.

Provided all of the necessary requirements are met, amalgamation is accomplished by registering a declaration and description amalgamating the corporations. In order to qualify for amalgamation, each amalgamating corporation must have:

- held its turn-over meeting;
- received the turn-over materials which were to be provided by the developer;
- completed a comprehensive (or updated) reserve fund study within the year prior to the owner's meeting to discuss amalgamation; and
- entered into an agreement with the other amalgamating corporation(s) dealing with the conduct of the corporation's affairs.

In addition to the stipulations above, there are certain other requirements that must be met prior to amalgamation:

- the Board of each amalgamating corporation must hold a meeting of owners to consider a declaration and description effecting the amalgamation;
- the owners of at least 90 per cent of the units of each corporation at the date of the meeting have, within 90 days of the meeting, consented in writing to the registration of the declaration and description; and
- the corporations have complied with all other requirements.

The regulations under the Act also provide for certain requirements that must be adhered to before an amalgamation can take place.

After amalgamation, the amalgamated corporations continue as one, and the units and common interests are also continued, as are leases and existing encumbrances. The Directors of the individual amalgamating corporations constitute the first Directors of the new amalgamated corporation, and hold office until the owners elect their successors (at a meeting that the first Directors must call and hold within 60 days of registration of the declaration and description).

The schedule to the amalgamating declaration must contain lists identifying units of the amalgamating corporations and what units they will become in the amalgamated corporation, and *vice versa*.

The directors of the amalgamating corporations become the first directors of the new amalgamated corporation, and hold office until the owners elect successors, which must occur within 60 days of registration. The amalgamated corporation must carry out a comprehensive reserve fund study within three years of the date upon which any of the amalgamated corporation completed its last study.

B. CO-OPERATIVES

i. The Basics

1. *Ownership Structure*

Next we will consider co-operatives, which — as compared to condominiums — are significantly further away from outright ownership, on the ownership-vs.-tenancy scale.

Essentially, co-operatives represent an attempt to satisfy the desire for home ownership through the use of a corporate vehicle. In particular, and unlike condominiums, *the buyer does not own his or her own unit*. Rather, he or she obtains shares of a private corporation which has been formed for the sole purpose of owning and managing the entire building and the land on behalf of its shareholders.

In addition to the shares, by virtue of either the shareholder's agreement, the exclusive licence agreement, or a proprietary lease, the buyer acquires a long-term, exclusive use leasehold interest in a specific suite. The owners share the use and enjoyment of common elements (*i.e.*, common areas), and are assessed a pro-rated share of the common expenses which — although technically the liability of the corporation — are apportioned amongst owners.

(Note that in a less common arrangement, the owner's shares entitle him or her to an equity ownership interest in the property, usually leading to the owner's actual purchase of the property as he or she accumulates shares over time. This is not the type of co-operative under consideration in this seminar. Also, it is important to distinguish between ownership co-operatives (sometimes known as "equity co-ops") and non-profit government-assisted housing co-operatives. This latter type of housing co-operative does not involve the purchase of shares at all; rather, the co-operative corporation's ownership in the land is made possible by provincial grants, and the residents of the co-operative become "members", not shareholders. In such non-profit co-operatives, and unlike ownership co-operatives, no member has any ownership interest in the corporation whatsoever.)

Existing co-operatives were generally intended and built as co-operatives from the outset; this is unlike co-ownerships, which are conversions from other types of ownership or rental. All in all, co-operatives usually represent a good real estate investment, since the cost to purchase the shares is generally lower than what it would cost to buy a comparable condominium unit. (Naturally, though, an owner who subsequently sells the shares will also receive less for them, than he or she would if selling a comparable condominium.)

2. *Governance Structure*

First of all, the Ontario *Condominium Act, 1998*[14] is wholly inapplicable to co-operatives. Instead, and because owners obtain shares in a corporation, the relationship between shareholders is governed in broad terms by Ontario corporate law (pursuant to the Ontario *Corporations Act*),[15] and by the rules embodied in the articles of incorporation, by-laws and rules of the particular co-operative corporation. Additional aspects of the relationship may also be governed by the occupancy licence, proprietary lease, and any shareholders' agreement that may apply to owners. The additional agreements and rules are all administered by the co-operative corporation, through its Board of Directors.

ii. **Owner's Rights and Obligations**

1. *Owner's Right to Deal with the Unit*

Selling or assigning the owner's interest — First of all, because the owner owns shares rather than an interest in the property, an owner

---

[14] S.O. 1998, c. 19.
[15] R.S.O. 1990, c. C.38.

who wants to divest him or herself of an interest in a co-operative corporation must sell the shares.

Furthermore, and unlike the significant liberty enjoyed by owners of a condominium unit, an owner of shares in a co-operative corporation is somewhat more limited in terms of his or her right to deal with those shares. More specifically, the consent of the Board of Directors of the co-operative corporation must almost always be obtained before an owner can sell his or her shares or assign the leasehold interest to someone else. This allows the Board to screen or veto who can buy into the building, in theory as a means to ensure that the new buyer is able to pay his or her share of utilities, municipal taxes, and other maintenance costs.

As a result, most agreements of purchase and sale will be conditional on obtaining approval of the Board of Directors, with the condition period usually being ten to 14 days from the date of the acceptance of the offer. (Note that in some cases, the consent of the Board may be arbitrarily or unreasonably withheld, which means that an owner's intent to sell shares to a specific new buyer could be completely frustrated. This tends to happen only rarely, however.)

Also, the sale of a unit in a co-operative is subject to the new buyer's receipt of a status certificate, which provides a glimpse as to the financial shape of the corporate entity. It also indicates whether there are any outstanding or pending payments or special assessments due to the co-operative corporation, the nature and extent of building insurance obtained, the amount of the monthly common expenses, the status of the building respecting Urea Formaldehyde Foam Insulation ("UFFI"), and whether there are any legal actions pending involving the particular unit or the co-operative corporation itself. A copy of the rules and regulations, plus the financial statements, is usually included as part of the package.

Leasing — First of all, some buildings have strict prohibitions on leasing, and in most cases the approval of the Board of Directors will be required.

Secondly, since the owner/shareholder in a co-operative corporation never actually "owns" the unit (rather, ownership remains with the co-operative corporation itself), an unusual legal issue arises for owners who decide to lease their unit to someone else.

Technically, the owner is merely a shareholder of the co-operative corporation that continues to own the unit. On the other hand, the corporation cannot actually physically "occupy" the unit itself. Because of the way the Ontario *Tenant Protection Act, 1997*[16] is worded, tenancies are defined to involve an owner *regaining the occupancy right* from the tenant after giving the required notice. With respect to co-operatives, it is technically impossible for the corporation to regain "occupancy", so strictly speaking it could be difficult for the owner/shareholder to actually obtain possession at some future date, in the event that he or she wants to regain occupation for his or her own personal use.

Owners who are contemplating leasing out their units should only do so after consulting their lawyers.

Financing — Likewise, co-operatives can give rise to certain hurdles in connection with financing. Because the co-operative structure does not involve ownership of the unit, an owner is not able to mortgage his or her specific suite. However, the owner can pledge and assign his or her shares as collateral security to a lender with the consent of the co-operative corporation (provided that the corporation has not imposed a prohibition on pledging shares as security).

2. *Owner Conduct and Maintenance Responsibilities*

The owner of shares in a co-operative corporation can be subject to an array of rules, much like in the case of condominium ownership.

Specifically, rules may be embodied in the by-laws, in the co-operative agreement, and/or in an exclusive licence, proprietary lease agreement, and/or shareholder agreement. They may cover a wide range of topics and owner conduct; they may impose restrictions on having pets, renovating, decorating, or using the property in certain ways. Essentially, the purposes behind these rules and agreements are to ensure that owners in a co-operative all share the same general "lifestyle".

One of the things that will be covered by these agreements is the owner's level of responsibility, if any, in connection with maintenance and repair. In some co-operatives, the unit owner is personally responsible for limited repairs and maintenance inside the unit, while in others, this responsibility remains with the corporation itself.

---

[16] S.O. 1997, c. 24.

3.   *How the Owner's Share of Common Expenses is Calculated*

The calculation of an owner's share of the common expenses of a co-operative is quite straightforward: each individual owner is assessed for percentage share of common expenses, based on the size of the unit in comparison to the entire building, just as in condominiums.

One noteworthy point about this ownership structure is that buildings owned by co-operative corporations receive a single tax bill that applies to the entire property. This means that all owners are jointly liable for the tax bill, and the proportion that each owner must pay is determined by the percentage interest that each owner has, in relation to the whole.

4.   *Owner Status and Participation in Management*

Upon purchasing a unit in a co-operative, each owner automatically becomes a member of the co-operative corporation. This, in turn, entitles an owner to vote at the Annual General Meeting, and to run for a position on the Board of Directors, which is elected from among owners and is responsible for the general management of the co-operative corporation.

In many co-operative corporations, members may also be able to join various volunteer committees.

5.   *Other Responsibilities of the Owner*

Because it relates to an "interest in land", the sale of shares in a co-operative corporation attracts Land Transfer Tax, calculated on the value of the shares purchased, based on the same formula as that for the purchase of any other form of real estate.

iii.   The Co-operative Corporation's Rights and Obligations

1.   *Financial Management*

As indicated above, co-operatives are not governed by the legislation that is applicable to condominiums. This means that there is no law requiring that a reserve monetary fund be set up, although in practice most co-operative agreements establish one nonetheless.

Otherwise, the requirement to report to members with annual financial reports, and the decision as to whether a co-operative is professionally managed or self-managed, will vary from co-operative to co-operative.

In many respects, co-operative corporations are run very much like any other corporation, with their governance decisions made, carried out and administered by the elected Board of Directors, but dictated by the provisions found in the by-laws, shareholder agreements, and other constating documents.

2.   *Building Management and Maintenance*

Because the co-operative corporation remains the actual owner of the building and land on which the building is situate, it remains responsible for the management of the property on behalf of the owner/shareholders. Although some co-operative corporations choose to self-manage, in many cases the day-to-day property management responsibilities are usually assigned to a property management firm, for a fee.

The maintenance and repair obligations will be governed by the co-operative agreement, a proprietary lease agreement, or shareholder's agreement entered into between the corporation and the owner. In most co-operatives, the corporation remains responsible for the majority of repairs to the unit.

iv.   What to Think about Before Buying Shares in a Co-operative Corporation

Many of the same considerations apply whether a potential buyer is interested in a condominium or a co-operative. However, buyers of shares in a co-operative tend to face their most difficult hurdle in connection with financing.

First of all, there are only a limited number of institutions willing to provide individual financing for this kind of arrangement. Secondly, even a willing lender will usually finance only up to a certain dollar and/or percentage limit, and one that is usually lower than with conventional transactions. This means that buyers must contribute a larger down payment than with other types of deals. In any event, lenders can take the security of a pledge and assignment of the purchaser's share interest in the corporation (provided that the corporation has not imposed a prohibition on pledging shares as security).

But notwithstanding these financing challenges, co-operative units are often more affordable than comparable condominium units, in recognition of the fact that the buyer must get the approval of the Board of Directors before selling the shares and/or financing their purchase, and because financing is more difficult to arrange. This means that buyers can enter the housing market at a monetary level that would not otherwise be available to them. While this may be an appealing incentive, it is still essential for potential buyers to "do their homework" about the co-operative corporation before buying. In particular, the status certificate will provide detailed information on a co-operative's financial shape.

The possibility of re-sales give rise to another issue for consideration: buyers should ascertain the specific criteria that the Board of Directors uses for giving its approval for re-sales. This is because a buyer would likely want to avoid purchasing a unit that may be subject to unreasonable or arbitrary restrictions on the subsequent re-sale of the unit.

Finally, although many co-operative corporations have their own purchase and sale agreements, for the most part these agreements do not adequately protect either the buyer or the seller. Buyers should review these agreements in detail with their sales representatives and/or lawyers to ensure that they understand all of the provisions, and any potential repercussions, that may arise from them.

Respecting the purchase and sale of units in a co-operative, the Toronto Real Estate Board has drafted a form of Agreement of Purchase and Sale aimed at these types of transactions, which goes a long way toward standardizing the protection of both buyers and sellers. However, the form still leaves room for improvement, and I would strongly recommend that the parties seek the advice of a lawyer experienced in dealing with co-ops, who will customize the form to ensure maximum protection for all parties.

C. CO-OWNERSHIPS

i. The Basics

1. Ownership Structure

Alongside condominiums and co-operative corporations, co-ownerships represent a third, unique combination of ownership rights and occupation rights.

Unlike condominiums, the buyer in a co-ownership does not own his or her specific unit. And unlike co-operatives, he or she generally does not obtain shares, either. Rather, in a co-ownership arrangement the buyer acquires an *undivided percentage ownership* in the building and the land on which it is located, and becomes what is known as an "owner in common". The buyer's interest is registered on title, and takes the form of a freehold interest, expressed as a percentage of the whole co-ownership property, for example "4.23 per cent".

In addition, by virtue of a registered co-ownership agreement, the owner then has the exclusive right to occupy a particular unit, suite, or apartment, and also has shared rights with each of the other owners with respect to the common elements of the property, and they are assessed a pro-rated share of the common expenses.

Many of the existing co-ownerships in Ontario were developed in the 1980s, and were originally built as single-owner apartment rental buildings. Since that time, there have been conversions of other buildings to the co-ownership structure, including duplexes, four-plexes, and larger buildings as well. Moreover, several co-ownership corporations have been converted to residential condominium buildings, which was achieved by making an application to amend the Official Plan.

Nonetheless, when available, co-ownerships often represent a good real estate investment, since the prices are generally lower than costs for a comparable condominium unit. On the flip side, however, owners stand to sell for less than they would for a comparable condominium, when it comes time to sell their co-ownership interest.

2. *Governance Structure*

Once again the Ontario *Condominium Act, 1998*[17] has no application to co-ownership corporations; rather, the relationship between owners is governed by private contracts, namely the articles of incorporation, by-laws, and rules of the co-ownership corporation, as well as by the co-ownership agreement and any occupancy or exclusive licence agreement.

However, and being that they are usually a form of corporation, co-ownerships are generally subject to the provisions of the Ontario *Corporations Act.*[18]

The co-ownership corporation administers the co-ownership agreement, the co-ownership by-laws, rules and regulations, and/or any private contracts with suppliers that may have been entered into by the co-ownership corporation.

ii. Owner's Rights and Obligations

1. *Owner's Right to Sell, Assign, or Finance*

Unlike the situation in co-operative corporations, in most cases an owner in a co-ownership corporation does not need the consent of the Board of Directors or of the other co-owners in order to rent, or mortgage his or her interest in the unit. This is also generally true for owners who intend to sell, although some co-ownership agreements do require the Board's consent to approve a prospective buyer.

Either way, the sale of the unit should be subject to the new buyer receiving a status certificate which identifies any outstanding or pending payments, assessments, or legal actions regarding either the specific unit, or the co-ownership corporation as a whole. It also provides information as to building insurance coverage, UFFI status, the amount of the monthly common expenses, and the identity of the Directors, whether the seller is current in his or her payments and other obligations, and whether the corporation is a party to any legal actions, among other things. A copy of the rules and regulations, plus the financial statements, is usually included as part of the package.

---

[17] S.O. 1998, c. 19.

[18] R.S.O. 1990, c. C.38.

Although many co-ownerships have their own purchase and sale agreement, buyers should review these agreements in detail with their sales representatives and/or lawyers, because these custom agreements do not always properly protect either the buyer or vendor.

It should be noted that the Toronto Real Estate Board does not currently have an Agreement of Purchase and Sale form geared toward purchases and sales involving co-ownership units. This means that the parties are responsible for safeguarding their own interests, so it is particularly important that a real estate lawyer experienced in co-ownerships be consulted to provide a form that adequately and thoroughly protects those interests.

Incidentally, the financing of co-ownerships can be very straight-forward: as with condominiums, owners are generally entitled to individually finance their interest in the unit, and the consent of the Board of Directors is not required. On the other hand, the *availability* of financing is limited, as few institutional lenders are willing to provide financing for this type of ownership model. Moreover, buyers who succeed in obtaining financing will face lending maximums (based on a maximum dollar amount, and/or on a percentage maximum, depending on the lender) and will have to supply a larger down payment. As with co-operatives, however, there is a considerable benefit, in that co-ownership units are often more affordable than comparable condominium units. On the other hand, co-ownership units tend to sell for lower prices than would be attained for similar condominium units.

2.   *Owner's Right to Lease*

Despite the lack of need for Board consent to lease, in most co-ownership corporations the renting out of the owner's co-ownership unit can be fraught with difficulties. An owner who has not occupied the unit initially may find it difficult to obtain possession for personal use after renting to a tenant. An owner should consult a lawyer before embarking on any attempts to rent out the unit.

In a similar vein, a new buyer of a unit that is occupied by an existing tenant may also have difficulty obtaining occupancy when needed. Potential purchasers in these circumstances would likewise benefit from legal advice before proceeding with the sale.

3.   *Owner Conduct and Maintenance Responsibilities*

As with condominiums and co-operatives, the conduct of an owner in a co-ownership will be governed primarily by the by-laws and rules of the co-ownership corporation and the co-ownership agreement. Again, these will cover a broad range of topics.

Among them will be the owner's obligation to effect repairs and maintenance inside the unit itself. In many co-ownerships, the corporation remains responsible for this type of work (and will usually hire a maintenance firm for these purposes, with costs being reflected in the common expenses). However, this will vary from corporation to corporation.

4.   *How the Owner's Share of Common Expenses is Calculated*

The owner is assessed his or her pro-rata share of those common expenses, in the same manner as for condominiums and co-operative owners.

As with co-operatives, co-owners receive a single tax bill that applies to the entire property. This means that all owners are jointly liable for the tax bill, and the proportion that each owner must pay is determined by the percentage interest that each owner has, in relation to the whole. Each co-owner's tax liability amount is included in the monthly common expenses payment.

5.   *Owner Status and Participation in Management*

In this form of ownership, the owner becomes a member of the co-ownership corporation. As such, the collective rights that an owner obtains will be embodied in the provisions of an occupancy agreement and/or the co-ownership agreement, by-laws and private contracts between the co-owners.

As with other forms of hybrid ownership already discussed, the owner can participate in management decisions by sitting on the Board of Directors and voting at the Annual General Meeting, and by getting involved with committees.

iii.   The Co-ownership Corporation's Rights and Obligations

1.   Management of the Building

In larger buildings, the co-ownership structure involves the participation of a co-ownership corporation, whose role is to manage the property on behalf of owners. The Board of Directors, which is elected by the owners, takes on the major decision-making responsibility for the corporation. However, day-to-day management is usually entrusted to a management company that takes care of maintenance, security, payment of accounts, landscaping, repairs, housekeeping and so on.

2.   Financial Management

The financial obligations and management requirements for co-ownership corporations are not governed by legislation, but rather are usually mandated by the specific co-ownership agreements that apply to particular projects. Some co-ownership agreements require that a reserve monetary fund be established for the ongoing maintenance of the building; others do not. Likewise, the requirement to report to members with annual financial reports, and the decision as to whether a co-ownership is professionally managed or self-managed, will vary from co-ownership to co-ownership.

In many respects, co-ownerships are simply run very much like any other corporation, with their governance decisions made, carried out, and administered by the elected Board of Directors, but dictated by the provisions found in the by-laws, co-ownership agreements, and other constating documents.

D.   SUMMARY — CONDOS, CO-OPS AND CO-OWNERSHIPS

i.   What Condos, Co-ops and Co-ownerships Have in Common

It's important to understand that, despite their differences, condominiums, co-operatives and co-ownerships all share one thing in common: they all involve a building, structure, or project that contains more than one unit.

Aside from that requirement, however, there are a wide variety of structures to which these three types of ownership can apply. For example, and despite the common misconception, condominiums are not strictly limited to high-rise buildings. Rather, they — and co-operatives and co-ownerships alike — can be high-rises, low-rises, townhouses, multiple dwellings, horizontal or vertical buildings, as well as buildings that are subject to different types of zoning (such as residential, commercial or industrial).

Secondly, and because condominiums, co-operatives and co-ownerships each represent a particular "blend" of rights, it is important to be aware of the distinction between "exclusive" rights on the one hand, and "shared" rights on the other.

"Exclusive" rights, as one would expect, represent a bundle of rights that can be exercised only by a single owner. Outright ownership in fee simple — whereby others are restricted from claiming ownership rights — is the most concrete example of exclusive rights. (However, even a mere tenant obtains the exclusive right to occupy the unit, by virtue of the tenancy agreement.)

"Shared" rights, on the other hand, mean that more than one party can assert an interest in a particular aspect of the property. An example is found in the common areas of a condominium high-rise, such as the lobby and hallway areas.

ii.   Checklist for These Kinds of Transactions

In Ontario, co-operatives and co-ownerships are a little less well known than the condominium model of ownership. As such, a prospective buyer must be careful to ask many questions.

The following is a sample list of questions that may apply to co-operatives, co-ownerships, or both:

- Is the seller conveying all of his or her allotted shares in the corporation?
- Is the seller the beneficial owner of record of those shares?
- Does the seller have good and marketable title, free of any pledge of the shares, or lien?
- Does the seller have the authority of the Board of Directors to sell the shares or assign the lease?
- What consents are needed to complete the transaction? Have they been obtained?

- Does the co-operative corporation or the seller have good title to the building?
- Has the corporation been validly incorporated, and is it in good standing?
- Have the shares been validly issued?
- Is the seller or any other shareholder/tenant in arrears for any common expenses that the owner may be responsible for?
- What are the parking and locker arrangements? Are they owned, or are owners merely entitled to exclusive use of the parking and locker facilities?
- Are there copies of the current financial statements and budgets or forecasts?
- Is the reserve fund adequate?
- Has a reserve fund study been completed, or has one been planned for?
- Is the corporation current in payment of its property taxes and utilities?
- What are the estimated common expenses?
- Is there a resident superintendent?
- What insurance arrangements does the co-operative corporation/ co-ownership corporation have in place?
- Has the co-operative corporation/co-ownership corporation set aside a reserve fund for emergencies or repairs?
- Who are the other shareholders and how many shares have been allocated to them, and what units do they occupy?
- Is the share allocation of the particular unit fair, relative to other units/suites/apartments?
- Has the buyer received copies of the status certificate, as well as copies of all major agreements and documents?
- Will the buyer acquire vacant possession?
- What conditions should be included in the Agreement of Purchase and Sale? For example:
  - Consent of the Board of Directors to the sale;
  - Consent of the Board of Directors to the pledging of shares;
  - Transfer of the shares on the corporate registry;
  - Assignment of the proprietary lease;
  - Vacant possession (if applicable);

- Review and approval of status certificates and financial statements, and other related documentation included in the status certificate package;
- Delivery of deed and/or share certificate;
- Buyer arranging financing on terms and conditions satisfactory to the buyer;
- Solicitors for both the seller and the buyer to review and approve the Agreement of Purchase and Sale;
- Warranty that there have not been any structural changes in the unit without the approval of the Board of Directors;
- For changes, additions or repairs to the unit, common elements or exclusive use areas that require the Board's consent, a warranty by the seller that (1) Board consent was obtained for any such changes; (2) no other changes were made without the Board's consent; and (3) the seller will provide a statutory declaration to this effect upon closing.
- If any changes, additions or repairs requiring the Board's consent have been carried out, then it is a condition of the agreement that the seller will provide a copy of the written consent of the corporation permitting such changes within six (6) days of the date that the offer is accepted; failing which, the offer will be at an end and the deposit will be returned by the seller immediately without deduction. The representation and warranty shall survive the closing of the transaction.
- Warranty as to the state and condition of the appliances, chattels and fixtures, as at the date of offer, and that the representation and warranty will survive the closing of the transaction.

iii.   **Important Features of Condominiums, Co-operative Corporations and Co-ownerships At-a-glance**

	Condominiums	Co-operatives	Co-ownerships
Individual ownership of unit	Yes	No; buyer owns shares in the corporation	No; buyer owns an undivided percentage ownership in the building and land
Easy to finance	Yes	Very limited	Limited
Consent needed to mortgage, finance or pledge (as applicable)	No	Yes	No
Consent needed to sell	No	Yes	Varies
Separate realty tax assessment	Yes	No	No
Sharing of common expenses on a pro-rated bases	Yes	Yes	Yes
Participate in management	Yes	Yes	Yes
Affected by default of others	No	No	No
Shareholder relationship	No	Yes	No

iv.   The Essentials of Condominiums, Co-operative Corporations, and Co-ownerships — Compared

	Condominiums	Co-operatives	Co-ownerships
Nature of unit ownership	(1) Buyer obtains ownership of individual unit (Deed) and is registered on title	(1) Co-operative corporation is the registered owner of the property; buyer does not own unit	(1) Buyer obtains ownership of a percentage interest by deed, which is registered on title
	(2) Buyer obtains exclusive ownership of the individual unit, and a percentage interest in the common areas of the building	(2) Buyer has long-term, exclusive use of the individual unit through a proprietary lease or occupancy agreement (not a deed)	(2) Buyer gains exclusive right to occupy a specific unit through a registered co-ownership agreement and through the provisions of that agreement
	(3) Buyer becomes a member of the condominium corporation	(3) Buyer acquires shares in the corporation and is a shareholder in the corporation	(3) Buyer becomes a member of the co-ownership corporation
Governing legislation	The *Condominium Act, 1998*	No specific Act; generally subject to the Ontario *Corporations Act*	No specific Act; generally subject to the Ontario *Corporations Act*
Buyer financing	Buyer can individually finance his or her own unit	Buyer can finance unit, using his or her corporation shares and leasehold interests in a unit (if there is no prohibition on pledging shares as security), with the Board's consent	Buyer can individually finance interest in his / her own unit

	Condominium	Co-operative	Co-ownership
Governing documents	The condominium corporation administers the declaration, by-laws, rules and regulations	The co-operative corporation administers the by-laws, rules and regulations, as well as the co-operative agreement, exclusive licence, proprietary lease agreement and/or shareholder agreement	The co-ownership corporation administers the co-ownership agreement, the co-ownership by-laws, rules and regulations, and / or private contracts
Owner obligations as to conduct	Owner is subject to the declaration, rules and by-laws of the condominium corporation	Owner is subject to the rules and by-laws of the co-operative agreement, exclusive licence, proprietary lease agreement and/or shareholder agreement	Owner is subject to the co-ownership agreement rules and by-laws and other contractual documentation of the co-ownership corporation
Owner participation in management	Owner can participate in management decisions by sitting on the Board of Directors and voting at the Annual General Meetings	Owner becomes a member of the co-operative corporation and can participate in management decisions by sitting on the Board of Directors and voting at the Annual General Meeting	Owner can participate in management decisions by sitting on the Board of Directors and voting at the Annual General Meeting
Limitations on owner's right to sell, rent or mortgage	Owner does not need the consent of the other owners or the condominium corporation to sell, rent or mortgage his or her unit	Owner needs the consent of the Board of Directors of the co-operative corporation to sell shares, assign the lease for the unit, finance, or rent the unit. In some cases, consent may be unreasonably withheld	Owner does not need consent of the other co-owners or co-ownership corporation to sell, rent or mortgage his or her unit in most cases
Status Certificate	The sale of the unit is subject to receipt of a status certificate which identifies any outstanding or pending payments, assessments, or legal actions regarding the unit or the corporation	The sale of the unit is subject to receipt of a status certificate which identifies any outstanding or pending payments, assessments, or legal actions, regarding the unit or the corporation	Sale of the unit is subject to receipt of a status certificate which identifies any outstanding or pending payments, assessments, or legal actions, regarding the unit or the corporation

How owner share of common expenses is calculated	Owner is assessed for a percentage share of common expenses (based on the size of the unit in comparison to the entire building)	Owner is assessed for percentage share of common expenses (based on the size of the unit in comparison to the entire building)	Owner is assessed for percentage share of common expenses (based on the size of the unit in comparison to the entire building)
Role of corporation / Management of building	The condominium corporation: (a) manages the affairs of the building according to the *Condominium Act, 1998*; and, (b) represents the interests of the owners. Often, a property management firm is hired for day-to-day management, although in some cases the corporation may self-manage	Co-operative corporation: (a) owns and manages the entire building and land on behalf of the shareholders; and, (b) grants exclusive occupation rights to shareholders of a specific unit. Often, a property management firm is hired for day-to-day management, although in some cases the corporation may self-manage	If a co-ownership corporation exists, it: (a) manages the affairs of the building according to the co-ownership agreement and/or private contracts; and, (b) represents the interests of the owners. Often, a property management firm is hired for day-to-day management, although in some cases the corporation may self-manage
Financial management	(1) The *Condominium Act, 1998* requires a reserve monetary fund to be established for the maintenance of the building (2) Condominium corporations must have yearly Audited Financial Statements issued to all owners and are managed by a professional management company.	(1) There is no legislation requiring a reserve monetary fund for the maintenance of the building (although many buildings have established one) (2) The co-operative corporation may or may not have yearly Audited Financial Statements issued to all shareholders, and are self-managed or managed by a professional management company	(1) There is no legislation requiring a reserve monetary fund for the maintenance of the building, but some co-ownership agreements require one (2) Co-ownerships may or may not have yearly Audited Financial Statements issued to all owners and are either managed by a professional management company, or are self-managed

E.   OIL TANKS

Oil leaks and spills from underground residential fuel tanks are a significant concern in Canada — both on the environmental front, and as a potential hurdle in real estate transactions.

Insurers now balk at insuring homes with older fuel tanks, and in some instances real estate deals have collapsed due to issues arising from the presence of a fuel tank on the property. Moreover, Ontario has passed strict new regulations and guidelines dealing with when the tanks must be replaced, and how they must be disposed of. These standards affect homeowners, who must be aware of them and comply.

All of this becomes the concern of the prudent real estate agent, as well. The following are the main points for agents to consider whenever acting for someone who is selling or buying a home with an underground fuel tank.

i.   The Particular Problem with Underground Fuel Tanks

1.   What are They?

A fuel tank is a container that holds fuel oil used in residential appliances, such as furnaces and boilers. When full, they usually weigh just over one tonne, and hold 1,000 litres of oil.

Approximately 1.5 million Canadian homes are heated by oil; while most of these have aboveground tanks, a certain proportion feature tanks that are buried underground instead. (Note that a tank installed in a home's basement is not considered an "underground" tank.)

Although precise figures are unavailable, there remain a significant number of homes in Ontario with underground fuel storage tanks.

2.   Corrosion and Leaks

The key problem with underground tanks is all of them corrode eventually. Indeed, several studies by provincial ministries have concluded that virtually all tanks — whether located aboveground or underground — experience an accumulation of sludge and water at the bottom, due to inevitable condensation. Because most tanks are constructed of unprotected steel, this accumulation causes the tanks to corrode from the inside, out.

And corrosion leads inevitably to leaks. These usually start small, and gradually increase over time, which means a pin-hole sized leak could go undetected for several years. It is only relatively recently that tank manufacturers have added leak deterrent and detection features; older tanks do not have this protection.

Leaking fuel is a significant, and serious, problem that gives rise to several safety, environmental, and health hazards. These include:

- fuel leaking into surface water;
- fuel leaking into drinking water;
- fuel contamination of surrounding soil;
- property damage; and
- fuel or its vapours generating a potentially explosive mixture.

Leaking oil can also migrate into nearby streams, rivers, and groundwater. It may also find its way into sump pumps or sewers and quickly contaminate drinking water. And even slight leaks can cause a major hazard — a single litre of leaked fuel oil can contaminate up to one million litres of water. This is a pressing and significant environmental concern; and Environment Canada estimates that there are currently thousands of leaking storage tanks in Ontario alone.

All of these concerns are heightened with underground tanks; they tend to corrode faster due to increased condensation arising from greater differentials in soil temperature. Also, their location in the ground prevents homeowners from conducting an inspection as to their condition.

3. The Insurance Problem

Clean-up after a leak is vital, but it may also be quite costly. It can involve replacing the leaking tank and supply lines, removing contaminated soil, and treating the groundwater. If the oil has leaked below the footings of the home, a portion of the foundation may have to be replaced. The total bill may amount to several thousand dollars.

In light of these potential repercussions, insurance companies are justifiably concerned about leaking older fuel tanks, and the very expensive clean-up operations which they necessitate. Some insurers are now flatly refusing to issue home insurance policies to homeowners with older underground storage tanks; others insure only physical damage to the dwelling, but not the cost of remediation to the soil and groundwater. In fact, the Insurance Bureau of Canada has decreed that any home with an exterior tank that is more than 15 years old (or an interior tank than is more than 25 years old) will not be insured. This may have repercussions for sellers, which will be discussed below.

4. *Other Concerns*

Even aside from the insurability question, the actual remediation of properties with underground oil tanks gives rise to additional concerns. For one thing, it is difficult to obtain competent, effective clean-up work at a reasonable price; there is currently no public roster of qualified, accredited clean-up contractors with appropriate liability insurance, and so it cannot be assumed that the contractors called in by the insurers are competent. Poorly-performed remediation work can serve to exacerbate the damage to the property.

Also, while some insurers will have the property cleaned up until there is no longer any detectable petroleum — which is considered a "pristine" state — others will only perform clean-up to the minimum standard set by government regulations. In the Ontario Court of Appeal decision in *Tridan Developments Ltd. v. Shell Canada Products Ltd.*,[19] the court accepted the proposition that a clean-up to government standards, rather than to pristine condition, could result in there being a stigma associated with the land, and that its value could be negatively affected as a result. Naturally, this could be a key issue when it comes time to sell the property.

ii.   Obligations on Both Sellers and Potential Buyers

In light of these potential environmental hazards that underground tanks can cause, the provincial government has implemented laws that govern virtually all aspects of underground tank use, repair, and replacement. As a result, homeowners — and especially sellers and potential buyers — should be aware of the requirements and regulations.

---

[19]   [2002] O.J. No. 1, 57 O.R. (3d) 503 (C.A.), leave to appeal to S.C.C. dismissed [2002] S.C.C.A. No. 98.

They can be summarized as follows:

1. Fuel Supply

Fuel oil distributors in Ontario are prohibited from supplying fuel oil to an underground tank unless it has been registered with the province's Technical Standards Safety Authority ("TSSA"). This body is an independent, not-for-profit organization responsible for the delivery of a range of safety services, including the administration of Ontario's *Technical Safety Standards and Safety Act, 2000,*[20] and the delivery of safety programs to the public.

Registration of the tank is free. Tank owners must simply complete the TSSA's Underground Fuel Oil Application Form, but — depending on the age of the tank — they may be required to upgrade the tank with specific leak and spill prevention equipment as well. (Note that tanks located in the basements of homes, or which are situated aboveground, are exempted; there is no registration requirement for these.)

If the TSSA approves the Application, then the tank will be assigned a registration number. This number must be provided to the fuel oil distributor each time fuel is supplied to the tank.

2. Tank Inspection

All fuel oil customers, including those with underground tanks, must have had at least a basic, visual inspection of the fuel oil tank system completed by May of 2004. Further, a comprehensive inspection must be completed by May of 2007, with additional comprehensive inspections taking place every ten years. These inspections must be carried out by a TSSA-certified technician, and may result in the homeowner having to upgrade the tank and/or heating system with spill and leak prevention equipment.

3. Tank Replacement, Repair and Removal

There are also a number of regulations that have been implemented in connection with tank replacement and removal. In short:

---

[20] S.O. 2000, c. 16.

- only licensed installers are allowed to place new aboveground or underground tanks in residential homes, or to replace existing tanks.
- depending on the age of the tank, existing tanks must be replaced pursuant to a defined schedule. In particular:
  - tanks that were installed 25 or more years ago[21] must be removed or upgraded by October 1, 2006;
  - tanks that were installed 20 to 24 years ago must be removed or upgraded by October 1, 2007;
  - tanks that were installed ten to 19 years ago must be removed or upgraded by October 1, 2008; and
  - tanks that were installed less than a year to nine years ago must be removed or upgraded by October 1, 2009;
- regardless of its age, a tank that is no longer in use must be removed within two years;
- the removal procedure respecting old underground tanks must be conducted by TSSA-registered fuel oil contractors. The soil around the tank must also be assessed for contamination, and any contaminated soil must be cleaned.

F. ACTING FOR A SELLER WITH AN UNDERGROUND FUEL TANK

In light of the potential hazards caused by underground tank leaks, as well as these regulatory obligations on owners, a real estate agent who has been asked to list a home with an underground tank should make certain inquiries and take precautionary steps before agreeing to do so.

This is for good reason. For one thing, if the home is uninsurable because an older underground tank is on the premises, it will likely be difficult to attract potential new buyers who are interested or willing to proceed under those circumstances.

Secondly, some real estate deals have fallen through entirely because of underground tanks; buyers have reneged on their offers after learning, late in the deal, that one exists on the property. Naturally, this can affect the individual real estate agent as well: in a Quebec case,[22] for

---

[21] As calculated from May 1, 2002, the date that the relevant legislation was enacted.

[22] *Immeubles Aimé Deslauriers Ltée v. 2413-4520 Québec Inc.*, [2000] Q.J. No. 328 (S.C. (Civ. Div.)), aff'd [2001] Q.J. No. 1930 (C.A.).

example, the agent was forced to sue for his commission. The deal collapsed after it was revealed that there were underground oil tanks on the property, and the vendor refused to allow an inspection to be conducted.

Finally, even if the deal closes, an unwary buyer who later discovers that an unused and/or leaky underground tank exists on the property will likely sue the seller, and possibly the agent, for misrepresentation (among other things), and will claim damages arising from cleaning up any contamination.

i.   Disclosure as the Best Prevention

So how can all of this be avoided?

Before accepting a listing on any home, you should make some simple inquiries of the owner as to how the home is heated, whether an underground fuel tank exists on the property, and whether a leak is suspected. Early and candid disclosure by the owner, and by you to any potential purchasers, is the best way to deal with the potential problems that can arise from the presence of the tank on the property. In fact, the Ontario Real Estate Association has created specific clauses that accompany the listing agreement, which encourage full disclosure for the protection of both the seller and the buyer.

If the oil tank isn't leaking, hasn't leaked, has been the subject of regular and thorough preventive maintenance, and is not otherwise subject to legislated removal in the short-term, then the owner need merely disclose the presence of the tank to the buyer. In these cases, the buyer will generally insist on obtaining a warranty from the seller, attesting to his or knowledge of the tank and its state of repair. The owner should also provide any tank maintenance and testing records, as well as fuel usage records, to the potential buyer.

If the owner is aware that an *unused* tank exists on the property, then he or she must empty the tank of oil, and must comply with the provincial regulations which mandate the removal of unused tanks within two years. The seller will then provide documentation to the buyer showing that the tank has been removed.

In some cases, however, the owner may genuinely not know whether an underground tank exists. In these cases, you and the owner may want to perform a quick inspection of the property, prior to listing, to try and determine the true state of affairs. This will involve looking for:

- an oil fill pipe, which is usually close to the ground, near where the furnace is located in the home; and
- a vent pipe. These are usually attached to the side of the house, are about 3-4 cm. in diameter and between one-half to two metres long.

Alternatively, the homeowner may want to hire someone to look for an underground tank. The cost is usually about $150, and reputable contractors who do this work can be found in the phone directory under "Tanks".

ii. Be Attuned to Signals of Potential Leaking

Even if an owner is aware of an underground tank's existence, he or she may not be attuned to the warning signals that point to potential leaks. Questions you may want to ask on behalf of your client are:

- is the homeowner using more fuel than normal?
- is the tank taking in water? (The homeowner can check for increases in the water level of more than one centimeter, for no less than an eight-hour period. A water-finding paste can be obtained from an oil burner technician.)
- are there signs of oil sheens in nearby streams, wetlands, or drainage ditches?
- is the vent whistle silent when the tank is being filled (the homeowner can ask the oil delivery person to confirm).
- are there signs of spills around the fill pipe or the vent pipe?

By asking these questions, you can satisfy yourself that the tank will not cause unexpected problems to a potential buyer, since this could lead to collapsed deals and/or acrimonious lawsuits after sale transaction has been concluded.

iii. Legal Obligation to Remedy Leaks

If your client suspects a leak in the underground fuel tank of the home, he or she should remedy the problem immediately, and prior to attempting to sell the home. (If the owner believes that the leak occurred before he or she bought the property, then there may be a claim for recovering costs from the previous owner.)

The first step is to contact a TSSA-registered fuel oil contractor who will determine the location of the leak and clean up any leaked fuel oil. Ontario homeowners are also required by law to call the Spills Action Centre of the Ministry of Environment if the spill causes, or is likely to cause, adverse effects such as ground or surface water contamination, or damage to a neighbour's property. The Spills Action Centre provides 24-hour assistance for spills and spill situations.

Owners of leaking underground fuel tanks have no choice — the tank must be removed. The process begins with an analysis of the surrounding soils for evidence of contamination. This analysis must be performed by a professional engineer, and usually costs about $1,500.

If the soil is not contaminated — If the soil sample does not show contamination, then the owner has fulfilled his or her obligation and nothing more needs to be done in terms of inspection. In such cases, the engineer's report becomes a very important document in the sale of the property, since it eliminates concern over further risk on the part of the seller.

An Ontario court decision[23] illustrates this point. The seller had five underground tanks removed from his property, because he thought this would improve the land's marketability. Prior to closing, he provided the buyer with copies of an engineer's report, verifying that the tanks had been removed, as well as copies of an environmental audit, which showed no contamination. He also gave the buyer:

- a declaration that, to his knowledge, there were no underground tanks and the land was not contaminated;
- an undertaking that, to his knowledge, all environmental laws had been complied with, there were no outstanding environmental work orders, and there were no hazardous substances on the property.

However, and despite these assurances, the agreement of purchase and sale itself expressly indicated that the buyer was purchasing the property "as is".

---

[23] *Holtby's Design Service Inc. v. Campbell Chevrolet Oldsmobile Inc.*, [2002] O.J. No. 2889, 115 A.C.W.S. (3d) 519 (S.C.J.).

After closing, and as part of his preparations to develop the property, the buyer had his own environmental studies done, which in fact showed significant contamination of the soil. The buyer sued the seller for $250,000 in clean-up costs, claiming (among other things) that the seller had misrepresented the condition of the land.

The court dismissed the buyer's claim, finding that the seller had not misled the buyer at all. Notwithstanding the seller's undertaking and declaration, there was no wording in the agreement of purchase and sale itself to suggest the seller was giving the buyer a legal *warranty* that the land was uncontaminated. The land was purchased "as is", and in fact the various reports from the seller should have put the buyer on notice that he should have his own independent environmental studies done before closing.

If the soil is contaminated — If the soil is indeed contaminated, then it must be removed or cleaned up under the guidance of a professional engineer.

Note that an owner whose tank leaks will be responsible not only for the damage and environmental clean-up of his or her property, but also for damage sustained by neighbouring properties. The scope of what is considered "damage" can be quite broad: in another court case,[24] which involved leaking oil from a neighbour's tank that found its way onto adjoining commercial property, the neighbour claimed damages for:

- the cost of restoring the soil;
- business interruption;
- increased mortgage finance payments (because lenders were now less willing to advance funds on the strength of a secured interest in land that had a "stigma");
- the reduction in the property's value; and
- for loss of management time in dealing with the problem.

The neighbour succeeded in getting damages in most of these categories, and even though the Court of Appeal later reduced the total,[25] the owner with the leaking tank was still liable to pay its commercial neighbour more than $500,000.

---

[24] *Tridan Developments Ltd. v. Shell Canada Products Ltd.*, [2000] O.J. No. 1741, 97 A.C.W.S. (3d) 246 (S.C.J.).

[25] *Tridan Developments Ltd. v. Shell Canada Products Ltd.*, [2002] O.J. No. 1, 57 O.R. (3d) 503 (C.A.).

For residential properties, the damages will usually not be so varied or extensive. However, depending on the type of residential property and the extent of the leak, the costs for such clean-up can sometimes be as high as $10,000. Moreover, because of insurers' increasing reluctance to insure against such occurrences, it may not be covered by the home-owner's policy.

iv. Anticipating the Questions

Even if both you and the owner are satisfied that the underground tank is in good repair and is unlikely to leak, its presence on the property may set off warning signals for savvy potential buyers. Therefore, you must anticipate and be prepared to answer questions such as:

- what is the age of the tank?
- where is it located?
- what are the approximate monthly fuel costs?
- has regular maintenance been performed, and is there documentary evidence to prove it?
- is there proof that the underground tank has been registered, in accordance with the mandatory provincial requirements? and
- is there proof that it meets all other provincial safety requirements?

A wise agent will have obtained this information and documentation prior to showing the property to potential buyers.

v. Acting for a Buyer

1. Disclosure and Inspection

Ideally, the existence of an underground tank on the property will normally be revealed through disclosure by the seller, as discussed above. However, in some cases the seller will genuinely be unaware of the tank's existence. Again, you or a home inspector may be able to identify the presence of an underground tank on the property, by means of either a visual inspection, a test dig, or the use of a metal detector.

A buyer who is interested in a home that has, or had, an underground fuel tank should take the following steps before closing:

For a property with a recently-removed fuel tank —

- If an old or unused fuel tank has been recently removed from the property, ask the seller to supply evidence that the work has been performed by a TSSA-registered professional.

- The buyer should also obtain documentation from the seller attesting to the fact that the soil has not been contaminated. He or she can also contact the Ministry of the Environment to determine whether there has been a previous leak reported and dealt with.

For a property with an unused fuel tank that is still on the premises —

- For an oil tank that is not in use, but which has not yet been removed in accordance with the legislated two-year deadline, the cost for removing the tank should be borne by the seller and incorporated into the deal. (The cost is usually several thousand dollars if the soil is not contaminated, but much higher if it is.)

For a property that has an operational underground tank in place —

- For a newer underground tank that is in use, the buyer should first and foremost insert a clause in the offer requiring the seller to remediate any problems with the tank prior to the sale. The buyer should then obtain the related documentation from the seller, attesting to the fact that the work was done, and that it was performed in compliance with the regulations.

- For older tanks that are subject to the specified removal deadlines imposed by provincial legislation (*i.e.*, deadlines ranging from 2006 to 2009, depending on the age of the tank), the buyer should insist that the seller assume responsibility for the removal of the tank, and any associated clean-up, prior to closing. The buyer will want to insert a clause in the offer accordingly. (Alternatively, a buyer comfortable with the risks may be willing to accept a disclaimer from the seller, which indicates that the property is being sold "as is", with no claims about its condition. However, it will be the rare buyer who is willing to purchase on these terms, and this should only be done after obtaining advice from an experienced real estate lawyer who can advise of the potential risks.)

A buyer contemplating a home that has an underground tank should also:

- obtain a disclosure statement from the seller, which indicates whether he or she is aware of any underground storage tanks or contaminated soil or water on the property;
- contact the TSSA to ensure the tank is registered;
- contact the Ministry of the Environment to determine whether there has been a previous leak and clean-up on the property;
- request fuel consumption and tank servicing records from the seller;
- hire a heating contractor to inspect the system, including the piping;
- contact the fuel oil supplier for that particular home, and determine whether the basic or comprehensive inspections of the tank and its components have been completed; and
- determine what servicing and inspection program is in place for that home. (This information will be available from the fuel oil supplier.)

Buyers will also be asked by their insurer to supply information as to the tank's age, location, and evidence that it complies with safety requirements. The buyer will also need to obtain this information from the seller.

2.   *A Note about Buyer Maintenance*

If your client has purchased a home with an underground oil tank, he or she should be encouraged to take some simple steps to optimize the tank's condition and prolong its life. Specifically:

- yearly inspections of the tank should be arranged, and any problems or recommended repairs should be dealt with promptly.
- the filters should be changed, and the sludge and water removed from the tank, on a yearly basis as well.
- the owner should regularly check the visible portions of the tank for rust, and clean it off whenever possible.
- he or she should also check for problems after each fuel delivery.
- the tank should be kept relatively full over the summer, as a means of helping prevent condensation from collecting inside.
- the tanks should be tested for leaks regularly, and owners should be alert to the warning signs that suggest a leak may have developed. Although it will be a rare residential tank that has a storage capacity of 5,000 litres or more, any underground

tanks of this size must be leak-tested annually, pursuant to the regulations.

- an unused tank should be emptied. (As discussed above, if there is no intention to use it in the future, serious consideration should be given to removing it even prior to the two-year deadline provided under Ontario regulations. In such cases, the soil must be tested for contamination, and contaminated soil must be removed and replaced with clean fill, which must be tilled level. All work must be performed by a TSSA-registered professional.)

Note that unless it is written into the deal, the new owner is responsible for the costs of maintaining and upgrading the tank purchased with the property.

But in light of the problems described, owners may want to consider replacing even a functioning underground tank with a new aboveground one. Some fuel suppliers even have special financing programs designed to assist homeowners in this regard.

CHAPTER 6

ESTATE PLANNING

A. What Comprises Estate Planning?
B. Wills
    i. Who Should Make a Will?
    ii. Choosing an Executor
    iii. Distributing Your Assets
    iv. Probate Fees
C. Dying Without a Will
D. Trusts
E. Powers of Attorney
F. Marriage Contracts

Real estate often comprises one of the major components of a person's estate. Normally, a person will not look to his or her agent for advice on estate planning, but it is not uncommon for the topic to arise on an informal basis. As a result, you should be generally aware of the steps and issues involved in making arrangements for proper estate planning; this will be useful not only in the context of dealing with your clients, but also for your own personal estate planning purposes as well!

A. WHAT COMPRISES ESTATE PLANNING?

There is much more to estate planning than the mere preparation of your will. A will only makes provisions in the event of your death, but an estate plan can also give effect to gifting or disposing of your assets, for the benefit of others while you are still alive. In fact, in addition to protecting and providing for your family members, employees and friends, a well-constructed estate plan can also maintain your family business, minimize taxes, avoid conflicts between your beneficiaries, and realize your charitable aims, among many other things.

Good estate planning actually consists of two primary elements: (1) attempting to ensure that your assets will last as long as you require them; and (2) attempting to ensure that upon your death, your estate will be transferred to your beneficiaries quickly, efficiently and with as little tax liability and other costs (including legal and accounting fees) as possible. These objectives are particularly important if you have a spouse or common-law spouse and children, or if you own a home or business, have significant assets or investments, or intend to pass along family possessions and heirlooms.

An estate plan is — and should be — a continuously evolving project. Periodically it will have to be updated to reflect changes in your life situation, including the arrival of additional children or grandchildren, changes in your marital status such as separation or divorce, or the death of a spouse or child. It may also need changing to take into account any asset growth and changes in relevant federal and/or provincial tax laws.

Not surprisingly, there is no specific formula for creating an estate plan; you must design your own personal estate plan to suit your needs and specific situation. But for most people, the initial steps are usually these:

- prepare an inventory of your assets and liabilities;
- define your estate planning objectives;
- evaluate your objectives based on your current situation;
- determine what arrangements are necessary to achieve your objectives; and
- consult the appropriate advisors to implement the components of your plan.

Respecting this last point, a good lawyer will recommend to his or her clients that they consult their accountant, life insurance consultant, financial advisor (if applicable). Ensure that you have adequate insurance to cover expenses on death, debts, taxes, professional fees and bequests if necessary in accordance with the provisions of your will. You will want to be certain that you have adequately provided for your spouse and children — especially children who are still dependent upon you.

Every estate plan will be unique, and so will the individual components that comprise the plan. Nonetheless, some common steps in estate planning include:

- the creation of Wills and Powers of Attorney;
- arranging for a marriage contract (if applicable);
- arranging for life, health and disability insurance;
- arranging for mortgage insurance;
- arranging for investment vehicles in various forms; and
- making any necessary trust arrangements.

Only a few of these components will be covered, namely: (1) Wills; (2) Dying Intestate; (3) Trusts; (4) Powers of Attorney; and (5) Marriage Contracts.

B. WILLS

One of the first steps in good estate planning is to make sure that you have a valid Will which sets out your wishes and intentions. A Will is a legal document in which you direct the manner in which you want your assets to be disposed of after your death, and it serves as written evidence of those wishes. It is not a legally binding document until death, and you are always free to change it as long as you are competent and able to do so.

To make a legally valid Will you must have "testamentary capacity" at the time it is made. That means the ability to understand the nature and extent of your assets and legal obligations (if any) to your dependents, coupled with the ability to have your will prepared accordingly. Also, for a Will to be legally valid, there are certain formalities which must be followed in its execution. For example, a Will that is typed or otherwise drafted must be signed in the presence of two witnesses who are of legal age and of sound mind, neither of whom are beneficiaries or spouses of the beneficiaries. Those two people must witness the signature in the presence of each other and in the presence of the person making the Will. Incidentally, it is strongly recommended that those witnesses be someone other than the executor or trustee, or their spouses.

i. Who Should Make a Will?

Regardless of your net worth or family status, having a Will is important. In fact, *everyone who has attained the age of majority should have a Will*. Even if you have only a few assets, the existence of a Will ensures a smooth transfer to your heirs or other designated beneficiaries. It is a common fallacy to think that making a Will is something which only the "rich" need worry about, but nothing could be further from the truth: a smaller estate cannot afford the added legal expenses and inconvenience incurred when there is no Will to guide the estate's distribution.

Wills are designed to provide for your loved ones by anticipating future events — even unlikely ones. Young people, for example, usually overlook the fact that the size of their estates could be increased dramatically by an inheritance from a relative, or — if they're really lucky — by winning the lottery. (Of course, young people often ignore the need for a Will because they don't think they are ever going to die anyway!)

The need for a Will comes into sharper focus if you have a spouse, common-law spouse, or children, or a specific beneficiary to whom you would like your estate to pass. For both married and single parents of under-aged children, having a Will is essential: if you have left no Will and both you and your spouse die in a common disaster, then for any children under 18 years of age their share of your estate is held in an interest-earning government bank account until they reach the age of majority, at which time they receive the entire inheritance as a lump sum. This leaves open the possibility that (1) your under-aged children will not be adequately provided for in the time before they reach 18; and (2) that once they reach the age of majority, they could unwisely spend much or all of the lump-sum inheritance that you left for them. Moreover, without a Will you cannot appoint a guardian to care for your minor children; rather, the government will appoint one for them, usually from among the next-of-kin. And until your children turn 18, that government-appointed guardian may have to apply to a provincial government agency for support payments to be taken from your children's inheritance.

This point bears repeating: making a Will is not just for "older" people — it should be a concern for people of all ages. It is important for anyone's personal career and financial planning that they take the time necessary to plan a Will, and to review it from time to time as part of an overall life planning strategy. A Will has two principle functions: (1) to appoint an executor to look after your affairs once you're gone;

and (2) to document how your estate will be distributed to your heirs and other parties you choose to leave something to.

ii.   Choosing an Executor

Selecting the executor(s) of your Will (which in Ontario is formally called the "Estate Trustee with a Will") is one of the most crucial elements of the Will-making process. You must trust and feel comfortable that the executor will act in the best interests of your estate, and will carry out your instructions. The executor you appoint in your Will has specific duties to perform, but the following list gives you an outline of only some of them:

- Make funeral arrangements (this is the duty of the executor named in a Will, if there is one, and not the next-of-kin; however, in many cases the executor or one of the executors is the next-of-kin. However, if there is no Will appointing an executor, then the task of making funeral arrangements falls on the next-of-kin). An executor named in a Will must remember, in arranging a funeral, that the funeral should be in keeping with your station in life. A personal representative who arranges an excessively lavish and expensive funeral, without written directions and indemnification from the beneficiaries of the estate, risks finding himself or herself personally liable for the funeral bill in excess of what would have been reasonable in the circumstances;

- Determine, locate and notify the beneficiaries;

- Locate the estate inventory, identify the value of assets for tax and distribution purposes and, where applicable, take the required steps to secure and safeguard the assets;

- Retain professional services such as a solicitor and accountant for advice;

- Determine, settle and pay the outstand debts of the deceased;

- File tax returns in all necessary jurisdictions, pay taxes owing and, following the payment and assessment of amounts owing from the estate, obtain appropriate tax clearances or releases;

- Distribute the assets as directed by the Will and obtain releases from the beneficiaries;

- Invest assets for the establishment of on-going trusts if so directed by the Will, in accordance with stated or statutory investment powers;

- Maintain proper accounting records for all capital assets of the estate and assets distributed from the estate, together with all expenditures made and income received;
- Prepare statements and reports periodically for the beneficiaries to keep them abreast of the progress of the estate administration.

Ideally, your executor should be someone you trust fully, and who has good common sense. It can be either an individual, or a trust company appointed to take on the role of making the necessary decisions in relation to your estate.

If choosing an individual, it is usually wise to choose someone younger than yourself, and who is in good health, since you will want them to be around when you are gone. Selecting someone who lives close by will also simplify matters when it comes time to settle your estate. If you don't know anyone who fits the bill, consider a professional executor, such as an accountant, lawyer, financial planner, or trust company. In any event, it is a good idea to appoint a back-up or alternate executor in your Will.

iii. Distributing your Assets

Your Will should specify when and to whom your assets should be distributed. This may not be an easy question to answer, but keep in mind that a fair distribution of your assets may not necessarily mean an *equal* distribution. For instance, some family members may have special needs that have to be taken into account.

If your Will is "airtight", it will consider and anticipate all the conceivable scenarios — even those that are unlikely to happen. As a starting point, when drafting your Will be sure to consider all of the following possibilities:

- your spouse might predecease you;
- you and your spouse could die together;
- there is a disaster involving the total immediate family;
- you might have another child or children;
- a child might predecease you leaving their children surviving them (*i.e.*, your grandchildren);
- you may have no children surviving who themselves left no children; or
- your executor might be unable to fulfil his or her responsibilities.

Finally, be sure to review your Will periodically, to make sure that it still accurately itemizes what you want to do with your estate; ideally, you should review your Will every three years. If there are no changes necessary, then leave the Will alone; but if there are changes required you need to contact your lawyer to have him or her make the appropriate modifications. Too many people make a Will, never change it, and on their death — and in light of a changed family and/or financial situation — it no longer represents their wishes.

iv. Probate Fees

"Probate" was the term used for the process of legally proving a Will and administering a deceased's estate; currently, the process of applying for probate is now called an "Application for a Certificate of Appointment of Estate Trustee with a Will". Despite this change, the more familiar and user-friendly term of "probate" will continue to be used here.

Probate fees arise whenever a person applies to prove the will as legally valid, and applies to be appointed as Estate Trustee. Essentially, probate fees are a tax on your estate, payable to the court. For the first $50,000 of your estate's value, the fees are currently set at $5 per $1000 in assets; for everything above $50,000, they are calculated at $15 per $1,000 in assets. Probate fees apply to the value of all assets belonging to your estate on a world-wide basis, as of the date of your death.

While minimizing probate fees is a worthwhile goal, there may be drawbacks to some of the steps required to do so. These drawbacks should be discussed at length with your lawyer, financial advisor and/or accountant. Having said that, the following are five strategies to reduce probate fees:

Hold an asset in joint tenancy: If an asset is held in joint tenancy with your spouse, the property will pass directly to your spouse upon your death, by-passing distribution under the terms of your Will, and avoiding probate fees. Transferring assets to someone other than your spouse carries with it certain implications that should be discussed prior to your making such provision.

Name the beneficiary directly: When it comes to your RRSP, RRIF, pension plan, annuity, or life insurance policy, you are able to name a beneficiary directly under the terms of those plans. By doing this, you will avoid probate fees on those assets, because those assets will pass to the named beneficiary directly, rather than under your Will.

Change the location of property: Move your assets to a province with lower probate fees by using a corporation; *e.g.*, move them to an Alberta corporation since there is a $6,000 limit on probate fees in that province, notwithstanding the size of the Estate.

Transfer debt to your real estate: Where you own mortgage-free real estate but you also have other debts, consider converting the debt to a mortgage or charge on the real estate, since the value of that real estate will be reduced by the debt when calculating probate fees.

Create a "Double Will": This is a relatively new method of estate planning which involves the making of two Wills; *i.e.*, "Double Wills". This technique has so far been approved by the courts in the few cases where this manner of estate planning has been challenged by the Ministry of Revenue for the Province of Ontario.

This type of planning allows parties with substantial estates to divide their assets into two groups — with one group passing to the beneficiaries without the necessity of obtaining probate and incurring the probate fees which are incurred upon filing for probate. The other group of assets will be included in the application for Certificate of Appointment of Estate Trustee with a Will which will be subject to probate fees; *i.e.*, a tax.

In the leading case the deceased left two Wills which I shall refer to as the "primary" and the "secondary" Wills respectively. The assets covered by the "primary" Will were valued at approximately $3 million and included the deceased's real estate and some personal property. The "secondary" Will, while similar in wording to the "primary" Will, covered assets having a value of nearly $25 million and included shares of a private closely-held company. The "primary" Will was probated while the "secondary" Will was not — thereby saving the estate approximately $375,000 in probate fees. To consider using this technique your "primary" Will should include real estate as well as shares of publicly traded companies — as probate is generally required to transfer real estate and shares of publicly traded companies. The "secondary" Will would hold the shares of any private companies you may own, together with other types of assets for which evidence of probate would not be required, for example, art, jewellery, *etc*. It is not advisable to transfer your principal residence to a privately held company as you will likely lose the principal residence exemption. To consider using this technique your estate, *excluding your principal residence*, should have a value of not less than approximately $2 million. There are other issues of a legal nature to be considered and discussed with your advisors, in addition to those set out above.

C. DYING WITHOUT A WILL

If you die without a Will, a situation referred to as dying "intestate", your estate will be distributed to your heirs-at-law or the next-of-kin in accordance with the provisions of the relevant legislation of the province you live in. In Ontario these individuals are determined by the *Succession Law Reform Act*.[1] Consequently, the distribution of your assets may bear little or no resemblance to what your wishes and intentions are. In an intestacy the government has made a Will for you which is absolutely rigid and inflexible. It provides for no exceptions!

Appointing An Estate Trustee Where There Is No Will — First of all, if you die intestate in Ontario, your estate is frozen until your next-of-kin (or if necessary, a close friend) apply to the court to appoint an estate administrator, who under Ontario law is formally called an "Estate Trustee Without a Will".

To make an application, the party applying (whether it is a next-of-kin or close friend) must be an Ontario resident, and must be either:

(a)   the person to whom you were married immediately before your death, or a person of the opposite sex with whom you were living in a conjugal relationship outside of a formal marriage immediately before your death;

(b)   your next-of-kin; or

(c)   the person mentioned in (a), and your next-of-kin.

In this regard, and particularly where more than one relative of equal degree claims for the administration of the estate, the court will use its discretion in making the appointment.

Moreover, in circumstances where there are no next-of-kin, or where they are unavailable to act or live out of province, the court also retains discretion to allow someone else to administer your estate, including a friend or even a creditor. If no one steps forward whatsoever, then a government official in the form of the Public Guardian and Trustee will take on the role.

---

[1]   R.S.O. 1990, c. S.26.

Those people entitled to share the assets of your estate must, among themselves, nominate a person who will be appointed the Estate Trustee of your estate. Hopefully, they can easily and quickly agree who that individual or individuals should be. If the next-of-kin cannot agree upon a person, then the court will decide that issue. This takes time and added effort which means increased costs in the form of legal fees to your estate.

Once someone is nominated by your next-of-kin to administer the estate, that person must apply to the court for a Certificate of Appointment of Estate Trustee Without a Will, and must post a bond during the Will's administration, except in limited circumstances. The bond is usually the equivalent of twice the estate's value, and serves as a means of protecting the beneficiaries and the creditors of the estate.

There is no need for an administration bond where a government agency (such as the Public Guardian and Trustee) acts as Estate Trustee. Likewise, where a trust company acts, it is customary for the court to waive the bond requirement. Also, where the spouse acts as Estate Trustee and the value of the estate is less than $200,000, no bond is required, provided that an affidavit setting out the debts of the estate is filed along with the application for administration.

In addition to these exceptions, it is always open to the Estate Trustee to apply to the court for a waiver or reduction of the bond. Whether or not the request is granted depends on the particular circumstances, including the size of the estate, the beneficiaries, the debts, the relationship of the Estate Trustee to the estate, and the willingness of the beneficiaries to consent to the request.

Distributing the Estate When There is No Will — Once an Estate Trustee has been appointed, your estate will be distributed according to certain statutory rules.

If you are only survived by a spouse upon your death, and there are no children of the marriage, then the outcome is straightforward: your surviving spouse is entitled to all of your estate. Even if you do have children, the first $200,000 or less in the estate after debts is called the "preferential share", and it goes to your surviving spouse in any event. In other words, your spouse has the first share of your estate.

If you die leaving an estate with a value of more than $200,000, and your spouse and one child survive you, then your spouse receives the preferential share of $200,000 and also receives 50 per cent of the excess, and the remaining 50 per cent of the residue is given to the child.

If you die leaving an estate that has a residue of more than $200,000, and your spouse and more than one child survive you, then your spouse receives the preferential share of $200,000 and also receives one-third of the residue. The remaining two-thirds of the estate is divided amongst your surviving children; if any of them have pre-deceased you but have had children of their own, then those surviving grandchildren of yours are entitled to receive their parent's share of your estate.

In the event that neither your spouse, children, nor grandchildren are alive at the date of your death, the Estate Trustee has to determine if there are any more distant relatives. The extent of each relative's entitlement to share in your estate is determined according to the closeness of their blood relationship to you, which is called their "degree of kinship". Generally speaking, (1) descendants inherit before ancestors; and (2) children, grandchildren, parents and grandparents take before brothers, sisters, nieces, nephews, aunts, uncles and cousins.

The following summarizes various degrees of kinship in a typical family situation, and dictates the various hierarchies that apply to the distribution of your estate if you die intestate.

Table of Consanguinity

(Note: Bracketed numbers () indicate ascendants, descendants' and collaterals' degree of kinship to the deceased intestate.)

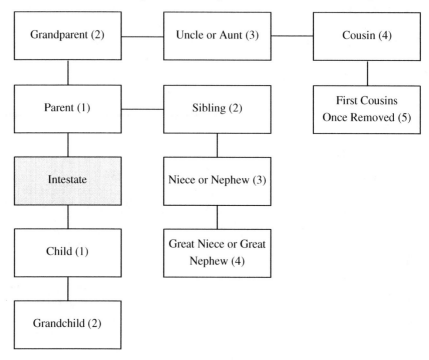

D. TRUSTS

What is a "trust"? First of all, it is not a contract, since a contract involves mutual promises between two or more parties. Rather, a trust is a method of transferring ownership of an asset from one person to another, for the benefit of a third. The person who establishes the trust vehicle allows the person known as the "trustee" to hold the asset in accordance with certain instructions; the person who benefits from the assets held by the trustee is called the "beneficiary". In establishing a trust, one separates the title holding and management of an asset from the enjoyment of the asset.

A trust can be very useful in cases where it is not feasible or advisable to give money or assets to your children directly. Often, parents who hold real property are inclined, as a means of gift-giving, to transfer that property outright into their children's names, as joint tenants or tenants-in-common. But this is frequently not the best course to take, because as long as the parents are alive this impairs their ability to deal with the property or encumber it with a mortgage, since the consent of the child (or children) becomes necessary. Moreover, if the child already owns another home, he or she cannot claim a principal residence exemption with regard to this gifted real property, and may be liable for capital gains tax. This being the case, the trust vehicle may be a better option for achieving the parents' gift-giving objectives.

(Having said that, it is important to note that the beneficiary of a trust arrangement may still find him or herself in an unanticipated situation: Ontario courts, for example, have consistently held that a beneficiary's interest in the capital or income of a trust constitutes an "asset" which, upon his or her marriage breakdown, is capable of being included in that person's assets in connection with dividing up the marital property.[2] This possibility must be borne in mind by any parent who intends to set up the trust for the benefit of the child or children.)

In a similar vein, a trust might be used where you as the parent want to provide your child not with a gift *per se*, but rather with a steady income source to cover his or her living expenses. In conjunction with a transfer of funds from you to a trustee, a trust agreement could be used to provide your child with an annual payment, perhaps until your child reaches a specified age.

Trusts come in essentially two forms: (1) an *inter vivos trust*, which is created during the lifetime of the creator, and takes effect as soon as it is signed; and (2) a *testamentary trust*, which is created pursuant to the terms of the Will of the party making provision for the trust, and takes effect only upon the death of that person.

Whether the trust is *inter vivos* or testamentary, the scope of your trustee's powers will vary depending on the specific type of trust that you have set up. In a *"discretionary" trust*, the trustee is given the broad power to administer all aspects of the trust, including:

- making decisions on the investment of trust funds;
- the timing of payments to the beneficiaries;
- the scope and duration of their entitlement; and
- the amounts payable to them.

---

[2]   See, for example, *Black v. Black*, [1988] O.J. No. 1975, 66 O.R. (2d) 643 (H.C.J.).

In contrast, in a *"non-discretionary" trust* the trustee has little or no decision-making authority; his or her duties will be specifically set out in the trust agreement itself.

There are various reasons for establishing trusts, and the following are four common ones:

Reducing taxes: Rather than leaving your assets directly in the hands of your spouse upon your death, create a spousal trust, naming your spouse as the sole beneficiary. The trust will pay tax on the future income earned on those assets, while your spouse can access the earnings by receiving a tax-free distribution of capital from the trust. Splitting income with the trust this way could save a significant amount in taxes each year.

Protecting assets: By setting up an asset protection trust, you will be able to shelter your assets from creditors or an ex-spouse. Remember, when an asset is held in a trust, you do not own it anymore, so others cannot take it from you. However, where your creditors are able to prove that you set up the trust, primarily if not solely, to avoid their claims, this idea may not work. Typically, these trusts are best set up offshore.

Meeting obligations: An *inter vivos* trust can be used in lieu of a power of attorney to look after your financial obligations if you are not able to. A trust in this case will enable you to be very specific about how you would like your assets dealt with. A testamentary family trust can be set up to provide regular income to your children upon your death, with specific instructions on when the assets should be given to them outright.

Ensuring privacy: Since assets held inside a trust are not registered in your name, a secret trust can be set up. With the assets in the name of the trust, privacy is insured.

It is important to recognize that trusts are complex legal instruments which require the input and advice of your accountant, financial advisor and lawyer.

E.   POWERS OF ATTORNEY

A power of attorney is a document which appoints one or more people to act on your behalf during a period of either physical and/or mental incapacity. There are essentially two kinds of Powers of Attorney.

"Power of Attorney for Property": is a document used to manage your affairs if — either temporarily or permanently — you cannot physically or mentally handle your own business or financial affairs, or if you are losing the ability to manage those affairs. This form of Power of Attorney essentially deals with all of your assets while you are alive; it is accordingly common and recommended for individuals to prepare a Power of Attorney for Property at the same time as they prepare a Will (since a Will deals with their assets after death).

"Power of Attorney for Personal Care": is a document used to enable decisions to be made for your physical and medical care if you have lost the mental ability to make decisions relating to your own health care. These include decisions relating to medical treatment, place of residence and other related matters. Although some people refer to it as a "Living Will", it really is a Power of Attorney for Personal Care. Again, it is recommended that a Power of Attorney for Personal Care is prepared at the same time as you prepare your Will.

Powers of attorney are discussed in detail in Chapter 4.

F.   MARRIAGE CONTRACTS

With the breakdown in marriage becoming more and more common-place in today's society, and because of the way the *Family Law Act*[3] applies in Ontario, marriage contracts have become an essential part of estate planning in many cases.

Essentially, marriage contracts are a means of avoiding the provisions of the *Family Law Act* respecting the division of property on death. By entering into a marriage contract either before marriage or during the course of your marriage, you and your spouse may agree that your assets will not be subject to division under the *Family Law Act*. This is entirely legal — and in fact the Act provides for it. (The only provisions that cannot be contracted out of are those dealing with a spouse's rights to the matrimonial home, including the surviving spouse's right to possess the home for a period of 60 days from the date of death, if the home was owned by the deceased spouse.)

This being the case, marriage contracts can be a useful and effective estate planning tool, but they are often overlooked by those who are

---

[3]   R.S.O. 1990, c. F.3.

marrying for the first time and/or who have few assets. They are particularly important for people who are marrying for a second time and who have children from their first marriage, since they may wish to have the majority, if not all, of their assets pass to those children or to other parties, rather than to their second spouse. Likewise, they are essential for people who have extensive business interests which they want to protect from claims by either a disgruntled spouse in the event of a marriage breakdown, or by a surviving spouse in the event that they might die during the course of a business relationship.

But whatever the factual scenario may be, all marriage contracts must be in writing, and must be properly executed and witnessed. Needless to say it is absolutely essential that both spouses obtain proper and independent legal advice and assistance in the preparation of such a contract.

CHAPTER 7

REAL ESTATE AGENTS' MISTAKES

A. The Agent Who Fails to Understand Exactly Who He or She Works For
    i.   Who is My Client?
    ii. Duty to Third Parties
    iii. Co-operating Agents
    iv. Dual Agents
    v.   Gratuitous Agents
B. The Agent Who Fails to Explain the Terms of the Agreement of Purchase and Sale, or Fails to Protect the Clients' Rights Under the Agreement
C. The Agent Who Makes Misrepresentations

No book geared toward real estate agents would be complete without a section devoted to the various and numerous pitfalls that can arise in the course of even the most average real estate transaction. Although this discussion is not comprehensive, it outlines some of the key and commonplace problem areas for agents.

A. THE AGENT WHO FAILS TO UNDERSTAND EXACTLY WHO HE OR SHE WORKS FOR

i. Who is My Client?

As was outlined in Chapter 2, in addition to statutory duties there are many general duties to which agents are subject, the main ones being those duties that arise from contract, plus fiduciary duties and duties of disclosure.

However, it is important to first acknowledge precisely *to whom* those duties are owed. Although it seems like a basic concept, problems arise when an agent fails to appreciate who the client really is, and what their corresponding obligations to that person will be.

On first blush, it may be tempting to assume that the person who pays your commission must inevitably be your client, in law. However, the courts have established that this is not necessarily so. The case of *Knoch Estate v. Jon Picken Ltd.*[1] involved a listing agent who helped procure an offer from a corporate buyer. However, the agent did not disclose that he himself had a 20 per cent interest in that corporation; he and the other shareholders re-sold the property at a substantial profit to another buyer who had originally expressed an interest in the property long before the initial sale, and who had disclosed the price that it would be willing to pay. Naturally, once the seller found out, he objected on the basis that the agent had a duty toward him to disclose the true state of affairs. The question was complicated by the fact that the listing agent had virtually no direct contact with the seller, and did not advise the seller on any aspect of the sale of the property whatsoever. Normally, the law had dictated that whoever pays the agent's commission is the agent's client, but applying that legal rule to this case, the agent would have been answerable to the client with whom he had virtually no contact, and would have had a duty to disclose the second, more lucrative offer to him. The Ontario Court of Appeal was therefore asked to determine whether the question of who pays the agent's commission is solely determinative of who the agent works for and is responsible to. Ultimately, the Court decided that payment of commission is *not* the only factor in determining who the agent works for.

As a result of this decision, most real estate boards now require, through their various Codes of Practice, that agents identify in writing who their client is, at the earliest stage of the transaction. In this context, some Boards now expressly recognize that there are three different types of agents in the real estate context:

- listing brokers, who are agents of the seller;
- co-operating brokers, who act as sub-agents of the seller (these were formerly called "selling agents"); and

---

[1]   [1991] O.J. No. 1394, 4 O.R. (3d) 385 (C.A.).

- buyer agents who work exclusively as agents of the buyer, but may be compensated by either the seller or the buyer (also formerly called "selling agents").

In most transactions, the agent represents the seller, and therefore has an obligation to market the property and represent the seller in negotiations that lead to a deal. Still, agents who independently represent *buyers* in real estate transaction have always been legally permissible, although that type of arrangement is relatively less common. Nonetheless, the fact that buyers can have a distinct role as clients in and of their own right is one of the key motivators behind the requirement for early and clear disclosure as to precisely which party the agent represents. When such an agency situation exists, the buyer's agent is obliged to act exclusively in the best interests of the buyer, and there is no relationship with the seller whatsoever. (This is true whether the Buyer's Agency Agreement provides that the agent is to be compensated by the seller directly, or through the listing agent.)

ii. Duty to Third Parties

Returning to the situation where a selling agent acts exclusively for the seller, the question still arises whether the agent has any obligation toward a buyer who has no independent representation by an agent of his or her own. The answer, unfortunately, is "sometimes". To be specific, selling agents may have duties to third parties who have not hired them, but who nonetheless reasonably rely on them to provide advice or guidance in the intended transaction.

There are several cases that deal with this, but it will be illustrative to highlight only one. *Bango v. Holt*[2] involved a potential buyer who approached a selling agent to find her a revenue-producing property. The property was advertised as an "Expired duplex, permit renewable", when in fact no permit could be obtained. After closing, the buyer sued the agent and the seller, and the agent resisted that lawsuit by claiming that he had no contractual relationship or duty toward the buyer whatsoever, and should not be held accountable to her. The court disagreed, finding that — to the agent's knowledge — the buyer had relied on the agent's professed special expertise in revenue-producing properties. In these circumstances, the agent owed a duty to the non-client buyer, and was

---

[2]   (1971), 21 D.L.R. (3d) 66 (B.C.S.C.).

required to exercise special skill and care, and to be honest in making statements to her.

iii. Co-operating Agents

Until relatively recently, Multiple Listing Service ("MLS") agreements could be the source of additional problems and confusion for agents and clients alike, because they add a new cast of characters to the real estate transaction. First of all, under these agreements the staff of the MLS (who take care of marketing the property) become the sub-agents of the seller. Secondly, because the listing agent invites other "co-operating agents" to bring prospective buyers to see the property and to procure an offer acceptable to the seller, those co-operating agents become entitled to share in the commission paid by the seller upon successful completion of the transaction. Usually in these cases (and absent a written agreement in which the buyer requests exclusive representation by the co-operating agent) the co-operating broker is considered to be a sub-agent of the *seller*, rather than an agent of the buyer. In this role, the co-operating agent's obligations toward the buyer are relatively limited, and correspond to the duties owed by any agent to *any* third party, namely the duty:

- to disclose all pertinent information about the seller's property;
- to not misrepresent their authority, or any facts about the property; and
- to honestly answer all questions about the property.

But the practical reality is that the co-operating agent and the buyer are usually in frequent contact with each other, and the co-operating agent may even be providing advice to the buyer on matters such as the values of comparable properties, the property's physical condition, zoning issues, and matters related to financing. Furthermore, buyers often freely express to co-operating agents their personal needs and preferences, their likes and dislikes, interests, personal financial situations, and other matters that normally would only be communicated to a trusted advisor.

And yet, from a legal standpoint the buyer's interests are not protected by the co-operating agent whatsoever, despite these appearances to the contrary. Naturally, this can lead to confusion and misunderstanding on the buyer's part, and may lead to three potentially volatile scenarios for the unwary agent: first, there is the likelihood that the co-operating agent can unwittingly breach his or her duty to the seller, for example in situations where information personal to the seller (such as motive for selling) has been disclosed. Secondly, the co-operating agent may err by failing to disclose to the seller pertinent information about the buyer (such as the terms on which the buyer is willing to do business, or the fact that the buyer is prepared to offer a higher price). Thirdly, there is the potential that an *implied* agency relationship between the buyer and the co-operating agent is created, in situations where words or conduct of the co-operating agent would lead the buyer to reasonably believe that their own best interests were being advanced by the co-operating agent. In other words, the buyer may have a unilateral belief that the co-operating agent is representing him or her, even when this was not intended by the co-operating agent to be the case.

Fortunately, these potential pitfalls led to practical changes affecting how these agents deal with each other and with their clients. As one example, TREB now publishes a pamphlet for clients called "Agency Relationships Explained", which outlines the nature of the agency relationship and the obligations that stem from it, and which contains a section for the buyer to sign by way of acknowledgment of having read and understood the document. This ensures that the buyer understands that the co-operating agent is not responsible for protecting the buyer's interests in the transaction.

(As an aside, there may be no downside to a co-operating agent acting for the buyer, and indeed it may be worthwhile for such agents to become buyer agents (to be compensated through the listing agent). For one thing, this is often consistent with the perceptions of the parties, and secondly no consents are needed to change a buyer agent's status to that of sub-agent for the seller at a later date. Conversely, a seller's sub-agent must obtain the consent of all parties if he or she wishes to switch to representing the potential buyer in a transaction.)

iv.   Dual Agents

In law, there is a general rule that an agent may not act for more than one party to a transaction. This is because to do so would be a patent breach of an agent's fiduciary duties, because (1) they are seeking to serve two "masters", and (2) because the interests of both the buyer and sellers as clients are being brought into direct conflict. (The most obvious one being that the seller naturally wants to obtain the highest price possible, while the buyer wants to pay as little as possible.)

There are narrow exceptions to this rule, and in the field of real estate the exception is actually quite common. The concept of "dual agency" involves an agent who acts for both a buyer and the seller, but with two important qualifications: (1) both clients must be advised of the dual agency (thus fulfilling the agent's duty of disclosure); and (2) they must each agree to have the agent act for both of them. In making the required disclosure the agent should point out (in writing) that:

- the dual agency situation involves an inherent conflict of interest;
- no information received by one party can remain confidential;
- the advice offered by the agent to one party might very well be prejudicial to the other; and
- in certain situations, the parties may have to seek independent expert advice.

In addition, after this initial disclosure each party should be given the opportunity to seek the services of other realtors, to obtain independent advice.

(Of course, this presupposes that the agent is aware that he or she is acting in a dual agent capacity in a transaction. Take note that it is no excuse that the agent believed that disclosure was not required in the situation, or that it was industry practice not to make such disclosure in the circumstances. It is therefore important for agents to turn their minds to the possibility that they act for both sides.)

Once a dual agency situation has been established, the agent's core duties to both of his or her clients remain the same as in any other agent-client relationship.

v.   Gratuitous Agents

The last category under the "Who is my client?" heading involves a concept known as "gratuitous agency", which arises when an agent unilaterally embarks upon a mandate to perform services for one party, and by doing so causes them not have those services performed by someone else. Agents performing such work can be found responsible and liable to these clients in the right circumstances, even though they are not being paid by them.

By way of illustration, the decision of *Spencer v. Invidiata*[3] involved an agent who had developed special expertise in lakefront properties. As a means of attracting new listings, he dropped off a pamphlet at the lake-front home of the Spencers, and they called him to set up a meeting. He provided them with an estimate for their own home, but also gave them a deliberately lowball valuation of a nearby home that they had expressed interest in buying. The agent did so because he was secretly interested in buying that nearby property for himself. Ultimately, the Spencers decided to list their own home for sale with someone else. Nonetheless, they later submitted a low offer on that nearby property, based on the agent's misleading evaluation. In keeping with the agent's plan, this caused the sellers of that property to re-evaluate the price they could get. After the Spencer's offer had expired, the agent ultimately snapped up their property for well under market value.

When the Spencers found out, they sued the agent, claiming that even though they listed their own home with someone else, his conduct in providing property valuations and counselling them on their potential purchase gave rise to certain obligations toward them, including a duty to disclose to them his own interest in and purchase of the other property. The court agreed with the Spencers. Even though the agent acted on a gratuitous basis, he nonetheless owed a duty to them in the same manner as he would have under a formal contract. In fact, the court found that the agent's conduct had deprived the Spencers of the opportunity to purchase the property, and ordered him to pay them the $95,000 in profit he made on the deal.

Fortunately, in the right circumstances gratuitous agency obligations can be short-lived. For example, in *Sandhu v. Shiell*[4] the sellers had two lots that they wanted to sell, and so they signed up with a listing agent. That agent worked in the same office as Shiell, who was contacted by some potential buyers. Shiell told them that because he lived in the area and was familiar with it, he would be prepared to help them, primarily by showing them the property and by physically taking their offer documen-tation to the listing agent. No buyer's agency agreement was signed. After the buyer's offer to buy both lots was rejected and negotiations failed, Shiell — who besides being an agent also ran a chicken farm — learned that the sellers were actually prepared to sell the lots *separately*, and decided to put in what turned out to be a successful offer on one of those

---

[3] [1994] O.J. No. 2189 (Gen. Div.).

[4] [1996] B.C.J. No. 507, 61 A.C.W.S. (3d) 850 (C.A.).

individual lots himself. Ultimately, the buyers succeeded in purchasing the other lot, but sued Shiell for breach of fiduciary duty, claiming he was their gratuitous agent. The court disagreed with this characterization, finding instead that Shiell was simply acting as a sub-agent of the listing agent, and not as a gratuitous agent of any kind. If he had any sort of fiduciary relationship to them, it ceased the moment the negotiations to buy both lots together came to an end.

Certainly, the concept that you could be liable to someone who is not paying you, and with whom you do not have a formal contract, is unsettling. Fortunately, these types of situations are relatively rare; but nonetheless, you should always be aware of duties that flow from the relationships that arise in the course of your dealing with others.

B.   THE AGENT WHO FAILS TO EXPLAIN THE TERMS OF THE AGREEMENT OF PURCHASE AND SALE, OR FAILS TO PROTECT THE CLIENTS' RIGHTS UNDER THE AGREEMENT

Increasingly, courts are acknowledging the important reality that in a standard real estate transaction, it is not the parties' lawyers but rather their agents that are on the "front line" of contact with the buyer or seller. As such, agents who take on an advisory role *vis-à-vis* the client can be held accountable for any poor advice that they give.

A primary decision on this point is from the Ontario Court of Appeal in *Wong v. 407527 Ontario Ltd.*[5] Wong bought a property from the numbered company. The sellers provided a warranty in the agreement of purchase and sale, as to the existing gross rental income. Unfortunately, the rental income turned to be much less than expected, and Wong sued his real estate agent (among others) for damages due to breach of that warranty. Ultimately, the real estate agent was found liable for failing to protect his client's interests, because he did not obtain security for the warranty in connection with that rental income. Of broader impact, however, was the court's conclusion that because the real estate agents are often the *only* professional advisors to the parties on the terms of an agreement of purchase and sale, they take on an advisory role, and are accountable for failing to protect their clients against the special risks of a transaction.

---

[5]   [1999] O.J. No. 3377, 26 R.P.R. (3d) 262 (C.A.).

A recent example occurs in the case of *Blais v. Cook.*[6] In that case, the agent acted for husband-and-wife buyers who were looking to purchase a home near the husband's work. The agent introduced them to a property, and they viewed it three times before submitting an offer. That offer was conditional on financing, on obtaining a home inspection, and on the buyers satisfying themselves as to the "quality and quantity of water". Because the property had a well, and the sellers were to supply an existing well certificate and a survey, which they did.

In fact, the agent took it upon himself to have the water tested, and phoned the buyers to advise that the water was "okay" or tested "zero zero". As such, the buyers waived the conditions and purchased the home. As it turned out, the water contained an extraordinarily high amount of salt, which made it undrinkable and unsuitable for domestic use. The buyers learned of the water situation only after closing; and ultimately sued their agent after unsuccessfully trying to remedy the situation with a water conditioner.

They were successful in their claim against the agent. The court found that respecting the salt content of the well water, there was certain documentation available to the buyers, but that it had not been brought to their attention and there was no evidence that they knew of the water problem prior to the sale. The court also pointed out that although the agent inserted conditions in the agreement that were designed to protect the buyers (specifically conditions entitling them to satisfy themselves as to the quantity and quality of water, and to conduct a home inspection), he did not advise them how to go about doing this. Instead, he simply had the water tested and told the buyers it was "okay", without mentioning either the salt problem or the fact that the testing by the department of health did not address the salt levels in particular. In the end, the court found the agent liable to the buyers for his lack of care, and for not fully apprising them of the special risks in the transaction.

Another good illustration of this principle is found in the case of *Wemyss v. Moldenhauer.*[7] The buyers retained the agent to help them find and purchase a home. During a tour of a home that looked promising, the buyers noticed a soggy area in the back yard, even though it had not rained recently. Suspecting septic system problems, the buyers asked the agent to submit an offer that contained a standard

---

[6]   [2005] O.J. No. 2643 (S.C.J.).

[7]   [2003] O.J. No. 38 (S.C.J.).

home inspection clause. After several subsequent offers and counter-offers were exchanged, the buyers accepted a counter-offer from the seller that contained several handwritten and initialled changes. One significant, but unnoticed amendment by the seller changed the home inspection clause to make the deal conditional only on an inspection revealing "no structural defects".

Soon after closing, it came to light that there was indeed a problem with the septic system, and the buyers tried unsuccessfully to cancel the deal. They sued the agent for breach of his duties toward them.

In the end, the court found that the agent failed to adequately explain the amendment in the counter-offer the buyers signed. In fact, he was obliged to show them not only the change, but to advise them that the inspection clause had been fundamentally altered. The agent was liable to the buyers for his failure to do so, and was ordered to compensate them for the $50,000 deposit they had lost to the seller.

Clearly, an agent who fails to explain the agreement of purchase and sale to his or her client can be held liable when things go wrong. Not surprisingly, agents who fail to adequately protect their clients' interests in agreements that they themselves prepare are also exposed to liability.

A recent example of this is found in *Winsham Fabrik Canada Ltd. v. Re/Max All Stars Realty Inc.*[8] The agent, who acted for the buyers, prepared an offer to purchase a particular property on behalf of his clients. The agent knew that the size of the property was of key importance to the buyer.

In preparing the offer and the agreement of purchase and sale, the agent made a litany of mistakes. In particular, he:

- did not obtain legal advice on how to prepare the agreement in the circumstances;
- relied on the description clause and marketing material provided by the seller's listing agents, to the effect that the building was 46,600 square feet;
- failed to obtain the architect's plans of the building so that the square footage could be ascertained, despite the buyer's repeated requests;
- failed to include a condition as to the size of building;

---

[8] [2001] O.J. No. 1478 (S.C.J.).

- failed to include a clause providing for a price adjustment if the size was different than claimed;
- did not review the agreement of purchase and sale with the buyer; and
- did not advise the buyer to take immediate steps to ascertain the size of the building.

To make matters worse, although the agreement contained an inspection condition, the buyer did not conduct an inspection, and in fact signed a waiver of the conditions in the agreement, based on the assurances as to size that he had received from both the agent and the seller's agents.

Ultimately, it was discovered that the property was 3,000 square feet smaller in size than the buyers were led to believe. The deal eventually closed, and the buyer sued all the real estate agents and their employers, claiming damages due to misrepresentation as to the building's size.

Even though no buyer's agent agreement was ever signed between the agent and the buyer, it was clear to all the parties that the agent was actually the exclusive agent for the buyer. The court found that the agent was negligent (as were the listing agents, who provided the original size estimate). The agent knew the accuracy of the marketing material from the listing agents was not guaranteed, but failed to follow up on the issue or at least protect the client as he should have. For example, he could have advised the buyer to retain his own surveyor to independently measure the building, or to consult a lawyer before signing a waiver of the inspection right. In any event, the agent should have reviewed the agreement with the client.

The court went out of its way to observe that the agent was an "honest and competent real estate agent", but for all these reasons found him liable to the buyer for negligence, to the tune of 50 per cent of the difference between the purchase price that was paid by the buyer, and its actual market value at the time of the sale.

The unfortunate agent in this case made a series of mistakes that most prudent agents would know to avoid. However, the decision in *Rankin v. Menzies*[9] demonstrates the level of knowledge that courts may assume an agent to possess.

---

[9] [2002] O.J. No. 51 (S.C.J.).

Roth was the president of a real estate agency. He also happened to own some land that he rented out to tenants. Gibson was a real estate agent employed by Roth, who was also responsible for collecting rent from those tenants. When Roth decided to sell the property, the tenant expressed interest in buying it, and negotiations were conducted through Gibson.

As the tenant was unable to raise the needed financing, the tenant's father agreed to buy the home so that the tenant could make payments to him and eventually acquire title.

The father never met the seller Roth, because all negotiations were conducted through the real estate agent Gibson. The father inquired of Gibson as to realty taxes for the property, and was told they were about $1,500 per year. There was no discussion about local improvement levies, and neither Gibson, the property appraiser, nor the solicitor for the parties took steps to ascertain whether such levies were or could become owing.

In fact, after closing the father learned that there was a significant local improvement levy in connection with the property, in the amount of $23,000. Gibson was unaware of the existence of the *Local Improvement Act* and admitted that he did not make inquiries with the tax department or with the seller, as he should have.

The court found that it was reasonable to infer that a knowledgeable and well-trained real estate agent would be expected to be aware of a local improvement levy. Gibson had a duty to make inquiries from the seller concerning the existence of levies charged at the time, or contemplated for the future. In the result, the real estate agent was found to have breached his fiduciary duty to the buyer.

C.   THE AGENT WHO MAKES MISREPRESENTATIONS

Misrepresentation is the next category of error by agents, and unfortunately it appears to be quite a prevalent form. Given the important role that the agent plays as intermediary between the buyer and the seller, and the often-informal nature of the interaction between agents and members of the public, this is not surprising.

In fact, misrepresentations often occur when the agent is eager to sell the property, and becomes careless in the language used or the information given to the potential buyer. In a case called *MacDonald v. Gerristen*,[10] the buyers had no prior experience in buying or selling homes, so they visited their local real estate office specifically to retain the services of an experienced agent. As it happened, they were greeted by an agent on staff that day who was a complete novice, and who had passed the required exams only a few days before. She did not want to "lose a sale", so she told them that she had been doing real estate on and off for several years and was familiar with the area. She showed them the property, and in response to several pointed questions about water seepage in the basement, repeatedly told them she was capable of identifying such problems and that "You two worry too much. You're being silly." In light of the agent's assurances, the buyers put in a successful offer for the home. Unfortunately for the agent, there were indeed serious water seepage problems in the basement, and after a three-day rainstorm it was completely flooded, and the newly-installed renovations to it were totally ruined. The agent arrived on the scene to find the buyer crying on the couch.

The court confirmed that when performing their duties, agents must not only be honest in expressing their opinions, but must also have some valid factual basis for the opinions they give. If the agent does not have a valid factual basis, then he or she ought to say so, or else should qualify the opinion so that the buyer can know how much reliance to place on it. Applying this concept to the novice agent, the court held her brokerage to be two-thirds liable for the buyer's damages, because the buyers relied completely on the agent's professed experience, and because her comments lulled them into believing that there were no patent or latent defects with the property.

In contrast, the recent decision of *Malpass v. Morrison*[11] involved an agent's culpable *silence* — this time as to the legality of a basement bedroom. In that case, the buyers had made it clear to the agent that they needed a retirement home with four bedrooms. The agent showed them a three-bedroom home with an added room in the basement that the sellers had furnished with a bed. In fact, this particular use for the room was contrary to a city by-law and therefore illegal. The feature sheet described that room as a "den".

The court found that the agent knew that having four bedrooms was crucial to the buyers, and that despite what the listing sheet said, that they erroneously considered the basement room to be a bedroom.

---

[10]   [1994] A.J. No. 468, 48 A.C.W.S. (3d) 490 (Q.B.).

[11]   [2004] O.J. No. 4596 (S.C.J.).

His decision not to correct the buyers' misapprehension — in the face of his duty to do so — cost the agent more than $50,000 in damages payable to them.

The recent case of *Hennessy v. Russell*[12] is another interesting example of how an agent's silence can be costly. There, the agent acted for both the buyer and the seller as a dual agent. The buyers had been interested in buying and building on a particular property which, unbeknownst to them, housed a nesting habitat for a certain endangered bird called a loggerhead shrike. They entered into an agreement of purchase and sale for a $34,000 sale price; the agreement also confirmed that the agent would not disclose "confidential information" received from either of the parties. After closing, when the buyers started making inquiries in connection with a building permit, they learned of the habitat's presence from the Ministry of the Environment. The Ministry informed the buyers that no house could be built within a 400-metre radius from the birds' nest, and that they might be subject to prosecution were they to go ahead and build anyway. After further inquiries the buyers determined that it would cost them more than $100,000 to prepare an alternative location on the land for their proposed building; although they did not go ahead and incur that cost, they nonetheless sued the agent for damages.

Although the agent initially denied it, he had in fact known of the nest's presence from the day the home was listed for sale, but had deliberately withheld the information from the buyers because he did not consider it to be "important enough". On these facts, the court found the agent liable for misrepresentation. He was fully aware of the buyers' intentions to build on the property, including the approximate location of the planned residence, and should therefore have conveyed the information about the shrike nest to them when they first expressed interest in the property. His unilateral and deliberate decision to withhold that necessary information deprived the buyers of the opportunity to make their own inquiries, and to assess the potential impact that the birds' presence would have on their construction plans.

(Fortunately, the court found that the agent's misrepresentation was *negligent*, rather than *fraudulent*, and awarded the buyers just $1,000 plus legal costs, representing the difference between what the buyers paid for the property, and what it was worth on appraisal.)

---

[12]   [2005] O.J. No. 2612 (S.C.J.).

As these cases demonstrate, an agent's failure to pass on vital information can attract liability. It is important to point out, however, that the obligation to disclose can be of a *continuing* nature, even right up until the buyers make an offer. In *Murray v. Tilley*,[13] the buyers viewed the property with the listing agent on two different occasions. During the second viewing, the husband got his foot wet when he stepped into some water on the basement floor. What happened next was the subject of dispute between the parties: the buyers said that the agent told them "not to worry" about it because the Town was doing temporary work on the water lines, and that this reassured them. The agent, in contrast, claimed that she made inquiries of the vendor that same evening, was told that the basement experience water flooding two or three times a year, and reported this information back to the buyers immediately. The buyers bought the property, but later sued the agent for their costs to fix subsequent damage caused by water seepage. Under these circumstances — and despite the buyers' claim that they "trusted" and "relied" on her — the court found that the listing agent had no fiduciary duty toward them. It also found that it was not reasonable for the buyers to rely on the agent's purported "not to worry" statement, and that it would not have served as an inducement for them to buy the house in the circumstances. However, once the agent had made inquiries of the vendor, and had learned from him that the basement flooded two or three times a year, she had a duty to pass this subsequently-obtained information on to the buyers, whom she knew were about to make an offer. Because of her failure to do so, she was found liable to them in negligence.

Misrepresentations also occur where the agent purports to offer valuation advice that is ill-founded. In *Lovell v. Century 21 Dome Realty Ltd.*,[14] the seller enlisted the help of an agent to sell a "fixer-upper" property. After showing the seller some comparables, the agent told his client the seller that if he could get "anything over $30,000 he should grab it and run". Based on this advice, the seller sold for $34,000. Shortly after, the new buyer asked the same agent to list it again, and this time it sold for $42,500. Asserting that there had been a negligent misrepresentation, the original seller successfully sued the agent for the difference, because agent's advice as to value had been negligently given, and the seller had relied on that advice to his detriment.

---

[13]   [2005] N.J. No. 5 (S.C. T.D.).

[14]   [2004] S.J. No. 366, 131 A.C.W.S. (3d) 372 (Prov. Ct.).

Obviously, agents can spread misinformation in several ways: on the one end of the spectrum is simply passing on inaccurate information; on the other end is deliberate falsehood. If the agent's misrepresentation is of this latter type, the outcome will be rather predictable. In *Athwal v. Sidhu*,[15] for example, the buyers bought a restaurant and cabaret from the sellers, who were represented by a listing agent. The issue was whether lights, speakers, a projector and screen, and a DJ system were included in the sale. The seller was motivated to sell, and the court found that in order to make the property as attractive as possible, he deliberately failed to correct the misapprehension by the buyers that the equipment was part of the deal. More importantly, when the real estate agent drew up the contract, he drafted the offer in such a way as to perpetuate the buyers' misconception as to what was included and what was excluded.

The court found that the real estate agent had a duty of care to draw up the contract in accordance with what he knew to be the facts. The buyers reasonably relied on this misrepresentation. The agent was liable, along with the sellers, for the buyers' damages.

But an agent's misrepresentation need not be *deliberate* to be potentially culpable, and there are many examples of this in the case law. Still, it is worth considering a few "happy ending" cases as well. The first is *Byrne Estate v. Berube*;[16] that case involved the sale of a particular property to what the court determined was a "sophisticated" buyer — she held several degrees, including a law degree, had her real estate licence, and had bought and sold several other properties in the area. Upon hearing from a local agent that there was a bidding war going on in connection with the property which was originally listed at $310,000, she started to investigate. She attended at an open house that was targeted at agents only, and had heard from another source that the highest offer was allegedly $325,000. She approached one of the two agents at the open house and asked them if that was true. One of the agents said, "You did not get that figure from me." She then put in an offer of $340,000 that was accepted. Ultimately, she reconsidered, and declined to go through with the deal unless there was a reduction in the purchase price. She claimed that she had been misled by the agent's comment as to whether $325,000 was the highest current offer. The sellers sued, and were successful at getting summary judgment against the buyer for the deficiency in price. The court found that there was

---

[15] [2002] B.C.J. No. 1596 (S.C.).
[16] [1995] O.J. No. 3497 (Gen. Div.).

nothing that the agents at the open house had said to mislead the buyer, and that a person in her position and with her experience would not have been misled into making a high offer by the agent's simple comment that "You did not get that figure from me."

The second "happy-ending" case is named *Colbourne v. Comerford*.[17] The issue was whether the seller's real estate agent could be liable for a misstatement he made to the buyer in the listing description of the home. This particular listing description was initially very matter-of-fact and indicated, among other things, that the buyer was to assume the lease on the furnace. However, at the request of one of the seller's relatives, the real estate agent revised the listing description to make the property more appealing, using words suggested by that relative such as "bright", and "appealing". The reference to the furnace was inadvertently deleted. The agent also made an error in measuring the lot size, and this error also appeared on the listing description.

The eventual buyers of the home sued the agent on the basis that they relied on the inaccurate information to their detriment. The court found that, in the first place, the buyers had many other sources of information to rely on besides the listing description, some of which contained accurate information. Secondly, the court acknowledged that the use of creativity was usual in such documents (and cautioned that the draftsperson still needed to ensure the accuracy of what was written), but concluded that the listing information sheet — which also bore a disclaimer — should not be taken as absolutely accurate. These were honest errors on the agent's part, said the court, and in any event it is the agreement of purchase and sale that ultimately binds the buyer and seller. Noting that "[r]eal estate agents are not omniscient", the court accordingly absolved this agent of liability.

---

[17]   [2001] N.J. No. 334 (Prov. Ct.).

APPENDICES

APPENDIX A

REAL ESTATE AND BUSINESS BROKERS ACT, 2002

S.O. 2002, c. 30, Schedule C

Amended by: S.O. 2004, c. 8, s. 46; S.O. 2004, c. 19, s. 18(1)-25, 24(2).

CONTENTS

PART I
INTERPRETATION

PART II
OFFICERS

PART III
PROHIBITIONS
RE: PRACTICE

PART IV
REGISTRATION

PART V
COMPLAINTS, INSPECTION
AND DISCIPLINE

PART VI
CONDUCT AND OFFENCES

PART I
INTERPRETATION

Interpretation

1. (1) In this Act,

"administrative authority" means the administrative authority as designated under section 3 of the Safety and *Consumer Statutes Administration Act, 1996* for the purpose of administering this Act;

"broker" means an individual who has the prescribed qualifications to be registered as a broker under this Act and who is employed by a brokerage to trade in real estate;

"brokerage" means a corporation, partnership, sole proprietor, association or other organization or entity that, on behalf of others and for compensation or reward or the expectation of such, trades in real estate or holds himself, herself or itself out as such;

"business" means an undertaking carried on for gain or profit and includes any interest in such undertaking;

"employ" means to employ, appoint, authorize or otherwise arrange to have another person act on one's behalf, including as an independent contractor;

"equity share" means, in respect of a corporation, a share of a class or series of shares of a corporation that carries a voting right either under all circumstances or under circumstances that have occurred and are continuing;

"Minister" means the Minister of Consumer and Business Services or such other member of the Executive Council to whom administration for this Act is assigned under the *Executive Council Act*;

"officer" includes the chair and any vice-chair of the board of directors, the president and any vice-president, the secretary and assistant secretary, the treasurer and assistant treasurer and the general manager and assistant general manager of the corporation or a partner or general manager and assistant general manager of a partnership, any other individual designated as an officer by by-law or resolution or any other individual who performs functions normally performed by an individual occupying such office and the manager of the real estate department of a trust corporation;

"prescribed" means prescribed by regulations made under this Act;

"real estate" includes leasehold interests and businesses, whether with or without premises, and fixtures, stock-in-trade and goods connected with the operation of a business;

"registrant" means a brokerage that is registered under this Act or a broker or salesperson who is registered under this Act;

"regulations" means regulations made under this Act;

"salesperson" means an individual who has the prescribed qualifications to be registered as a salesperson under this Act and who is employed by a brokerage to trade in real estate;

"trade" includes a disposition or acquisition of or transaction in real estate by sale, purchase, agreement for purchase and sale, exchange, option, lease, rental or otherwise and any offer or attempt to list real estate for the purpose of such a disposition, acquisition or transaction, and any act, advertisement, conduct or negotiation, directly or indirectly, in furtherance of any disposition, acquisition, transaction, offer or attempt, and the verb "trade" has a corresponding meaning;

"Tribunal" means the Licence Appeal Tribunal established under the *Licence Appeal Tribunal Act, 1999* or such other tribunal as may be prescribed;

"year" means a period of 365 consecutive days or, if the period includes February 29, 366 consecutive days.

Associated persons

(2) For purposes of this Act, one person is associated with another person in any of the following circumstances:

1. One person is a corporation of which the other person is an officer or director.

2. One person is a partnership of which the other person is a partner.

3. Both persons are partners of the same partnership.

4. One person is a corporation that is controlled directly or indirectly by the other person.

5. Both persons are corporations and one corporation is controlled directly or indirectly by the same person who controls directly or indirectly the other corporation.

6. Both persons are members of the same voting trust relating to shares of a corporation.

7. Both persons are associated within the meaning of paragraphs 1 to 6 with the same person.

[S.O. 2002, c. 30, Sched. C, s. 1, in force March 31, 2006 (O. Gaz. 2005, p. 3251); S.O. 2004, c. 19, ss. 18(1) and (2), 24(2), in force March 31, 2006]

PART II
OFFICERS

Director

2. (1) Subject to subsection (2), a director shall be appointed for the purposes of this Act and a maximum of two deputy directors may be appointed,

(a) by the board of the administrative authority; or

(b) by the Minister if there is no designated administrative authority.

Director cannot be registrar

(2) A person appointed as the registrar or a deputy registrar under subsection 3 (1) shall not be appointed as the director or a deputy director under subsection (1).

Deputy director, duties

(3) A deputy director shall perform such duties as are assigned by the director and shall act as director in his or her absence.

Deputy director

(4) If more than one deputy director is appointed, only one deputy director may act as the director under subsection (3) at any one time.

[S.O. 2002, c. 30, Sched. C, s. 2, in force March 31, 2006 (O. Gaz. 2005, p. 3251)]

Registrar

3. (1) Subject to subsection (2), a registrar shall be appointed for the purposes of this Act and a maximum of two deputy registrars may be appointed,

(a) by the board of the administrative authority; or

(b) by the deputy minister to the Minister if there is no designated administrative authority.

Registrar cannot be director

(2) A person appointed as the director or a deputy director under subsection 2 (1) shall not be appointed as the registrar or a deputy registrar under subsection (1).

Powers and duties

(3) The registrar shall exercise the powers and perform the duties imposed on him or her under this Act under the supervision of the

director, and a deputy registrar shall perform such duties as are assigned by the registrar and shall act as the registrar in the registrar's absence.

Deputy registrar

(4) If more than one deputy registrar is appointed, only one deputy registrar may act as the registrar under subsection (3) at any one time.

[S.O. 2002, c. 30, Sched. C, s. 3, in force March 31, 2006 (O. Gaz. 2005, p. 3251)]

PART III
PROHIBITIONS RE: PRACTICE

Prohibition against trade in real estate unless registered

4. (1) No person shall,

(a) trade in real estate as a brokerage unless the person is registered as a brokerage;

(b) trade in real estate as a broker unless he or she is registered as a broker of a brokerage;

(c) trade in real estate as a salesperson unless he or she is registered as a salesperson of a brokerage; or

(d) trade in real estate unless registered under this Act.

Unregistered persons

(2) A person who is not registered as a brokerage, broker or salesperson shall not,

(a) directly or indirectly hold himself, herself or itself out as being a brokerage, broker or salesperson, respectively; or

(b) perform any of the functions of a brokerage, broker or salesperson as provided in this Act.

Change in partnership

(3) A change in the membership of a partnership shall be deemed to create a new partnership for the purpose of registration.

Change in corporation

(4) A change in the officers or directors of a corporation registered as a brokerage may be made only with the consent of the registrar.

[S.O. 2002, c. 30, Sched. C, s. 4, in force March 31, 2006 (O. Gaz. 2005, p. 3251)]

Exemptions

5. (1) Despite section 4, registration shall not be required in respect of any trade in real estate by,

    (a) an assignee, custodian, liquidator, receiver, trustee or other person acting under the *Bankruptcy and Insolvency Act* (Canada), the *Corporations Act*, the *Business Corporations Act*, the *Courts of Justice Act*, the *Winding-up and Restructuring Act* (Canada), or a person acting under the order of any court, or an executor or trustee selling under the terms of a will, marriage settlement or deed of trust;

    (b) an auctioneer if the trade is made in the course of and as part of the auctioneer's duties as auctioneer;

    (c) a person who is registered under the *Securities Act* if the trade is made in the course of and as part of the person's business in connection with a trade in securities;

    (d) a bank or authorized foreign bank within the meaning of section 2 of the *Bank Act* (Canada), a credit union as defined in the *Credit Unions and Caisses Populaires Act, 1994* or a loan, trust or insurance corporation trading in real estate owned or administered by the corporation;

    (e) a person in respect of any mine or mining property within the meaning of the *Mining Act* or in respect of the real estate included in a Crown grant or lease, a mining claim or mineral lands under the *Mining Act* or any predecessor of that Act;

    (f) a full-time salaried employee of a party to a trade if the employee is acting for or on behalf of his or her employer in respect of land situate in Ontario;

    (g) a solicitor of the Superior Court of Justice who is providing legal services if the trade in real estate is itself a legal service or is incidental to and directly arising out of the legal services;

    (h) a person, on the person's own account, in respect of the person's interest in real estate unless,

        (i) the trade results from an offer of the person to act or a request that the person act in connection with the trade or any other trade, for or on behalf of the other party or one of the other parties to the trade, or

        (ii) the interest of the person in the real estate was acquired after the offer or request referred to in subclause (i) whether or not the trade is the result of the offer or request;

(i) a person in respect of the provision for another, for remuneration other than by commission, of all consultations, undertakings and services necessary to arrange for the routing of a right of way including the acquisition of land or interests in land for the purpose, and the person's employees engaged in the project;

(j) a person who trades in real estate solely for the purpose of arranging leases to which the *Tenant Protection Act, 1997* applies; or

(k) such persons or classes of persons that are prescribed as exempt from registration in respect of any class of trades in real estate.

Independent contractor not an employee

(2) An independent contractor is not an employee for the purpose of clauses (1) (f) and (i).

[S.O. 2002, c. 30, Sched. C, s. 5, in force March 31, 2006 (O. Gaz. 2005, p. 3251)]

Notification of registration required

6. Subject to subsection 14 (8), no brokerage, broker or salesperson shall trade in real estate until notified in writing by the registrar that the brokerage, broker or salesperson, as the case may be, is registered.

[S.O. 2002, c. 30, Sched. C, s. 6, in force March 31, 2006 (O. Gaz. 2005, p. 3251)]

Prohibition against multiple offices unless registered

7. (1) No brokerage shall conduct a business of trading in real estate from more than one place to which the public is invited unless the brokerage is registered in respect of each place, one of which shall be designated as the main office and the remainder as branch offices.

Branch offices

(2) Every branch office of a brokerage shall be under the supervision of a broker and each such office having more than one salesperson shall be under the direct management of a broker or of a salesperson who has been registered for at least two years and who is under the supervision of a broker.

[S.O. 2002, c. 30, Sched. C, s. 7, in force March 31, 2006 (O. Gaz. 2005, p. 3251)]

Specialist certification

8. (1) No registrant shall hold himself, herself or itself out as a specialist in trading in any type of real estate unless,

> (a) the trading in that type of real estate is prescribed as an area of specialization; and
>
> (b) the registrant is certified, as prescribed, as a specialist in trading in that area of specialization.
>
> *Brokerage categories*
>
> (2) A regulation under this section may differentiate among brokerages and between brokerages and brokers and salespersons and may provide that brokerages that are corporations may not be certified as specialists.
>
> [S.O. 2002, c. 30, Sched. C, s. 8, not yet proclaimed in force.]

Registration a requirement to bring action

9. No action shall be brought for commission or other remuneration for services in connection with a trade in real estate unless at the time of rendering the services the person bringing the action was registered or exempt from registration under this Act and the court may stay any such action upon motion.

[S.O. 2002, c. 30, Sched. C, s. 9, in force March 31, 2006 (O. Gaz. 2005, p. 3251)]

PART IV
REGISTRATION

Registration prohibited

9.1 (1) If an applicant for registration or renewal of registration does not meet the prescribed requirements, the registrar shall refuse to grant or renew the registration.

Non-application

(2) Section 14 does not apply to a refusal under subsection (1) to grant or renew a registration.

Notice of refusal

(3) The registrar shall give the applicant written notice of a refusal under subsection (1), setting out the reasons for the refusal and subsection 45 (3) does not apply to the notice.

[S.O. 2004, c. 19, ss. 18(3), 24(2), in force March 31, 2006]

Registration

10. (1) An applicant that meets the prescribed requirements is entitled to registration or renewal of registration by the registrar unless,

(a) the applicant is not a corporation and,

   (i)   having regard to the applicant's financial position or the financial position of an interested person in respect of the applicant, the applicant cannot reasonably be expected to be financially responsible in the conduct of business,

   (ii) the past conduct of the applicant or of an interested person in respect of the applicant affords reasonable grounds for belief that the applicant will not carry on business in accordance with law and with integrity and honesty, or

   (iii) the applicant or an employee or agent of the applicant makes a false statement or provides a false statement in an application for registration or for renewal of registration;

(b) [Repealed: S.O. 2004, c. 19, ss. 18 (5), 24 (2)]

(c) [Repealed: S.O. 2004, c. 19, ss. 18 (5), 24 (2)]

(d) the applicant is a corporation and,

   (i)   having regard to its financial position or the financial position of an interested person in respect of the corp-oration, the applicant cannot reasonably be expected to be financially responsible in the conduct of its business,

   (ii) having regard to the financial position of its officers or directors or an interested person in respect of its officers or directors, the applicant cannot reasonably be expected to be financially responsible in the conduct of its business,

   (iii) the past conduct of its officers or directors or of an interested person in respect of its officers or directors or of an interested person in respect of the corporation affords reasonable grounds for belief that its business will not be carried on in accordance with the law and with integrity and honesty, or

   (iv) an officer or director of the corporation makes a false statement or provides a false statement in an application for registration or for renewal of registration.

(e) the applicant or an interested person in respect of the applicant is carrying on activities that are, or will be if the applicant is registered, in contravention of this Act or the regulations, other than the code of ethics established under section 50;

(f) the applicant is in breach of a condition of the registration; or

(g) the applicant fails to comply with a request made by the registrar under subsection (1.1).

Request for information

(1.1) The registrar may request an applicant for registration or renewal of registration to provide to the registrar, in the form and within the time period specified by the registrar,

   (a)   information specified by the registrar that is relevant to the decision to be made by the registrar as to whether or not to grant the registration or renewal;

   (b)   verification, by affidavit or otherwise, of any information described in clause (a) that the applicant is providing or has provided to the registrar.

Conditions

(2) A registration is subject to such conditions as are consented to by the applicant or registrant, as are applied by the registrar under section 13, as are ordered by the Tribunal or as are prescribed.

Registration not transferable

(3) A registration is not transferable.

Interested person

(4) For the purposes of this section, a person shall be deemed to be an interested person in respect of another person if the person is associated with the other person or if, in the opinion of the registrar,

   (a)   the person has or may have a beneficial interest in the other person's business;

   (b)   the person exercises or may exercise control either directly or indirectly over the other person; or

   (c)   the person has provided or may have provided financing either directly or indirectly to the other person's business.

[S.O. 2002, c. 30, Sched. C, s. 10, in force March 31, 2006 (O. Gaz. 2005, p. 3251); S.O. 2004, c. 19, ss. 18(4)-(8), 24(2), in force March 31, 2006]

Registration of corporation

11. (1) When it registers and on each renewal of its registration, a brokerage that is a corporation shall disclose to the registrar the identity of,

   (a)   each person that beneficially owns or controls 10 per cent or more of the equity shares issued and outstanding at the time of the registration or the renewal of registration, as the case may be; and

(b) persons that are associated with each other and that together beneficially own or control 10 per cent or more of the equity shares issued and outstanding at the time of the registration or the renewal of registration, as the case may be.

Calculating number of shares

(2) In calculating the total number of equity shares of the corporation beneficially owned or controlled for the purposes of this section, the total number shall be calculated as the total number of all shares beneficially owned or controlled, but each share that carries the right to more than one vote shall be calculated as the number of shares equalling the total number of votes carried.

[S.O. 2002, c. 30, Sched. C, s. 11, in force March 31, 2006 (O. Gaz. 2005, p. 3251); S.O. 2004, c. 19, ss. 18(9), 24(2), in force March 31, 2006]

Broker of record

12. (1) Every brokerage shall,

(a) designate a broker who is employed by the brokerage as the broker of record and notify the registrar of his or her identity; and

(b) notify the registrar if the broker of record changes, within five days of the change.

Duties

(2) The broker of record shall ensure that the brokerage complies with this Act and the regulations.

Sole proprietor

(3) If a brokerage is a sole proprietorship, it shall designate the sole proprietor as the broker of record even though other brokers may be employed by the brokerage.

[S.O. 2002, c. 30, Sched. C, s. 12, in force March 31, 2006 (O. Gaz. 2005, p. 3251)]

Refusal to register, etc.

13. (1) Subject to section 14, the registrar may refuse to register an applicant or may suspend or revoke a registration or refuse to renew a registration if, in his or her opinion, the applicant or registrant is not entitled to registration under section 10.

Conditions

(2) Subject to section 14, the registrar may,

(a) approve the registration or renewal of a registration on such conditions as he or she considers appropriate; and

(b) at any time apply to a registration such conditions as he or she considers appropriate.

[S.O. 2002, c. 30, Sched. C, s. 13, in force March 31, 2006 (O. Gaz. 2005, p. 3251); S.O. 2004, c. 19, ss. 18(10), 24(2), in force March 31, 2006]

Notice re: refusal, suspension, etc.

14. (1) The registrar shall notify an applicant or registrant in writing if he or she proposes to,

(a) refuse under subsection 13(1) to grant or renew a registration;

(b) suspend or revoke a registration; or

(c) apply conditions to a registration or renewal to which the applicant or registrant has not consented.

Content of notice

(2) The notice of proposal shall set out the reasons for the proposed action and shall state that the applicant or registrant is entitled to a hearing by the Tribunal if the applicant or registrant mails or delivers, within 15 days after service of the notice, a written request for a hearing to the registrar and to the Tribunal.

Service

(3) The notice of proposal shall be served on the applicant or registrant in accordance with section 45.

If no request for hearing

(4) If an applicant or registrant does not request a hearing in accordance with subsection (2), the registrar may carry out the proposal.

Hearing

(5) If a hearing is requested, the Tribunal shall hold the hearing and may by order direct the registrar to carry out the registrar's proposal or substitute its opinion for that of the registrar and the Tribunal may attach conditions to its order or to a registration.

Parties

(6) The registrar, the applicant or registrant and such other persons as the Tribunal may specify are parties to the proceedings under this section.

Voluntary cancellation

(7) The registrar may cancel a registration upon the request in writing of the registrant and this section does not apply to the cancellation.

Continuation pending renewal

(8) If, within the time prescribed or, if no time is prescribed, before the expiry of the registrant's registration, the registrant has applied for renewal of a registration and paid the required fee, the registration shall be deemed to continue,

(a) until the renewal is granted;

(b) until the registrar gives the registrant written notice of the registrar's refusal under section 9.1 to grant the renewal; or

(c) if the registrant is served notice that the registrar proposes to refuse under subsection 13 (1) to grant the renewal, until the time for requesting a hearing has expired or, if a hearing is requested, until the Tribunal makes its order.

Immediate effect

(9) Even if a registrant appeals an order of the Tribunal under section 11 of the *Licence Appeal Tribunal Act, 1999*, the order takes effect immediately but the Tribunal may grant a stay until the disposition of the appeal.

[S.O. 2002, c. 30, Sched. C, s. 14, in force March 31, 2006 (O. Gaz. 2005, p. 3251); S.O. 2004, c. 19, ss. 18(11), (12), 24(2), in force March 31, 2006]

Immediate suspension

15. (1) If the registrar proposes to suspend or revoke a registration under section 14 and if the registrar considers it in the public interest to do so, the registrar may by order temporarily suspend the registration.

Immediate effect

(2) An order under subsection (1) takes effect immediately.

Expiry of order

(3) If a hearing is requested under section 14,

(a) the order expires 15 days after the written request for a hearing is received by the Tribunal; or

(b) the Tribunal may extend the time of expiration until the hearing is concluded, if a hearing is commenced within the 15-day period referred to in clause (a).

Same

(4) Despite subsection (3), if it is satisfied that the conduct of the registrant has delayed the commencement of the hearing, the Tribunal may extend the time of the expiration for the order,

(a) until the hearing commences; and

(b) once the hearing commences, until the hearing is concluded.

[S.O. 2002, c. 30, Sched. C, s. 15, in force March 31, 2006 (O. Gaz. 2005, p. 3251)]

Requirements for hearing request

16. (1) A request for a hearing under section 14 is sufficiently served if delivered personally or sent by registered mail to the registrar and to the Tribunal.

Same

(2) If service is made by registered mail, it shall be deemed to be made on the third day after the day of mailing.

Other methods

(3) Despite subsection (1), the Tribunal may order any other method of service.

[S.O. 2002, c. 30, Sched. C, s. 16, in force March 31, 2006 (O. Gaz. 2005, p. 3251)]

Further application

17. A person whose registration is refused, revoked or refused renewal may reapply for registration only if,

(a) the time prescribed to reapply has passed since the refusal, revocation or refusal to renew; and

(b) new or other evidence is available or it is clear that material circumstances have changed.

[S.O. 2002, c. 30, Sched. C, s. 17, in force March 31, 2006 (O. Gaz. 2005, p. 3251)]

Notice of issue or transfer of shares

18. (1) In addition to the disclosure required under section 11, every brokerage that is a corporation shall notify the registrar in writing within 30 days after the issue or transfer of any equity shares of the corporation, if the issue or transfer results in,

(a) any person, or any persons that are associated with each other, acquiring or accumulating beneficial ownership or control of 10 per cent or more of the total number of all issued and outstanding equity shares of the corporation; or

(b) an increase in the percentage of issued and outstanding equity shares of the corporation beneficially owned or controlled by any person, or any persons who are associated with each other, where the person or the associated persons already beneficially owned or controlled 10 per cent or more of the total number of all issued and outstanding equity shares of the corporation before the issue or transfer.

Same

(2) Despite subsection (1), if a registrant that is a corporation becomes aware of a transfer that otherwise falls into subsection (1) after the transfer has taken place, it shall notify the registrar in writing within 30 days after knowledge of the transfer comes to the attention of its officers or directors.

Calculation of total number of equity shares

(3) In calculating the total number of equity shares of the corporation beneficially owned or controlled for the purpose of this section, the total number shall be calculated as the total of all the shares beneficially owned or controlled, but each share that carries the right to more than one vote shall be calculated as the number of shares equalling the total number of votes it carries.

[S.O. 2002, c. 30, Sched. C, s. 18, in force March 31, 2006 (O. Gaz. 2005, p. 3251); S.O. 2004, c. 19, s. 18(13), 24(2), in force March 31, 2006]

PART V
COMPLAINTS, INSPECTION AND DISCIPLINE

Complaints

19. (1) If the registrar receives a complaint about a registrant, the registrar may request information in relation to the complaint from any registrant.

Request for information

(2) A request for information under subsection (1) shall indicate the nature of the complaint.

Duty to comply with request

(3) A registrant who receives a written request for information shall provide the information as soon as practicable.

Procedures

(4) In handling complaints, the registrar may do any of the following, as appropriate:

1. Attempt to mediate or resolve the complaint.

2. Give the registrant a written warning that if the registrant continues with the activity that led to the complaint, action may be taken against the registrant.

3. Require the broker or salesperson to take further educational courses.

4. Refer the matter, in whole or in part, to the discipline committee.

5. Take an action under section 13, subject to section 14.

6. Take further action as is appropriate in accordance with the Act.

[S.O. 2002, c. 30, Sched. C, s. 19, in force March 31, 2006 (O. Gaz. 2005, p. 3251)]

Inspection by registrar

20. (1) The registrar or a person designated in writing by the registrar may conduct an inspection and may, as part of that inspection, enter and inspect at any reasonable time the business premises of a registrant, other than any part of the premises used as a dwelling, for the purpose of,

(a) ensuring compliance with this Act and the regulations;

(b) dealing with a complaint under section 19; or

(c) ensuring the registrant remains entitled to registration.

Powers on inspection

(2) While carrying out an inspection, an inspector,

(a) is entitled to free access to all money, valuables, documents and records of the person being inspected that are relevant to the inspection;

(b) may use any data storage, processing or retrieval device or system used in carrying on business in order to produce information in any form; and

(c) may, upon giving a receipt for them, remove for examination and may copy anything relevant to the inspection including any data storage disk or other retrieval device in order to produce information, but shall promptly return the thing to the person being inspected.

Identification

(3) An inspector shall produce, on request, evidence of his or her authority to carry out an inspection.

Assistance to be given

(4) An inspector may, in the course of an inspection, require a person to produce a document or record and to provide whatever assistance is reasonably necessary, including using any data storage, processing or retrieval device or system to produce information in any form, and the person shall produce the document or record or provide the assistance.

Obstruction prohibited

(5) No person shall obstruct an inspector conducting an inspection or withhold from him or her or conceal, alter or destroy any money, valuables, documents or records that are relevant to the inspection.

Use of force prohibited

(6) An inspector shall not use force to enter and inspect premises under this section.

Admissibility of copies

(7) A copy of a document or record certified by an inspector to be a true copy of the original is admissible in evidence to the same extent as the original and has the same evidentiary value.

[S.O. 2002, c. 30, Sched. C, s. 20, in force March 31, 2006 (O. Gaz. 2005, p. 3251)]

Discipline proceedings

21. (1) A discipline committee shall be established to hear and determine, in accordance with the prescribed procedures, if a registrant has failed to comply with the code of ethics established by the Minister.

Appeals committee

(2) An appeals committee shall be established to consider, in accordance with the prescribed procedures, appeals from the discipline committee.

Appointment of members

(3) The board of the administrative authority or, if there is no designated administrative authority, the Minister shall appoint the members of the discipline committee and the members of the appeals

committee and, in making the appointments, shall ensure that the prescribed requirements for the composition of each committee are met.

Result of a determination

(4) If the discipline committee makes a determination under subsection (1) that a registrant has failed to comply with the code of ethics, it may order any of the following as appropriate:

1. Require the broker or salesperson to take further educational courses.

2. In accordance with the terms that may be specified by the committee, require the brokerage to fund educational courses for brokers and salespersons employed by the brokerage or to arrange and fund such educational courses.

3. Despite subsection 12 (1) of the *Safety and Consumer Statutes Administration Act, 1996*, impose such fine as the committee considers appropriate, to a maximum of $25,000, or such lesser amount as may be prescribed, to be paid by the registrant to the administrative authority or to the Minister of Finance if there is no designated administrative authority.

4. Suspend or postpone the taking of further educational courses, the funding or the funding and arranging of educational courses or the imposition of the fine for such period and upon such terms as the committee designates.

5. Fix and impose costs to be paid by the registrant to the administrative authority or to the Minister of Finance if there is no designated administrative authority.

Appeal

(5) A party to the discipline proceeding may appeal the final order of the discipline committee to the appeals committee.

Power of the appeals committee

(6) The appeals committee may by order overturn, affirm or modify the order of the discipline committee and may make an order under subsection (4).

Payment of fine

(7) The registrant shall pay any fine imposed under subsection (4),

(a) on or before the day specified in the order of the discipline committee or, if the fine is the subject of an appeal, on or before the day specified in the order of the appeals committee; or

(b) on or before the 60th day after the date of the last order made in respect of the fine, if no day is specified in that order.

Taking of educational course

(8) The registrant shall take the educational course required under subsection (4),

(a) within the time period specified in the order of the discipline committee or, if the requirement is the subject of an appeal, within the time period specified in the order of the appeals committee; or

(b) at the first reasonable opportunity after the last order made in respect of the educational course, if no time period is specified in that order.

Arranging and funding educational courses

(9) The brokerage shall arrange and fund educational courses for brokers and salespersons employed by the brokerage as required under subsection (4) within the time period specified in the order of the discipline committee or, if the requirement is the subject of an appeal, within the time period specified in the order of the appeals committee.

Funding educational courses

(10) The brokerage shall fund the educational courses for brokers and salespersons employed by the brokerage as required under subsection (4),

(a) within the time period specified in the order of the discipline committee or, if the requirement is the subject of an appeal, within the time period specified in the order of the appeals committee; or

(b) at the first reasonable opportunity after the last order made in respect of the educational course, if no time period is specified in that order.

Public access

(11) Decisions of the discipline committee and the appeals committee shall be made available to the public in such manner as may be prescribed.

[S.O. 2002, c. 30, Sched. C, s. 21, in force March 31, 2006 (O. Gaz. 2005, p. 3251); S.O. 2004, c. 19, ss. 18(14), 24(2), in force March 31, 2006]

Appointment of investigators

22. (1) The director may appoint persons to be investigators for the purposes of conducting investigations.

Certificate of appointment

(2) The director shall issue to every investigator a certificate of appointment bearing his or her signature or a facsimile of the signature.

Production of certificate of appointment

(3) Every investigator who is exercising powers under section 23 shall, upon request, produce the certificate of appointment as an investigator.

[S.O. 2002, c. 30, Sched. C, s. 22, in force March 31, 2006 (O. Gaz. 2005, p. 3251)]

Search warrant

23. (1) Upon application made without notice by an investigator appointed under this Act, a justice of the peace may issue a warrant, if he or she is satisfied on information under oath that there is reasonable ground for believing that,

(a) a person has contravened or is contravening this Act or the regulations or has committed an offence under the law of any jurisdiction that is relevant to the person's fitness for registration under this Act; and

(b) there is,

(i) in any building, dwelling, receptacle or place anything relating to the contravention of this Act or the regulations or to the person's fitness for registration, or

(ii) information or evidence relating to the contravention of this Act or the regulations or the person's fitness for registration that may be obtained through the use of an investigative technique or procedure or the doing of anything described in the warrant.

Powers under warrant

(2) A warrant obtained under subsection (1) authorizes an investigator appointed under subsection 22 (1),

(a) upon producing his or her appointment, to enter or access the building, dwelling, receptacle or place specified in the warrant and examine and seize anything described in the warrant;

(b) to use any data storage, processing or retrieval device or system used in carrying on business in order to produce information or evidence described in the warrant, in any form;

(c) to exercise any of the powers specified in subsection (10); and

(d)   to use any investigative technique or procedure or do anything described in the warrant.

Entry of dwelling

(3) Despite subsection (2), an investigator shall not exercise the power under a warrant to enter a place, or part of a place, used as a dwelling, unless,

(a)   the justice of the peace is informed that the warrant is being sought to authorize entry into a dwelling; and

(b)   the justice of the peace authorizes the entry into the dwelling.

Conditions on search warrant

(4) A warrant obtained under subsection (1) shall contain such conditions as the justice of the peace considers advisable to ensure that any search authorized by the warrant is reasonable in the circumstances.

Expert help

(5) The warrant may authorize persons who have special, expert or professional knowledge to accompany and assist the investigator in respect of the execution of the warrant.

Time of execution

(6) An entry or access under a warrant issued under this section shall be made between 6 a.m. and 9 p.m., unless the warrant specifies otherwise.

Expiry of warrant

(7) A warrant issued under this section shall name a date of expiry, which shall be no later than 30 days after the warrant is issued, but a justice of the peace may extend the date of expiry for an additional period of no more than 30 days, upon application without notice by an investigator.

Use of force

(8) An investigator may call upon police officers for assistance in executing the warrant and the investigator may use whatever force is reasonably necessary to execute the warrant.

Obstruction

(9) No person shall obstruct an investigator executing a warrant under this section or withhold from him or her or conceal, alter or

destroy anything relevant to the investigation being conducted pursuant to the warrant.

Assistance

(10) An investigator may, in the course of executing a warrant, require a person to produce the evidence or information described in the warrant and to provide whatever assistance is reasonably necessary, including using any data storage, processing or retrieval device or system to produce, in any form, the evidence or information described in the warrant and the person shall produce the evidence or information or provide the assistance.

Return of seized items

(11) An investigator shall return any item seized under this section or section 23.1 within a reasonable time.

Admissibility

(12) A copy of a document or record certified by an investigator as being a true copy of the original is admissible in evidence to the same extent as the original and has the same evidentiary value.

[S.O. 2002, c. 30, Sched. C, s. 23, in force March 31, 2006 (O. Gaz. 2005, p. 3251); S.O. 2004, c. 19, ss. 18(15), 24(2), in force March 31, 2006]

Seizure of things not specified

23.1 An investigator who is appointed under this Act and who is lawfully present in a place pursuant to a warrant or otherwise in the execution of his or her duties may, without a warrant, seize anything that the investigator believes on reasonable grounds will afford evidence relating to a contravention of this Act or the regulations.

[S.O. 2004, c. 19, ss. 18(15), 24(2), in force March 31, 2006]

Searches in exigent circumstances

24. (1) An investigator may exercise any of the powers described in subsection 23 (2) without a warrant if the conditions for obtaining the warrant exist but by reason of exigent circumstances it would be impracticable to obtain the warrant.

Dwellings

(2) Subsection (1) does not apply to a building or part of a building that is being used as a dwelling.

Use of force

(3) The investigator may, in executing any authority given by this section, call upon police officers for assistance and use whatever force is reasonably necessary.

Applicability of s. 23

(4) Subsections 23 (5), (9), (10), (11) and (12) apply with necessary modifications to a search under this section.

[S.O. 2002, c. 30, Sched. C, s. 24, in force March 31, 2006 (O. Gaz. 2005, p. 3251); S.O. 2004, c. 19, ss. 18(15), 24(2), in force March 31, 2006]

Freeze order

25. (1) If the conditions in subsection (2) are met, the director may in writing,

(a)   order any person having on deposit or controlling any assets or trust funds of a registrant or former registrant to hold those funds or assets;

(b)   order a registrant or former registrant to refrain from withdrawing any asset or trust fund from a person having it on deposit or controlling it; or

(c)   order a registrant or former registrant to hold any asset or trust fund of a client, customer or other person in trust for the person entitled to it.

Conditions

(2) The director may make an order under subsection (1) if he or she believes that it is advisable for the protection of the clients or customers of a registrant or former registrant and,

(a)   a search warrant has been issued under this Act; or

(b)   criminal proceedings or proceedings in relation to a contravention under this Act or under any other Act are about to be or have been instituted against the registrant or former registrant in connection with or arising out of the business in respect of which the registrant or former registrant is or was registered.

Limitation

(3) In the case of a bank or authorized foreign bank within the meaning of section 2 of the *Bank Act* (Canada), a credit union within the meaning of the *Credit Unions and Caisses Populaires Act, 1994* or

a loan or trust corporation, the order under subsection (1) applies only to the offices and branches named in the order.

Release of assets

(4) The director may consent to the release of any particular asset or trust fund from the order or may wholly revoke the order.

Exception

(5) Subsection (1) does not apply if the registrant or former registrant files with the director, in such manner and amount as the director determines,

   (a)   a personal bond accompanied by collateral security;

   (b)   a bond of an insurer licensed under the *Insurance Act* to write surety and fidelity insurance;

   (c)   a bond of a guarantor accompanied by collateral security; or

   (d)   another prescribed form of security.

Application to court

(6) An application may be made to the Superior Court of Justice for a determination in respect of the disposition of an asset or trust fund,

   (a)   by a person in receipt of an order under subsection (1), if that person is in doubt as to whether the order applies to the asset or trust fund; or

   (b)   by a person who claims an interest in the asset or trust fund that is subject to the order.

Notice

(7) If an order is made under this section, the director may register in the appropriate land registry office a notice that an order under subsection (1) has been issued and that the order may affect land belonging to the person referred to in the notice, and the notice has the same effect as the registration of a certificate of pending litigation, except that the director may in writing revoke or modify the notice.

Cancellation or discharge application

(8) A registrant or former registrant in respect of which an order is made under subsection (1) or any person having an interest in land in respect of which a notice is registered under subsection (7) may apply to the Tribunal for cancellation in whole or in part of the order or for discharge in whole or in part of the registration.

Disposition by Tribunal

(9) The Tribunal shall dispose of the application after a hearing and may cancel the order or discharge the registration in whole or in part if the Tribunal finds,

(a) that the order or registration is not required in whole or in part for the protection of clients or customers of the applicant or of other persons having an interest in the land; or

(b) that the interests of other persons are unduly prejudiced by the order or registration.

Parties

(10) The applicant, the director and such other persons as the Tribunal may specify are parties to the proceedings before the Tribunal.

Court application

(11) If the director has made an order under subsection (1) or registered a notice under subsection (7), he or she may apply to the Superior Court of Justice for directions or an order relating to the disposition of assets, trust funds or land affected by the order or notice.

Notice not required

(12) An application by the director under this section may be made without notice to any other person.

[S.O. 2002, c. 30, Sched. C, s. 25, in force March 31, 2006 (O. Gaz. 2005, p. 3251)]

Freeze orders, non-registrants

25.1 (1) The director may make an order described in subsection (2) in respect of the money or assets of a person who is not registered under this Act and who is alleged to have conducted business for which registration is required under this Act at a time when the person was not registered to do so if,

(a) the director receives an affidavit in which it is alleged, and in which facts are set out supporting the allegation, that the person who is not registered under this Act,

(i) is subject to criminal proceedings or proceedings in relation to a contravention under this Act or any other Act that are about to be or have been instituted against the person in connection with or arising out of conducting business for which registration is required under this Act, or

> (ii) owns a building, dwelling, receptacle or place, or carries on activities in a building, dwelling, receptacle or place, in respect of which a search warrant has been issued under section 23; and
>
> (b) the director, based on the affidavit referred to in clause (a), finds reasonable grounds to believe that,
>
> > (i) in the course of conducting business for which registration is required under this Act, the person who is the subject of the allegation referred to in clause (a) has received money or assets from clients or customers, and
> >
> > (ii) the interests of those clients or customers require protection.

Order

(2) In the circumstances described in subsection (1), the director may, in writing,

> (a) order any person having on deposit or controlling any money or asset of the person who is the subject of the allegation referred to in clause (1) (a) to hold the money or asset; or
>
> (b) order the person who is the subject of the allegation referred to in clause (1) (a),
>
> > (i) to refrain from withdrawing any money or asset from a person having it on deposit or controlling it, or
> >
> > (ii) to hold any money or asset of a client, customer or other person in trust for the person who is entitled to it.

Application

(3) Subsections 25 (3) to (12) apply with necessary modifications to an order made under this section.

[S.O. 2004, c. 19, ss. 18(17), 24(2), in force March 31, 2006]

PART VI
CONDUCT AND OFFENCES

Duty of brokerage

26. A brokerage shall ensure that every salesperson and broker that the brokerage employs is carrying out their duties in compliance with this Act and the regulations.

[S.O. 2002, c. 30, Sched. C, s. 26, in force March 31, 2006 (O. Gaz. 2005, p. 3251)]

Trust account

27. (1) Every brokerage shall,

(a) maintain in Ontario an account designated as a trust account, in,

   (i) a bank, or an authorized foreign bank, within the meaning of section 2 of the *Bank Act* (Canada),

   (ii) a loan or trust corporation, or

   (iii) a credit union, as defined in the *Credit Unions and Caisses Populaires Act, 1994*;

(b) deposit into the account all money that comes into the brokerage's hands in trust for other persons in connection with the brokerage's business;

(c) at all times keep the money separate and apart from money belonging to the brokerage; and

(d) disburse the money only in accordance with the terms of the trust.

Disclosure

(2) Brokerages shall fully and clearly disclose in writing to a person depositing trust money the terms on which the brokerage deposits the money, including whether the money is deposited in an interest bearing account and the interest rate that the brokerage receives on the money.

Interest

(3) Unless otherwise provided by contract, all interest on the trust money referred to in subsection (1) shall be paid to the beneficial owner of the trust money.

Entitlement unclear

(4) If a brokerage holds money in trust for a period of two years and entitlement to the money has not been determined or is unclear, the brokerage shall pay the money to,

(a) the administrative authority; or

(b) if there is no designated administrative authority, the Minister of Finance.

Unclaimed trust money

(5) If a brokerage holds money in trust for a period of one year after the person for whom it is held first became entitled to payment of the money and the person cannot be located, the brokerage shall pay the money to,

(a) the administrative authority; or

(b)   if there is no designated administrative authority, the Minister of Finance.

Attempt to locate person entitled to payment of money

(6) Before the brokerage pays the money under subsection (5), the brokerage shall use reasonable efforts to locate the person entitled to the money being held in trust.

Information on entitlement

(7) When a brokerage pays money over under subsection (4) or (5), the brokerage shall provide to the administrative authority or to the Minister of Finance, as the case may be, as much information as the brokerage has in order to determine who is entitled to the trust money.

Money held in trust

(8) If the administrative authority has been paid money under clause (4) (a) or (5) (a), it shall hold the money in trust until the money is claimed by the person who is entitled to it or the money is transferred to the Minister of Finance under subsection (11).

Use of interest

(9) If money has been paid to the administrative authority under clause (4) (a) or (5) (a), the administrative authority shall allocate any interest that is earned after it has received the money to a separate account and may use the money from that account only to cover the costs of administering the trust fund and processing claims for the recovery of money held in trust.

Same

(10) If money to which clause (4) (a) or (5) (a) applies is held in an interest bearing account and the money is paid to the administrative authority, the administrative authority shall treat the money that is paid as a capital amount, and for purposes of subsection (9), interest shall be deemed not to be earned on the money until after the administrative authority has received it.

Unclaimed trust money to Minister of Finance

(11) If the administrative authority holds money that has been paid under clause (4) (a) or (5) (a) for a period of five years, the administrative authority shall pay the money to the Minister of Finance within one year after it has been held for the five-year period.

Attempt to locate person entitled to money

(12) The Minister or the administrative authority, as the case may be, shall use reasonable efforts to locate the person entitled to the money paid under subsection (5).

Rights preserved

(13) The payment of money held in trust to the Minister of Finance or the administrative authority is made without any prejudice to the rights of any person to claim entitlement to the trust money.

Payment

(14) The Minister of Finance or the administrative authority that receives money under subsection (4) or (5) shall pay it to the person entitled to the money.

Transition

(15) If a person who was registered as a broker under the *Real Estate and Business Brokers Act* immediately before that Act is repealed is holding money to which subsection (4) or (5) would apply if they were in force for the period specified in the subsection or for a longer period immediately before this section is proclaimed into force, within one year after this section has come into force, the person deemed to be a brokerage under subsection 49 (2) shall pay the money to,

    (a)   the administrative authority; or

    (b)   if there is no designated administrative authority, the Minister of Finance.

[S.O. 2002, c. 30, Sched. C, s. 27, in force March 31, 2006 (O. Gaz. 2005, p. 3251); S.O. 2004, c. 19, ss. 18(18), 24(2), in force March 31, 2006]

Notice of changes to registrar

28. (1) Every brokerage shall, within five days after the event, notify the registrar in writing of,

    (a)   any change in address for service;

    (b)   in the case of a corporation or partnership, any change in the officers or directors; and

    (c)   the date of commencement or termination of the employment of every broker and salesperson and, in the case of termination of employment of a broker or salesperson, the reason for the termination.

Same

(2) Every broker or salesperson shall, within five days after the event, notify the registrar in writing of,

    (a)   any change in address for service; and

    (b)   the commencement or termination of his or her employment by a brokerage and the date of the commencement or termination.

Timing

(3) The registrar shall be deemed to have been notified on the day on which he or she is actually notified or, where the notification is by mail, on the day of mailing.

Financial statements

(4) Every brokerage shall, when required by the registrar with the approval of the director, file a financial statement showing the matters specified by the registrar and signed by the broker of record and certified by a person licensed under the *Public Accounting Act, 2004.*

Confidential

(5) The information contained in a financial statement filed under subsection (4) is confidential and no person shall otherwise than in the ordinary course of the person's duties communicate any such information or allow access to the financial statement.

[**Editor's note:** Subsection 28 (4) was amended before being brought into force, by S.O. 2004, c. 8, s. 46, in force November 1, 2005 (O. Gaz. 2005, p. 3006).]

[S.O. 2002, c. 30, Sched. C, s. 28, in force March 31, 2006 (O. Gaz. 2005, p. 3251)]

Carrying on business as sole proprietor

29. (1) A brokerage carrying on business alone through an individual broker shall carry on business in the name of the broker and shall not use any description or device that would indicate that the brokerage's business is being carried on by more than one person or by a corporation.

Exception

(2) Despite subsection (1), a surviving or remaining partner may carry on business in the name of the original partnership if the surviving or remaining partner publishes on all letterhead, circulars and

advertisements used in connection with the business the fact that the surviving or remaining partner is the sole proprietor.

[S.O. 2002, c. 30, Sched. C, s. 29, in force March 31, 2006 (O. Gaz. 2005, p. 3251)]

Restrictions re: employees

30. No brokerage shall,

(a) employ another brokerage's broker or salesperson to trade in real estate or permit such broker or salesperson to act on the brokerage's behalf;

(b) employ an unregistered person to perform a function for which registration is required; or

(c) pay any commission or other remuneration to a person referred to in clause (a) or (b).

[S.O. 2002, c. 30, Sched. C, s. 30, in force March 31, 2006 (O. Gaz. 2005, p. 3251)]

31. (1) No broker or salesperson shall trade in real estate on behalf of any brokerage other than the brokerage which employs the broker or salesperson.

Same

(2) No broker or salesperson is entitled to or shall accept any commission or other remuneration for trading in real estate from any person except the brokerage which employs the broker or salesperson.

[S.O. 2002, c. 30, Sched. C, s. 31, in force March 31, 2006 (O. Gaz. 2005, p. 3251)]

Acquisition or divestiture by registrant

32. (1) Unless the registrant first delivers to all other parties to the agreement the notice described in subsection (2) and the other parties have acknowledged in writing receipt of the notice, no registrant shall, directly or indirectly,

(a) purchase, lease, exchange or otherwise acquire for himself, herself, or itself, any interest in real estate, or make an offer to do so; or

(b) divest himself, herself, or itself of any interest in real estate, or make an offer to do so.

Contents of notice

(2) The notice referred to in subsection (1) shall be in writing and shall include,

(a)   a statement that the registrant is a brokerage, broker or salesperson, as the case may be;

(b)   full disclosure of all facts within the registrant's knowledge that affect or will affect the value of the real estate; and

(c)   in the case of a transaction described in clause (1) (a), the particulars of any negotiation, offer or agreement by or on behalf of the registrant for the subsequent sale, lease, exchange or other disposition of an interest in the real estate to any other person.

[S.O. 2002, c. 30, Sched. C, s. 32, in force March 31, 2006 (O. Gaz. 2005, p. 3251); S.O. 2004, c. 19, ss. 18(21), 24(2), in force March 31, 2006]

Prohibition re: breaking contract

33. (1) No registrant shall induce any party to an agreement for purchase and sale or an agreement for rental of real estate to break the agreement for the purpose of entering into another such agreement.

Date of signing

(2) Every salesperson and broker shall make all reasonable efforts to ensure that a person signing an agreement in respect of a trade in real estate sets out the date upon which the signature was affixed.

Commission

(3) Unless agreed to in writing by the seller, no brokerage is entitled to claim commission or other remuneration from the seller in respect of a trade in real estate if the real estate is, to the knowledge of the brokerage, covered by an unexpired listing agreement with another brokerage.

[S.O. 2002, c. 30, Sched. C, s. 33, in force March 31, 2006 (O. Gaz. 2005, p. 3251); S.O. 2004, c. 19, ss. 18(22), 24(2), in force March 31, 2006]

Falsifying information

34. No registrant shall falsify, assist in falsifying or induce or counsel another person to falsify or assist in falsifying any information or document relating to a trade in real estate.

[S.O. 2002, c. 30, Sched. C, s. 34, in force March 31, 2006 (O. Gaz. 2005, p. 3251)]

Furnishing false information

35. No registrant shall furnish, assist in furnishing or induce or counsel another person to furnish or assist in furnishing any false or deceptive information or documents relating to a trade in real estate.

[S.O. 2002, c. 30, Sched. C, s. 35, in force March 31, 2006 (O. Gaz. 2005, p. 3251)]

Commission and remuneration, scale

36. (1) All commission or other remuneration payable to a brokerage in respect of a trade in real estate shall be either an agreed amount or percentage of the sale price or rental price, as the case may be, but not both and, if there is no agreement as to the amount of the commission, the rate of commission or other remuneration or other basis or amount of remuneration shall be that generally prevailing in the community where the real estate is located.

Same

(2) If the commission payable in respect of a trade in real estate is expressed as a percentage of the sale price or rental price, the percentage does not have to be fixed but may be expressed as a series of percentages that decrease at specified amounts as the sale price or rental price increases.

Same

(3) No registrant shall request or enter into an arrangement for the payment of a commission or any other remuneration based on the difference between the price at which real estate is listed for sale or rental and the actual sale price or rental price, as the case may be, of the real estate, nor is a registrant entitled to retain any commission or other remuneration computed upon any such basis.

[S.O. 2002, c. 30, Sched. C, s. 36, in force March 31, 2006 (O. Gaz. 2005, p. 3251)]

False advertising

37. No registrant shall make false, misleading or deceptive statements in any advertisement, circular, pamphlet or material published by any means relating to trading in real estate.

[S.O. 2002, c. 30, Sched. C, s. 37, in force March 31, 2006 (O. Gaz. 2005, p. 3251)]

Order of registrar re: false advertising

38. (1) If the registrar believes on reasonable grounds that a registrant is making a false, misleading or deceptive statement in any advertisement, circular, pamphlet or material published by any means, the registrar may,

    (a) order the cessation of the use of such material;

    (b) order the registrant to retract the statement or publish a correction of equal prominence to the original publication; or

(c)   order both a cessation described in clause (a) and a retraction or correction described in clause (b).

Procedures

(2) Section 14 applies with necessary modifications to an order under this section in the same manner as to a proposal by the registrar to refuse a registration.

Effect

(3) The order of the registrar shall take effect immediately, but the Tribunal may grant a stay until the registrar's order becomes final.

Pre-approval

(4) If the registrant does not appeal an order under this section or if the order or a variation of it is upheld by the Tribunal, the registrant shall, upon the request of the registrar, submit all statements in any advertisement, circular, pamphlet or material to be published by any means to the registrar for approval before publication for such period as the registrar specifies.

Specified period

(5) The registrar shall not specify under subsection (4) a period,

(a)   that exceeds such period as may be prescribed; or

(b)   any part of which falls outside such period as may be prescribed.

[S.O. 2002, c. 30, Sched. C, s. 38, in force March 31, 2006 (O. Gaz. 2005, p. 3251); S.O. 2004, c. 19, ss. 18(23) and (24), 24(2), in force March 31, 2006]

Restraining orders

39. (1) If it appears to the director that a person is not complying with this Act or the regulations or an order made under this Act, the director may apply to the Superior Court of Justice for an order directing that person to comply, and, upon the application, the court may make such order as the court thinks fit.

Same

(2) Subsection (1) applies in addition to any other procedures that may be available to the director, whether or not the director has exercised his or her rights under such procedures.

Appeal

(3) An appeal lies to the Divisional Court from an order made under subsection (1).

[S.O. 2002, c. 30, Sched. C, s. 39, in force March 31, 2006 (O. Gaz. 2005, p. 3251)]

Offence

40. (1) A person is guilty of an offence who,

(a)   furnishes false information in any application under this Act or in any statement or return required under this Act;

(b)   fails to comply with any order, other than an order made under section 21, direction or other requirement under this Act; or

(c)   contravenes or fails to comply with any section of this Act or the regulations made under the Act, other than a code of ethics established by the Minister under section 50.

Brokerages

(2) An officer or director of a brokerage is guilty of an offence who fails to take reasonable care to prevent the brokerage from committing an offence mentioned in subsection (1).

Penalties

(3) An individual who is convicted of an offence under this Act is liable to a fine of not more than $50,000 or to imprisonment for a term of not more than two years less a day, or both, and a corporation that is convicted of an offence under this Act is liable to a fine of not more than $250,000.

Limitation

(4) No proceeding under this section shall be commenced more than two years after the facts upon which the proceeding is based first came to the knowledge of the director.

[S.O. 2002, c. 30, Sched. C, s. 40, in force March 31, 2006 (O. Gaz. 2005, p. 3251)]

Orders for compensation, restitution

41. (1) If a person is convicted of an offence under this Act, the court making the conviction may, in addition to any other penalty, order the person convicted to pay compensation or make restitution.

If insurance has paid

(2) If an order is made in a person's favour under subsection (1) and that person has already received compensation or restitution from an insurer, the person ordered to pay the compensation or make restitution shall deliver the amount to the insurer.

[S.O. 2002, c. 30, Sched. C, s. 41, in force March 31, 2006 (O. Gaz. 2005, p. 3251)]

Default in payment of fines

42. (1) If a fine payable as a result of a conviction for an offence under this Act is in default for at least 60 days, the director may disclose to a consumer reporting agency the name of the defaulter, the amount of the fine and the date the fine went into default.

If payment made

(2) Within 10 days after the director has notice that the fine has been paid in full, the director shall inform the consumer reporting agency of the payment.

Transition

(3) If a fine is payable as a result of a conviction under the *Real Estate and Business Brokers Act*, despite the repeal of that Act, the director may treat the fine as if it is payable as a result of a conviction under this Act, and subsections (1) and (2) apply to such a fine in like manner as they apply to a fine payable for a conviction under this Act.

[S.O. 2002, c. 30, Sched. C, s. 42, in force March 31, 2006 (O. Gaz. 2005, p. 3251)]

Liens and charges

43. (1) If a fine payable as a result of a conviction for an offence under this Act is in default for at least 60 days, the director may by order create a lien against the property of the person who is liable to pay the fine.

Liens on personal property

(2) If the lien created by the director under subsection (1) relates to personal property,

(a) the *Personal Property Security Act*, except Part V, applies with necessary modifications to the lien, despite clause 4 (1) (a) of that Act;

(b) the lien shall be deemed to be a security interest that has attached for the purposes of the *Personal Property Security Act*; and

(c)   the director may perfect the security interest referred to in clause (b) for the purposes of the *Personal Property Security Act* by the registration of a financing statement under that Act.

Liens and charges on real property

(3) If the lien created by the director under subsection (1) relates to real property, the director may register the lien against the property of the person liable to pay the fine in the proper land registry office and on registration, the obligation under the lien becomes a charge on the property.

Initiation of sale proceedings prohibited

(4) The director shall not initiate sale proceedings in respect of any real property against which he or she has registered a lien under subsection (3).

Proceeds of sale

(5) If a lien is perfected by registration under subsection (2) or is registered against real property under subsection (3) and the related real or personal property is sold, the director shall ensure that the funds he or she receives as a result of the sale are used to pay the fine.

Discharge of lien

(6) Within 10 days after the director has knowledge of the payment in full of the fine, the director shall,

(a)   discharge the registration of any financing statement registered under clause (2) (c); and

(b)   register a discharge of a charge created on registration of a lien under subsection (3).

[S.O. 2002, c. 30, Sched. C, s. 43, in force March 31, 2006 (O. Gaz. 2005, p. 3251)]

PART VII
GENERAL

Confidentiality

44. (1) A person who obtains information in the course of exercising a power or carrying out a duty related to the administration of this Act or the regulations shall preserve secrecy with respect to the information and shall not communicate the information to any person except,

(a) as may be required in connection with a proceeding under this Act or in connection with the administration of this Act or the regulations;

(b) to a ministry, department or agency of a government engaged in the administration of legislation similar to this Act or legislation that protects consumers or to any other entity to which the administration of legislation similar to this Act or legislation that protects consumers has been assigned;

(c) to a prescribed entity or organization, if the purpose of the communication is consumer protection;

(d) to a law enforcement agency;

(e) to his, her or its counsel; or

(f) with the consent of the person to whom the information relates.

Testimony

(2) Except in a proceeding under this Act, no person shall be required to give testimony in a civil proceeding with regard to information obtained in the course of exercising a power or carrying out a duty related to the administration of this Act or the regulations.

[S.O. 2002, c. 30, Sched. C, s. 44, in force March 31, 2006 (O. Gaz. 2005, p. 3251); S.O. 2004, c. 19, ss. 18(25), 24(2), in force March 31, 2006]

Service

45. (1) Any notice, order or request is sufficiently given or served if it is,

(a) delivered personally;

(b) sent by registered mail; or

(c) sent by another manner if the sender can prove receipt of the notice, order or request.

Deemed service

(2) If service is made by registered mail, the service shall be deemed to be made on the third day after the day of mailing unless the person on whom service is being made establishes that the person did not, acting in good faith, through absence, accident, illness or other cause beyond the person's control, receive the notice or order until a later date.

Exception

(3) Despite subsections (1) and (2), the Tribunal may order any other method of service it considers appropriate in the circumstances.

[S.O. 2002, c. 30, Sched. C, s. 45, in force March 31, 2006 (O. Gaz. 2005, p. 3251)]

Fees

46. (1) The Minister may by order establish fees that are payable under this Act in respect of registration, renewal of registration, late filings and other administrative matters.

Exception

(2) Subsection (1) does not apply if there is a designated administrative authority.

Non-application of the Regulations Act

(3) An order made under this section is not a regulation for the purposes of the Regulations Act.

[S.O. 2002, c. 30, Sched. C, s. 46, in force March 31, 2006 (O. Gaz. 2005, p. 3251)]

Certificate as evidence

47. (1) For all purposes in any proceeding, a statement purporting to be certified by the director is, without proof of the office or signature of the director, admissible in evidence as proof in the absence of evidence to the contrary, of the facts stated in it in relation to,

(a)   the registration or non-registration of any person;

(b)   the filing or non-filing of any document or material required or permitted to be filed with the registrar;

(c)   the time when the facts upon which the proceedings are based first came to the knowledge of the director; or

(d)   any other matter pertaining to registration or non-registration of persons or to filing or non-filing of information.

Proof of document

(2) Any document made under this Act that purports to be signed by the director or a certified copy of the document is admissible in evidence in any proceeding as proof, in the absence of evidence to the contrary, that the document is signed by the director without proof of the office or signature of the director.

[S.O. 2002, c. 30, Sched. C, s. 47, in force March 31, 2006 (O. Gaz. 2005, p. 3251)]

Names of and information concerning registrants

48. (1) As required by regulation, the registrar shall make available to the public the names of registrants and other information, as prescribed, in respect of registrants.

Same

(2) The names of registrants shall be made available in the prescribed form and manner and with such information as is prescribed.

S.O. 2002, c. 30, Sched. C, s. 48, in force March 31, 2006 (O. Gaz. 2005, p. 3251).

Transition

49. (1) Despite the repeal of the *Real Estate and Business Brokers Act*, any person who was registered as a broker or salesperson under that Act immediately before this Act is proclaimed into force shall be deemed to be registered as a broker or salesperson, as the case may be, under this Act until the person is required to renew their registration under this Act.

Same

(2) If a person was registered as a broker under the *Real Estate and Business Brokers Act* immediately before this Act is proclaimed into force and the person would be required to be registered as a brokerage under this Act, the person shall be deemed to be registered as a brokerage under this Act until the person is required to renew their registration under this Act.

[S.O. 2002, c. 30, Sched. C, s. 49, in force March 31, 2006 (O. Gaz. 2005, p. 3251)]

PART VIII
REGULATIONS

Minister's regulations

50. (1) The Minister may make regulations,

    (a) establishing a code of ethics for the purposes of subsection 21 (1);

    (b) governing the jurisdiction and procedures of any committee established under this Act;

    (c) respecting any matter that is delegated by the Lieutenant Governor in Council to the Minister under paragraph 25 of subsection 51 (1).

Code of ethics

(1.1) A regulation under clause (1) (c) may be made as part of the code of ethics established under clause (1) (a).

Delegation

(2) Despite subsection 3 (4) of the *Safety and Consumer Statutes Administration Act, 1996*, the Minister may, by regulation, delegate to the board of the administrative authority the power to make some or all of the regulations under subsection (1), subject to the approval of the Minister.

Approval

(3) The Minister may approve or refuse to approve the regulations but approval shall not be given unless, in his or her opinion, they have been made in accordance with the consultation criteria and process set out in the administrative agreement described in subsection 4 (1) of the *Safety and Consumer Statutes Administration Act, 1996*.

Revocation, transition

(4) The Minister may, by regulation, revoke a delegation to the board of the administrative authority under subsection (2), but the revocation of a delegation does not result in the revocation of any regulation made by the board of the administrative authority under the delegated power before the revocation of the delegation, and the board's regulation remains valid.

Conflicts

(5) If there is a conflict between a regulation made under this section and a regulation made by the Lieutenant Governor in Council under section 51, the latter prevails.

General or particular

(6) A regulation under this section may be general or particular in its application.

[S.O. 2002, c. 30, Sched. C, s. 50, in force November 7, 2005 (O. Gaz. 2005 p. 3251); S.O. 2004, c. 19, s. 18 (26-28)]

Lieutenant Governor in Council regulations

51. (1) The Lieutenant Governor in Council may make regulations,

1. exempting any person or class of persons or class of trades from any provision of this Act or the regulations and attaching conditions to an exemption;

2. respecting applications for registration or renewal of registration and prescribing conditions of registration;

2.1 prescribing requirements for the purposes of subsections 9.1 (1) and 10 (1);

3. governing educational requirements for applicants for registration, applicants for renewal of registration and registrants, including,

   i. establishing areas of specialization and prescribing different educational requirements for each area,

   ii. establishing a certification process in respect of an area of specialization,

   iii. requiring applicants for registration, applicants for renewal of registration and registrants to meet educational requirements specified by the board of the administrative authority, the Minister, the director or the registrar or to complete a program of studies that has been, or take one or more courses that have been, designated by the board of the administrative authority, the Minister, the director or the registrar,

   iv. authorizing the board of the administrative authority, the Minister, the director or the registrar to designate organizations that are authorized to provide the programs and courses designated under subparagraph iii, and

   v. requiring that all educational requirements specified under subparagraph iii and the list of all programs and courses designated under that subparagraph be made available to the public;

4. governing specialization in respect of brokerages that are corporations, including restricting or prohibiting the certification of corporations as specialists;

5. [REPEALED: S.O. 2004, c. 19, s. 18 (31)]

6. respecting financial security requirements for brokerages, brokers and salespersons, including requiring them to be bonded or insured or have collateral security, and prescribing the forfeiture of bonds, the disposition of proceeds and other terms related to the financial security requirements;

7. governing the insurance that brokerages, brokers or salespersons must have, including,

   i. prescribing the types of insurance they must have,

      ii.   prescribing the minimum amounts for which they must be insured under each type of insurance,

     iii.   governing group insurance for brokerages, brokers or salespersons, including,

         A. authorizing the board of the administrative authority or, if there is no designated administrative authority, the Minister to arrange for and administer group insurance on behalf of brokerages, brokers or salespersons and to act as named insured, and

         B. requiring brokerages, brokers or salespersons to participate in group insurance;

8.   governing the documents, records and trust accounts that must be kept by brokerages, including the manner and location in which they are kept and the time periods for retaining such information and authorizing the registrar to specify the location at which they must be kept;

9.   prescribing the responsibilities of brokers of record, brokerages, brokers or salespersons;

10. requiring registrants to provide information to the registrar concerning persons other than the registrants in order to assist in determining whether such persons are or may be interested persons;

11. prescribing procedures and other matters related to complaints under section 19;

12. respecting inspections and investigations under this Act;

13. governing the composition of the discipline committee and the appeals committee and, subject to subsection 21 (3), governing matters relating to the appointment of the members of those committees;

14. requiring registrants to provide, on request and in the prescribed circumstances, proof of registration and prescribing the nature of the proof and the manner in which it is to be provided;

15. respecting the manner in which and the frequency with which decisions of the discipline committee and appeals committee are made available to the public;

16. varying the manner in which a notice under subsection 25 (7) or a lien under subsection 43 (3) is registered as a result of technological or electronic changes in the filing of documents in the land registry office;

17. prescribing information that must be provided to the registrar and requiring that specified information be verified by affidavit;

18. governing the activities of registrants including,

    i.   prescribing matters that must be disclosed and when they must be disclosed in the course of a trade in real estate, including matters related to any holdings in brokerages other than the brokerage by which they are employed, in the case of salespersons and brokers, or in other brokerages, in the case of brokerages and the conditions under which such disclosures may be required,

    ii. setting out the manner in which trust accounts are wound down when a brokerage's registration ends,

    iii. regulating advertising and representations or promises intended to induce a trade in real estate,

    iv. regulating listing agreements, representation agreements and specific types of representation agreements,

    v.   prescribing conditions that must be met before commissions or other remuneration may be charged or collected,

    vi. prescribing statements that are to be provided in respect of any trade in real estate, the content of the statement, the manner in which the statement is to be provided, the circumstances under which a statement is not required and the consequences of failing to provide a statement,

    vii. setting out obligations of a brokerage, broker and salesperson that follow the acceptance of an offer to sell, purchase, exchange, lease or rent real estate;

19. governing the conduct of registrants when they represent more than one party in a trade;

20. requiring that any information required under this Act be in a form approved by the director, the registrar or the Minister, as specified in the regulation;

21. prescribing matters that must be disclosed by brokers and salespersons to the brokerages by which they are employed and to brokerages that are prospective employers and the conditions under which such disclosures are required;

22. requiring the registrar to make available to the public the names of registrants and prescribing the form and manner in which the names of registrants are made available and prescribing other information in respect of registrants that may be made available to the public;

23. requiring registrants to maintain business premises that comply with the prescribed rules;

24. providing for any transitional matter necessary for the effective implementation of this Act or the regulations;

25. delegating any matter that may be the subject of a regulation under this section to the Minister;

26. prescribing rules relating to addresses for service under the Act;

27. prescribing any matter or thing that this Act refers to as being prescribed or in accordance with the regulations;

28. governing the application of the *Electronic Commerce Act, 2000* or any part of that Act to this Act.

29. defining, for the purposes of this Act and the regulations, any word or expression that is used in this Act but not defined in this Act;

30. authorizing the director or the board of the administrative authority to conduct quality assurance programs in relation to the administration of this Act or the regulations and to use information collected under this Act for the purposes of those programs.

Residual authority to act

(2) Despite any delegation to the Minister under paragraph 25 of subsection (1) and without having to revoke the delegation, the Lieutenant Governor in Council continues to have authority to make regulations in respect of the matter that is the subject of the delegation.

Revocation, transition

(3) The Lieutenant Governor in Council may, by regulation, revoke a delegation to the Minister under paragraph 25 of subsection (1), but the revocation of a delegation does not result in the revocation of any regulation that was made, before the revocation of the delegation,

(a) by the Minister under the delegated power; or

(b) by the board of the administrative authority pursuant to a delegation by the Minister under subsection 50 (2),

and the Minister's or board's regulation remains valid.

Making regulation not revocation

(4) The making of a regulation to which subsection (2) applies by the Lieutenant Governor in Council shall not constitute the revocation of a delegation under this section unless the regulation so specifies.

General or particular

(5) A regulation under this section may be general or particular in its application.

[S.O. 2002, c. 30, Sched. C, s. 51, in force November 7, 2005 (O. Gaz. 2005, p. 3251); S.O. 2004, c. 19, s. 18 (29-35)]

APPENDIX B

GENERAL REGULATION

O. Reg. 567/05

CONTENTS

Interpretation

Registration

Copies of Agreements

Trust Money

Termination of Brokerage's Registration

Exemptions

Miscellaneous

Interpretation

Definitions: Act and regulations

1. (1) In the Act,

"client" means,

    (a) with respect to a brokerage and a trade in real estate, a person who, in the trade, is represented under a representation agreement by the brokerage, and

    (b) with respect to a broker or salesperson and a trade in real estate, a person who, in the trade, is represented under a representation agreement by the brokerage that employs the broker or salesperson, if the broker or salesperson represents the person pursuant to the agreement;

"customer" means,

    (a) with respect to a brokerage and a trade in real estate, a person who, in the trade,

        (i) has an agreement with the brokerage under which the brokerage provides services to the person, and

        (ii) is not represented under a representation agreement by the brokerage or any other brokerage, and

(b) with respect to a broker or salesperson and a trade in real estate, a person who, in the trade, obtains services under an agreement, other than a representation agreement, from the brokerage that employs the broker or salesperson, if the broker or salesperson provides services to the person pursuant to the agreement;

"organization" includes an individual or other person;

"representation agreement" means a written, oral or implied agreement between a brokerage and a person under which the brokerage and the person agree that the brokerage will represent the person in respect of a trade in real estate;

"sell" means dispose of or seek to dispose of an interest in real estate, and "seller" has a corresponding meaning, but "sale" does not have a corresponding meaning.

(2) In the regulations,

"client" means,

(a) with respect to a brokerage and a trade in real estate, a person who, in the trade, is represented under a representation agreement by the brokerage, and

(b) with respect to a broker or salesperson and a trade in real estate, a person who, in the trade, is represented under a representation agreement by the brokerage that employs the broker or salesperson, if the broker or salesperson represents the person pursuant to the agreement;

"customer" means,

(a) with respect to a brokerage and a trade in real estate, a person who, in the trade,

(i) has an agreement with the brokerage under which the brokerage provides services to the person, and

(ii) is not represented under a representation agreement by the brokerage or any other brokerage, and

(b) with respect to a broker or salesperson and a trade in real estate, a person who, in the trade, obtains services under an agreement, other than a representation agreement, from the brokerage that employs the broker or salesperson, if the broker or salesperson provides services to the person pursuant to the agreement;

"organization" includes an individual or other person;

"representation agreement" means a written, oral or implied agreement between a brokerage and a person under which the brokerage and the person agree that the brokerage will represent the person in respect of a trade in real estate;

"sell" means dispose of or seek to dispose of an interest in real estate, and "seller" has a corresponding meaning, but "sale" does not have a corresponding meaning.

(3) For the purposes of the definition of "broker" in subsection 1 (1) of the Act, the following qualifications are prescribed:

1.   The individual must have successfully completed any relevant educational requirements set out in a regulation made under clause 50 (1) (c) of the Act.

(4) For the purposes of the definition of "salesperson" in subsection 1 (1) of the Act, the following qualifications are prescribed:

1.   The individual must have successfully completed any relevant educational requirements set out in a regulation made under clause 50 (1) (c) of the Act.

(5) Subsection (6) applies only if Bill 190 (An Act to promote good government by amending or repealing certain Acts and by enacting one new Act, introduced in the Legislative Assembly of Ontario on April 27, 2005) receives Royal Assent.

(6) On the later of March 31, 2006 and the date Bill 190 receives Royal Assent, subsections (1) and (2) are revoked and the following substituted:

(1) In the Act and the regulations,

"client" means,

(a)   with respect to a brokerage and a trade in real estate, a person who, in the trade, is represented under a representation agreement by the brokerage, and

(b)   with respect to a broker or salesperson and a trade in real estate, a person who, in the trade, is represented under a representation agreement by the brokerage that employs the broker or salesperson, if the broker or salesperson represents the person pursuant to the agreement;

"customer" means,

(a)   with respect to a brokerage and a trade in real estate, a person who, in the trade,

(i) has an agreement with the brokerage under which the brokerage provides services to the person, and

(ii) is not represented under a representation agreement by the brokerage or any other brokerage, and

(b) with respect to a broker or salesperson and a trade in real estate, a person who, in the trade, obtains services under an agreement, other than a representation agreement, from the brokerage that employs the broker or salesperson, if the broker or salesperson provides services to the person pursuant to the agreement;

"organization" includes an individual or other person;

"representation agreement" means a written, oral or implied agreement between a brokerage and a person under which the brokerage and the person agree that the brokerage will represent the person in respect of a trade in real estate;

"sell" means dispose of or seek to dispose of an interest in real estate, and "seller" has a corresponding meaning, but "sale" does not have a corresponding meaning.

Definitions: this Regulation

2. In this Regulation,

"buy" means acquire or seek to acquire an interest in real estate, and "buyer" has a corresponding meaning;

"buyer representation agreement" means a representation agreement between a brokerage and a buyer.

Registration

Application, form and fee

3. An application for registration or for renewal of registration as a brokerage, broker or salesperson shall contain all the required information, in a form approved by the registrar, and shall be accompanied by the relevant fee set by the administrative authority under clause 12 (1) (b) of the *Safety and Consumer Statutes Administration Act, 1996*, payable to the administrative authority.

Requirements for registration as broker or salesperson

4. (1) For the purposes of subsection 9.1 (1) of the Act, the following requirements are prescribed for an applicant for registration or renewal of registration as a broker or salesperson:

1. The applicant must be at least 18 years of age.
2. The applicant must be a resident of Canada.
3. If the application is for registration as a broker and the applicant has never been registered as a broker, the applicant must,
   i. have been registered and employed as a salesperson for at least 24 of the 36 months immediately preceding the date of the application, or
   ii. have experience that, in the opinion of the registrar, is equivalent to the requirement in subparagraph i.
4. The applicant must have paid any group insurance premiums and applicable taxes, and any expenses associated with a group insurance policy, including contributions to reserve funds, that he or she is required to pay by any regulation made under clause 50 (1) (c) of the Act.
5. The applicant must have paid the fee referred to in section 3.

(2) For the purposes of subsection 10 (1) of the Act, the following requirement is prescribed for an applicant for registration or renewal of registration as a broker or salesperson:

1. The registrar must not have refused to grant or renew the registration under subsection 9.1 (1) of the Act.

Conditions of registration as broker or salesperson

5. For the purposes of subsection 10 (2) of the Act, the following are prescribed as conditions of registration for a broker or salesperson:

1. The broker or salesperson must be a resident of Canada.
2. The broker or salesperson must pay any group insurance premiums and applicable taxes, and any expenses associated with a group insurance policy, including contributions to reserve funds, that he or she is required to pay by any regulation made under clause 50 (1) (c) of the Act.

Requirements for registration as brokerage

6. (1) For the purposes of subsection 9.1 (1) of the Act, the following requirements are prescribed for an applicant for registration or renewal of registration as a brokerage:

1. The applicant must have a broker of record.
2. The applicant must have a trust account for the purpose of section 27 of the Act.
3. The applicant must have paid the fee referred to in section 3.

(2) For the purposes of subsection 10 (1) of the Act, the following requirement is prescribed for an applicant for registration or renewal of registration as a brokerage:

1. The registrar must not have refused to grant or renew the registration under subsection 9.1 (1) of the Act.

Conditions of registration as brokerage

7. For the purposes of subsection 10 (2) of the Act, the following are prescribed as conditions of registration for a brokerage:

1. The brokerage must have a broker of record.
2. The brokerage must comply with section 27 of the Act.

Name

8. (1) A registrant may be registered in only one name.

(2) An applicant for registration or renewal of registration as a broker or salesperson shall provide the registrar with one of the following names as the name in which the applicant is to be registered:

1. The complete legal name of the applicant.
2. One or more of the legal given names of the applicant, in the correct order, followed by his or her legal surname.

(3) An applicant for registration or renewal of registration as a brokerage shall provide the registrar with one of the following names as the name in which the applicant is to be registered:

1. The complete legal name of the applicant.
2. One or more of the legal given names of the applicant, in the correct order, followed by his or her legal surname, if the applicant is an individual.
3. A name registered under the *Business Names Act* by the applicant.

(4) For the purpose of paragraph 2 of subsection (2) and paragraph 2 of subsection (3), the following may be substituted for a given name:

1. An initial or commonly recognized short form of the given name.

2.   A name by which the applicant is commonly known.

(5) A registrant may apply to the registrar, in a form approved by the registrar, to change the name in which the registrant is registered, and subsections (2), (3) and (4) apply with necessary modifications.

(6) A registrant shall not trade in real estate in a name other than the name in which the registrant is registered.

(7) Subsection 2 (6) of the *Business Names Act* applies despite this section.

Certificate of registration

9. (1) If a registrant is a broker or salesperson, the registrar shall give the registrant a certificate of registration that includes the following information:

1.   The registrant's complete legal name and, if the registrant is registered in another name, the name in which the registrant is registered.

2.   An indication whether the registrant is a broker or salesperson.

3.   The employer's name.

4.   The registration number of the registrant.

5.   The expiration date of the registration.

(2) If a registrant is a brokerage that is registered in respect of only one place, the registrar shall give the registrant a certificate of registration that includes the following information:

1.   The registrant's complete legal name and, if the registrant is registered in another name, the name in which the registrant is registered.

2.   An indication that the registrant is a brokerage.

3.   The place to which the certificate of registration relates.

4.   The registration number of the registrant.

5.   The expiration date of the registration.

(3) If a registrant is a brokerage that is registered in respect of more than one place, the registrar shall give the registrant a certificate of registration for each of those places that includes the following information:

1.   The registrant's complete legal name and, if the registrant is registered in another name, the name in which the registrant is registered.

2.   An indication that the registrant is a brokerage.

3.   The place to which the certificate of registration relates.

4.   The registration number of the registrant and, in addition, if the certificate is for a branch office of the brokerage, a separate registration number that relates specifically to that branch office.

5.   The expiration date of the registration.

(4) When the registrar gives a certificate of registration to a broker or salesperson under subsection (1), he or she shall give a duplicate original of the certificate to the brokerage that employs the broker or salesperson.

(5) If the registrar revokes, suspends, cancels or refuses to renew the registration of a brokerage, the brokerage shall immediately return to the registrar,

(a)   all certificates of registration that relate to the brokerage and its branch offices, if any; and

(b)   all certificates of registration in the brokerage's possession that relate to brokers and salespersons employed by the brokerage.

(6) When a suspension of the registration of a brokerage ends, the registrar shall immediately return to the brokerage all certificates of registration referred to in subsection (5).

(7) If the registrar revokes, suspends, cancels or refuses to renew the registration of a broker or salesperson, or a broker or salesperson ceases to be employed by a brokerage,

(a)   the broker or salesperson shall immediately return his or her certificate of registration to the registrar; and

(b)   the brokerage that employs the broker or salesperson shall immediately return to the registrar the certificate of registration of the broker or salesperson that is in the brokerage's possession.

(8) When a suspension of the registration of a broker or salesperson ends, the registrar shall immediately return the broker's or salesperson's certificates of registration to the person who returned them to the registrar under subsection (7).

(9) A person who is required to return a certificate of registration to another person under this section shall return it using a form of delivery that provides proof of delivery.

Re-employment within specified period

10. (1) If a broker or salesperson ceases to be employed by a brokerage and, within the period described in subsection (2), is employed by that brokerage or another brokerage, the broker or salesperson may, during that period, make an application for registration in a form that the registrar has approved for use in those circumstances.

(2) The period referred to in subsection (1) is the period that begins on the day the broker or salesperson ceased to be employed and ends on the earlier of the following dates:

1. The date that is 60 days after the day the broker or salesperson ceased to be employed.

2. The date that the previous registration of the broker or salesperson would have expired if he or she had not ceased to be employed.

(3) Despite any regulation made under clause 50 (1) (c) of the Act that relates to the expiration of registration, if an application under subsection (1) is approved, the registration expires on the date that the previous registration of the broker or salesperson would have expired if he or she had not ceased to be employed.

Information available to public

11. (1) The registrar shall make the following information available to the public:

1. The complete legal name of every registrant and, if a registrant is registered in another name, the name in which the registrant is registered.

2. For every registrant,
    i. the registrant's business address and business telephone number, and
    ii. if known to the registrar, the registrant's business fax number and business e-mail address.

3. For every registrant, whether the registrant is registered as a brokerage, broker or salesperson.

4. If a proposal by the registrar to revoke a registrant's registration has not yet been disposed of, an indication of that fact.

5. If a proposal by the registrar to refuse to renew a registrant's registration has not yet been disposed of, an indication of that fact.

6.   If a proposal by the registrar to suspend a registrant's registration has not yet been disposed of, an indication of that fact.

7.   If a proposal by the registrar to apply conditions to a registrant's registration has not yet been disposed of, an indication of that fact.

8.   If, within the preceding 24 months, a former registrant's registration was revoked or a former registrant was refused renewal of registration, an indication of that fact.

9.   If a registrant's registration is currently suspended, an indication of that fact.

10. If conditions, other than conditions prescribed by the regulations or consented to by the registrant, currently apply to a registrant's registration, a description of the conditions.

11. For every registrant, whether or not the registrant has paid any group insurance premiums and applicable taxes, and any expenses associated with a group insurance policy, including contributions to reserve funds, that he or she is required to pay by any regulation made under clause 50 (1) (c) of the Act.

12. If an order described in subsection 38 (1) of the Act has been made against a registrant and is currently in effect, a copy of the order.

13. For every registrant, former registrant and director or officer of a brokerage who is currently charged with an offence as a result of an information laid by an employee of the administrative authority,

   i.   the Act that creates the offence,

   ii.   a description of the charge, and

   iii. the date on which the information was laid.

14. For every registrant, former registrant and director or officer of a brokerage who has been found guilty of an offence as a result of an information laid by an employee of the administrative authority,

   i.   the Act that creates the offence,

   ii.   a description of the offence, and

   iii. a description of the disposition of the charge, including any sentence that was imposed and any order to pay compensation or make restitution.

15. Any information that relates to a registrant, a former registrant, a director or officer of a registrant or a person who is trading in real estate, if the registrar is of the opinion that making the

information available to the public could assist in protecting the public.

(2) The registrar shall make information described in paragraph 12 of subsection (1) available to the public for at least 60 months after,

(a) the date the registrar made the order under subsection 38 (1) of the Act, if the registrant did not appeal the order; or

(b) the date the Tribunal made its order, if the registrant appealed the order made by the registrar under subsection 38 (1) of the Act.

(3) The registrar shall make information described in paragraph 14 of subsection (1) available to the public for at least 60 months after the registrant was found guilty.

(4) The registrar,

(a) shall publish the information described in subsection (1) on the Internet on the administrative authority's website; and

(b) shall make the information described in subsection (1) available to the public in at least one other manner that the registrar considers appropriate.

(5) In making any information available to the public under this section, the registrar shall ensure that the information does not include the name of an individual, unless,

(a) the individual is an applicant for registration, a registrant, a former registrant, a director or officer of a brokerage or a person who is required to be registered; or

(b) the name of the individual is otherwise available to the public in connection with the information.

(6) The information that this section requires the registrar to make available shall not be disclosed in bulk to any person except as required by law or to a law enforcement authority.

Waiting period for reapplication

12. For the purpose of clause 17 (a) of the Act, 12 months is prescribed as the time to reapply.

Copies of Agreements

Copies of agreements

13. (1) If a broker or salesperson represents a client who enters into a written agreement that deals with the conveyance of an interest in real estate, the broker or salesperson shall use his or her best efforts to deliver a copy of the agreement at the earliest practicable opportunity to the brokerage that employs the broker or salesperson.

(2) Subsection (1) applies, with necessary modifications, to a broker or salesperson who has a customer, if the customer and the brokerage that employs the broker or salesperson have an agreement that provides for the brokerage to provide services to the customer in respect of any agreement that deals with the conveyance of an interest in real estate.

Trust Money

One account

14. A brokerage shall not maintain more than one trust account for the purpose of section 27 of the Act, unless the registrar consents in writing.

Real Estate Trust Account

15. A brokerage shall ensure that each account maintained under section 27 of the Act is designated as a Real Estate Trust Account.

Variable interest rate trust accounts

16. A brokerage that complies with section 27 of the Act through a variable interest rate account shall, on the request of a person for whom money is held in trust, inform the person of the current interest rate.

Deposit within five business days

17. (1) If an amount of money comes into a brokerage's hands in trust for another person in connection with the brokerage's business, the brokerage shall deposit the amount in the trust account maintained under section 27 of the Act within five business days.

(2) In subsection (1),

"business day" means a day that is not,

(a)   Saturday, or

(b) a holiday within the meaning of subsection 29 (1) of the *Interpretation Act.*

Requests for disbursements

18. If a brokerage receives a request for a disbursement from the trust account maintained under section 27 of the Act and the disbursement is required by the terms of the applicable trust, the brokerage shall disburse the money as soon as practicable, subject to the terms of the applicable trust.

Authorization of transactions

19. A brokerage shall not engage in any transaction involving money that comes into the brokerage's hands in trust for other persons in connection with the brokerage's business unless the transaction is authorized by the brokerage's broker of record.

Other Property in Trust

Other property in trust

20. (1) If property other than money comes into a brokerage's hands in trust for another person in connection with the brokerage's business, the brokerage shall preserve the property in a safe manner.

(2) A brokerage shall not engage in any transaction involving property that is not money and that comes into the brokerage's hands in trust for other persons in connection with the brokerage's business unless the transaction is authorized by the brokerage's broker of record.

(3) If a brokerage receives a request to withdraw all or any part of the property held in trust and the withdrawal is required by the terms of the applicable trust, the brokerage shall withdraw the property requested as soon as practicable, subject to the terms of the applicable trust.

Purchase of Business

Purchase of business: statements to be delivered

21. (1) The definitions of "buy" and "buyer" in section 2 do not apply to this section.

(2) If the purchase of a business is negotiated by a brokerage on behalf of the person disposing of the business, the brokerage shall

provide to the purchaser, before a binding agreement of purchase and sale is entered into, the following statements signed by or on behalf of the person disposing of the business:

1. A profit and loss statement for the business for the preceding 12 months or since the acquisition of the business by the person disposing of it.

2. A statement of the assets and liabilities of the business.

3. A statement containing a list of all fixtures, goods, chattels, other assets and rights relating to or connected with the business that are not included in the trade.

(3) If the brokerage fails to provide the statement mentioned in paragraph 3 of subsection (2) in accordance with that subsection and the agreement of purchase and sale does not expressly deal with whether a fixture, good, chattel, other asset or right relating to or connected with the business is included in the trade, the fixture, good, chattel, other asset or right shall be deemed to be included in the trade.

(4) Paragraphs 1 and 2 of subsection (2) do not apply if a statement is signed by or on behalf of the purchaser and is delivered to the brokerage indicating that the purchaser has received and read a statement under oath or affirmation of the person disposing of the business that sets out the following:

1. The terms and conditions under which the person disposing of the business holds possession of the premises in which the business is being carried on.

2. The terms and conditions under which the person disposing of the business has sublet a part of the premises in which the business is being carried on.

3. All liabilities of the business.

4. A statement that the person disposing of the business has made available the books of account of the business that the person possesses for inspection by the purchaser, or that the person disposing of the business has refused to do so or has no books of account of the business, as the case may be.

Other Registrant Responsibilities

Multiple representation

22. A registrant shall not represent more than one client in respect of the same trade in real estate unless all of the clients represented by the registrant in respect of that trade consent in writing.

Commissions

23. (1) Subject to subsection 33 (3) of the Act and subsection (2), a registrant shall not charge or collect a commission or other remuneration in respect of a trade in real estate unless,

- (a) the entitlement to the commission or other remuneration arises under a written agreement that is signed by or on behalf of the person who is required to pay the commission or other remuneration; or
- (b) the entitlement to the commission or other remuneration arises under an agreement that is not referred to in clause (a) and,
  - (i) the registrant has conveyed an offer in writing that is accepted, or
  - (ii) the registrant,
    - (A) shows the property to the buyer, or
    - (B) introduces the buyer and the seller to one another for the purpose of discussing the proposed acquisition or disposition of an interest in real estate.

(2) Unless agreed to in writing by the buyer, a registrant shall not charge or collect a commission or other remuneration from a buyer in respect of a trade in real estate if the registrant knows that there is an unexpired buyer representation agreement between the buyer and another registrant.

Office in Ontario

24. (1) A registrant shall not trade in real estate in Ontario from an office that is located outside Ontario.

(2) A registrant shall maintain an address for service that is in Ontario.

(3) A registrant shall keep the registrant's business records in Ontario if they relate to trading in real estate in Ontario.

Inducements

25. (1) The definitions of "sell" and "seller" in section 1 and the definitions of "buy" and "buyer" in section 2 do not apply to this section.

(2) A registrant shall not, as an inducement to purchase, lease or exchange real estate, make any representation or promise that the registrant or any other person will sell, lease or exchange the real estate.

(3) A registrant shall not, as an inducement to purchase real estate, make any representation or promise that the registrant or any other person will,

 (a) purchase or sell any of the purchaser's real estate;

 (b) procure for the purchaser a mortgage or extension of a mortgage or a lease or extension of a lease; or

 (c) purchase or sell a mortgage or procure a loan.

(4) A registrant shall not, as an inducement to sell real estate, make any representation or promise that the registrant or any other person will,

 (a) purchase any of the seller's real estate;

 (b) procure a mortgage, extension of a mortgage, lease or extension of a lease; or

 (c) purchase or sell a mortgage or procure a loan.

(5) Subsections (2), (3) and (4) do not apply to a representation or promise if the registrant has entered into a written contract with the person to whom the representation or promise is made that obligates the registrant to ensure that the promise or representation is complied with.

Notice of insurance

26. (1) Before a brokerage enters into an agreement with a buyer or seller in respect of trading in real estate, the broker or salesperson acting on behalf of the brokerage shall, at the earliest practicable opportunity, inform the buyer or seller, in writing, of whether or not the broker or salesperson is insured under any regulation made under clause 50 (1) (c) of the Act that relates to insurance.

(2) If a broker or salesperson, other than the broker or salesperson referred to in subsection (1), represents or provides services to the buyer or seller pursuant to the agreement referred to in that subsection, the broker or salesperson shall, at the earliest practicable opportunity, inform the buyer or seller, in writing, of whether or not the broker or salesperson is insured under any regulation made under clause 50 (1) (c) of the Act that relates to insurance.

(3) If the insured status of a broker or salesperson referred to in subsection (1) or (2) changes and the agreement referred to in subsection (1) subsists, the broker or salesperson shall, as soon as practicable, inform the buyer or seller, in writing, of the change and of what his or her status is after the change.

Complaints

Public summaries

27. (1) If an attempt to mediate or resolve a complaint under paragraph 1 of subsection 19 (4) of the Act is resolved to the satisfaction of the registrar, the registrar shall prepare a written summary of the complaint and the result of the complaint and shall make the summary available to the public.

(2) The registrar shall ensure that the summary does not identify any person without that person's written consent.

Corporate Structure of Brokerages

Changes in officers or directors

28. A request for consent under subsection 4 (4) of the Act to a change in the officers or directors of a corporation registered as a brokerage shall be in a form approved by the registrar.

Notice of issue or transfer of shares

29. A notice under subsection 18 (1) or (2) of the Act shall be in a form approved by the registrar and shall identify,

  (a) the person, or the persons that are associated with each other, who, as a result of the issue or transfer of equity shares of the corporation, are acquiring or accumulating beneficial ownership or control of 10 per cent or more of the total number of all issued and outstanding equity shares of the corporation; or

  (b) the person, or the persons that are associated with each other, who already beneficially own or control 10 per cent or more of the total number of all issued and outstanding equity shares of the corporation before the issue or transfer and who, as a result of the issue or transfer of equity shares of the corporation, are increasing that percentage.

Management of Brokerage

Broker of record

30. (1) A broker of record shall,

  (a) actively participate in the management of the brokerage;

(b) ensure an adequate level of supervision for the brokers, salespersons and other persons employed by the brokerage; and

(c) take reasonable steps to deal with any failure to comply with the Act or the regulations by a broker, salesperson or other person employed by the brokerage.

(2) A brokerage that is not a sole proprietorship shall designate another broker employed by the brokerage who, when the broker of record is absent or unable to act, shall exercise and perform the powers and duties of the broker of record under sections 19 and 20.

(3) A brokerage that is not a sole proprietorship shall promptly inform the registrar in writing of the designation under subsection (2) and of any change in the designation under that subsection.

Branch offices with more than one salesperson

31. If a branch office of a brokerage has more than one salesperson and is under the direct management of a broker or salesperson under subsection 7 (2) of the Act, the broker or salesperson shall,

(a) ensure an adequate level of supervision for the brokers, salespersons and other persons employed in the branch office;

(b) take reasonable steps to deal with any failure to comply with the Act or the regulations by a broker, salesperson or other person employed in the branch office; and

(c) manage all records relating to the branch office.

Brokerages and their Employees

Disclosure by brokers and salespersons to brokerages

32. (1) A broker or salesperson who is registered as a broker or salesperson shall, at the earliest practicable opportunity, disclose the following matters to the brokerage with which he or she is employed:

1. Any ownership interest that the broker or salesperson has in another brokerage.

2. Any conviction, absolute discharge or conditional discharge received by the broker or salesperson for an offence under any Act.

3. Any professional discipline proceeding under any Act that resulted in an order against the broker or salesperson.

4.   Whether or not the broker or salesperson is insured under any regulation made under clause 50 (1) (c) of the Act that relates to insurance.

(2) A broker or salesperson who is registered as a broker or salesperson shall also make the disclosure required by paragraph 4 of subsection (1) whenever he or she is required to renew the insurance.

(3) A broker or salesperson who is registered as a broker or salesperson and who communicates with another brokerage with respect to possible employment with the other brokerage shall, at the earliest practicable opportunity, disclose the matters referred to in subsection (1) to the other brokerage.

(4) A broker or salesperson who, under paragraph 4 of subsection (1) or subsection (2) or (3), discloses to a brokerage that he or she is insured shall provide proof of the insurance to the brokerage.

(5) A broker or salesperson who is not registered as a broker or salesperson shall disclose the matters listed in paragraphs 1, 2 and 3 of subsection (1) to a brokerage that is a prospective employer.

Termination of employment

33. (1) A broker or salesperson who initiates the termination of his or her employment with a brokerage shall give the brokerage written notice of the termination, including the date the termination takes effect, and shall forward a copy of the notice to the registrar within five days after the termination takes effect.

(2) A brokerage that initiates the termination of the employment of a broker or salesperson shall give the broker or salesperson written notice of the termination, including the date the termination takes effect, and shall forward a copy of the notice to the registrar within five days after the termination takes effect.

Notice to registrar re certain changes

34. (1) If there is a change to any of the information that was included in the registrant's application under section 3, the registrant shall notify the registrar, in writing, within five days after the change takes place and shall set out the nature of the change.

(2) Subsection (1) does not apply if notice of the change is required to be given to the registrar by any other provision of the Act or the regulations.

Termination of Brokerage's Registration

Information for registrar

35. (1) If a brokerage knows that it will cease to be registered, it shall provide the following to the registrar at the earliest practicable opportunity:

1. A letter setting out the exact date that the brokerage will cease to be registered.

2. A copy of a letter that has been sent to all clients and customers of the brokerage, advising them that the brokerage will cease to be registered and will be prohibited from trading in real estate as a brokerage.

(2) If a brokerage has ceased to be registered, it shall provide the following to the registrar at the earliest practicable opportunity:

1. A letter setting out the exact date the brokerage ceased to be registered, if a letter setting out that date was not provided under paragraph 1 of subsection (1).

2. A copy of a letter that has been sent to all clients and customers of the brokerage, advising them that the brokerage has ceased to be registered and is prohibited from trading in real estate as a brokerage, if a copy of a letter was not provided under paragraph 2 of subsection (1).

3. For each trust account maintained under section 27 of the Act, a statement from the financial institution in which the account is maintained that indicates the balance in the account on the date the brokerage ceased to be registered, together with a trust account reconciliation statement prepared by the brokerage that identifies the following as of the date the brokerage ceased to be registered:

    i.   The differences, if any, between the brokerage's records and the records of the financial institution.

    ii. The balances in the trust account.

    iii. The real estate, if any, to which each balance relates.

    iv. The persons, if known, who are entitled to each balance.

    v.   Each balance for which it is not known what persons are entitled to it.

4. If the brokerage holds property other than money in trust for another person in connection with the brokerage's business, a statement prepared by the brokerage that, for each of the properties held in trust, describes the property and identifies

the following as of the date the brokerage ceased to be registered:

    i.   The place where the property is kept.

    ii. The real estate, if any, to which the property relates.

    iii. The person who is entitled to the property, if the person is known, or an indication that the person who is entitled to the property is not known, if the person is not known.

5.   A statement prepared by the brokerage that identifies any changes that occur after the date the brokerage ceases to be registered to the information that is set out in a statement under paragraph 3 or 4 or this paragraph.

6.   A list of all trades in real estate that were pending on the date the brokerage ceased to be registered and that relate to the balance in a trust account maintained under section 27 of the Act or to other property held in trust by the brokerage.

7.   The names, addresses, telephone numbers and other contact information that is on file with the brokerage for all clients and customers of the brokerage who were involved in business that was outstanding on the date the brokerage ceased to be registered.

8.   A financial statement that sets out the assets and liabilities of the brokerage as of the date the brokerage ceased to be registered and a list of the brokerage's creditors and the amounts that are owed to them as of that date.

9.   A letter setting out the location where the brokerage's business records relating to trading in real estate will be kept.

Exemptions

Brokerages registered under the *Loan and Trust Corporations Act*

36. Subsection 4 (4) of the Act does not apply to a brokerage that is registered in the Loan Corporations Register or the Trust Corporations Register under the *Loan and Trust Corporations Act*.

Public Guardian and Trustee

37. For the purpose of clause 5 (1) (k) of the Act, the Public Guardian and Trustee or a person authorized to act on his or her behalf is prescribed as exempt from registration in respect of any class of trades in real estate.

Compliance with Code of Ethics

38. Subsection 12 (2) and section 26 of the Act do not apply to compliance with the code of ethics established under clause 50 (1) (a) of the Act.

Unclear or unclaimed trust obligations: amounts under $25

39. (1) Subsections 27 (4) to (15) of the Act do not apply if the amount of money involved is less than $25.

(2) Despite subsection (1), a brokerage may choose to pay an amount less than $25 in accordance with subsection 27 (4) or (5) of the Act, in which case subsections 27 (6) to (15) of the Act do apply.

Miscellaneous

Notice of changes under s. 28 of the Act

40. A brokerage, broker or salesperson who gives a notice under subsection 28 (1) or (2) of the Act shall do so in a form approved by the registrar.

Registrar's order re false advertising

41. For the purpose of clause 38 (5) of the Act, the prescribed period is one year from the date the registrar makes the request referred to in subsection 38 (4) of the Act.

Publication of committee decisions

42. (1) Subject to subsections (2) and (4), the discipline committee, shall publish a copy of its final decision or order in each proceeding, including the reasons if any have been given,

(a) on the Internet on the administrative authority's website; and

(b) in at least one other manner that the discipline committee considers appropriate.

(2) If something is published under subsection (1), the discipline committee shall publish it for at least 60 months.

(3) Subsections (1) and (2) also apply, with necessary modifications, to the appeals committee.

(4) The discipline committee and the appeals committee shall ensure that nothing published under subsection (1) or (3) identifies any person unless the person consents in writing.

(5) Subsection (4) does not apply to the identification of a registrant
if,

(a) the discipline committee has made a determination that the registrant failed to comply with the code of ethics established under clause 50 (1) (a) of the Act and,

   (i) the time for commencing an appeal has expired and no appeal has been commenced, or

   (ii) an appeal was commenced but has been withdrawn or abandoned; or

(b) the appeals committee has made a determination that the registrant failed to comply with the code of ethics established under clause 50 (1) (a) of the Act.

APPENDIX C

CODE OF ETHICS REGULATION

O. Reg. 580/05

CONTENTS

19. Properties that meet buyer's criteria
20. Seller property information statement
21. Material facts
22. Agreements with third parties
23. Steps taken by registrant
24. Conveying offers
25. Agreements relating to commission
26. Competing offers
27. Written and legible agreements
28. Copies of agreements
29. Delivery of deposits and documents
30. Business records
31. Certificate of registration: broker or salesperson
32. Certificate of registration: brokerage
33. Certificates of registration for brokers and salespersons kept by brokerage
34. Current forms
35. Financial responsibility
36. Advertising
37. Inaccurate representations
38. Error, misrepresentation, fraud, etc.
39. Unprofessional conduct, etc.
40. Abuse and harassment
41. Duty to ensure compliance

Procedures of Discipline Committee and Appeals Committee
42. Composition and appointment of committees
43. Assignment of discipline committee panels
44. Parties: discipline committee
45. Notice of hearing
46. Disclosure of evidence
47. Disclosure from closed hearing
48. Notice of decision to complainant
49. Notice of appeal rights
50. Commencement of appeals
51. Assignment of appeal committee panels

52. Parties: appeals committee
53. Application of ss. 45 to 48

Interpretation

Interpretation

1. (1) In this Regulation,

"buy" means acquire or seek to acquire an interest in real estate, and "buyer" has a corresponding meaning;

"buyer representation agreement" means a representation agreement between a brokerage and a buyer;

"material fact" means, with respect to the acquisition or disposition of an interest in real estate, a fact that would affect a reasonable person's decision to acquire or dispose of the interest;

"seller representation agreement" means a representation agreement between a brokerage and a seller, and includes a listing agreement that is a representation agreement.

(2) A person is related to another person for the purposes of this Regulation if,

(a) one person is associated with the other person within the meaning of subsection 1 (2) of the Act; or

(b) one person is related to the other person by blood, adoption or conjugal relationship.

(3) For the purposes of this Regulation,

(a) a person is related to another person by blood if,

(i) one is the child or other descendant of the other, or

(ii) one is the brother or sister of the other;

(b) a person is related to another person by adoption if,

(i) neither is related to the other by blood, and

(ii) one would be related to the other by blood if all adopted children were deemed to be the natural children of their adoptive parents; and

(c) a person is related to another person by conjugal relationship if,

(i) one is married to the other or to a person who is related by blood or adoption to the other, or

    (ii)   one lives in a conjugal relationship outside marriage with the other or with a person who is related by blood or adoption to the other.

Obligations of Registrants

Brokers and salespersons

2. (1) A broker or salesperson shall not do or omit to do anything that causes the brokerage that employs the broker or salesperson to contravene this Regulation.

(2) Subsection (1) does not apply to a contravention by the brokerage of section 32, 33 or 41.

Fairness, honesty, etc.

3. A registrant shall treat every person the registrant deals with in the course of a trade in real estate fairly, honestly and with integrity.

Best interests

4. A registrant shall promote and protect the best interests of the registrant's clients.

Conscientious and competent service, etc.

5. A registrant shall provide conscientious service to the registrant's clients and customers and shall demonstrate reasonable knowledge, skill, judgment and competence in providing those services.

Providing opinions, etc.

6. (1) A registrant shall demonstrate reasonable knowledge, skill, judgment and competence in providing opinions, advice or information to any person in respect of a trade in real estate.

(2) Without limiting the generality of subsection (1) or section 5,

(a)   a brokerage shall not provide an opinion or advice about the value of real estate to any person unless the opinion or advice is provided on behalf of the brokerage by a broker or salesperson who has education or experience related to the valuation of real estate; and

(b)   a broker or salesperson shall not provide an opinion or advice about the value of real estate to any person unless the broker or salesperson has education or experience related to the valuation of real estate.

Dealings with other registrants

7. (1) A registrant who knows or ought to know that a person is a client of another registrant shall communicate information to the person for the purpose of a trade in real estate only through the other registrant, unless the other registrant has consented in writing.

(2) If a broker or salesperson knows or ought to know that a buyer or seller is a party to an agreement in connection with a trade in real estate with a brokerage other than the brokerage that employs the broker or salesperson, the broker or salesperson shall not induce the buyer or seller to break the agreement.

Services from others

8. (1) A registrant shall advise a client or customer to obtain services from another person if the registrant is not able to provide the services with reasonable knowledge, skill, judgment and competence or is not authorized by law to provide the services.

(2) A registrant shall not discourage a client or customer from seeking a particular kind of service if the registrant is not able to provide the service with reasonable knowledge, skill, judgment and competence or is not authorized by law to provide the service.

Commissions, etc.

9. A registrant shall not indicate to any person, directly or indirectly, that commissions or other remuneration are fixed or approved by the administrative authority, any government authority, or any real estate board or real estate association.

Information before agreements

10. (1) Before entering into an agreement with a buyer or seller in respect of trading in real estate, a brokerage shall, at the earliest practicable opportunity, inform the buyer or seller of the following:

1. The types of service alternatives that are available in the circumstances, including a representation agreement or another type of agreement.

2. The services that the brokerage would provide under the agreement.

3. The fact that circumstances could arise in which the brokerage could represent more than one client in respect of the same trade in real estate, but that the brokerage could not do this

unless all of the clients represented by the brokerage in respect of that trade consented in writing.

4. The nature of the services that the brokerage would provide to each client if the brokerage represents more than one client in respect of the same trade in real estate.

5. The fact that circumstances could arise in which the brokerage could provide services to more than one customer in respect of the same trade in real estate.

6. The fact that circumstances could arise in which the brokerage could, in respect of the same trade in real estate, both represent clients and provide services to customers.

7. The restricted nature of the services that the brokerage would provide to a customer in respect of a trade in real estate if the brokerage also represents a client in respect of that trade.

(2) The brokerage shall, at the earliest practicable opportunity and before an offer is made, use the brokerage's best efforts to obtain from the buyer or seller a written acknowledgement that the buyer or seller received all the information referred to in subsection (1).

Contents of written agreements

11. (1) A brokerage shall not enter into a written agreement with a buyer or seller for the purpose of trading in real estate unless the agreement clearly, comprehensibly and prominently,

(a) specifies the date on which the agreement takes effect and the date on which it expires;

(b) specifies or describes the method for determining,

(i) the amount of any commission or other remuneration payable to the brokerage, and

(ii) in the case of an agreement with a seller, the amount of any commission or other remuneration payable to any other brokerage;

(c) describes how any commission or other remuneration payable to the brokerage will be paid; and

(d) sets out the services that the brokerage will provide under the agreement.

(2) A brokerage shall not, for the purpose of trading in real estate, enter into a written agreement with a buyer or seller that provides that the date on which the agreement expires is more than six months after the date on which the agreement takes effect unless,

(a) the date on which the agreement expires is prominently displayed on the first page of the agreement; and

(b) the buyer or seller has initialled the agreement next to the date referred to in clause (a).

(3) A brokerage shall ensure that a written agreement that is entered into between the brokerage and a buyer or seller for the purpose of trading in real estate contains only one date on which the agreement expires.

Copies of written agreements

12. If a brokerage and one or more other persons enter into a written agreement in connection with a trade in real estate, the brokerage shall ensure that each of the other persons is immediately given a copy of the agreement.

Seller representation agreements

13. If a brokerage enters into a seller representation agreement with a seller and the agreement is not in writing, the brokerage shall, at the earliest practicable opportunity and before any buyer makes an offer, reduce the agreement to writing, have it signed on behalf of the brokerage and submit it to the seller for signature.

Buyer representation agreements

14. If a brokerage enters into a buyer representation agreement with a buyer and the agreement is not in writing, the brokerage shall, before the buyer makes an offer, reduce the agreement to writing, have it signed on behalf of the brokerage and submit it to the buyer for signature.

Agreements with customers

15. If a brokerage enters into an agreement with a customer in respect of a trade in real estate and the agreement is not in writing, the brokerage shall, at the earliest practicable opportunity, reduce the agreement to writing, have it signed on behalf of the brokerage and submit it to the customer for signature.

Disclosure before multiple representation

16. A brokerage shall not represent more than one client in respect of the same trade in real estate unless it has disclosed the following matters to the clients or prospective clients at the earliest practicable opportunity:

1.   The fact that the brokerage proposes to represent more than one client in respect of the same trade.

2.   The differences between the obligations the brokerage would have if it represented only one client in respect of the trade and the obligations the brokerage would have if it represented more than one client in respect of the trade, including any differences relating to the disclosure of information or the services that the brokerage would provide.

Nature of relationship

17. If a registrant represents or provides services to more than one buyer or seller in respect of the same trade in real estate, the registrant shall, in writing, at the earliest practicable opportunity and before any offer is made, inform all buyers and sellers involved in that trade of the nature of the registrant's relationship to each buyer and seller.

Disclosure of interest

18. (1) A registrant shall, at the earliest practicable opportunity and before any offer is made in respect of the acquisition or disposition of an interest in real estate, disclose in writing the following matters to every client represented by the registrant in respect of the acquisition or disposition:

1.   Any property interest that the registrant has in the real estate.

2.   Any property interest that a person related to the registrant has in the real estate, if the registrant knows or ought to know of the interest.

(2) A brokerage shall, at the earliest practicable opportunity and before any offer is made in respect of the acquisition or disposition of an interest in real estate, disclose in writing the matters referred to in paragraphs 1 and 2 of subsection (1) to every customer with whom the brokerage has entered into an agreement in respect of the acquisition or disposition.

(3) A broker or salesperson shall, at the earliest practicable opportunity and before any offer is made in respect of the acquisition or disposition of an interest in real estate, disclose in writing the matters referred to in paragraphs 1 and 2 of subsection (1) to every customer of the broker or salesperson with whom the brokerage that employs the broker or salesperson has entered into an agreement in respect of the acquisition or disposition.

(4) A registrant shall disclose in writing to a client, at the earliest practicable opportunity, any direct or indirect financial benefit that the registrant or a person related to the registrant may receive from another person in connection with services provided by the registrant to the client, including any commission or other remuneration that may be received from another person.

(5) A brokerage that has entered into an agreement with a buyer or seller that requires the buyer or seller to pay the brokerage a commission or other remuneration in respect of a trade in real estate shall not charge or collect any commission or other remuneration under another agreement entered into with another person in respect of the same trade unless,

    (a) the brokerage discloses at the earliest practicable opportunity to the other person, in writing, the terms of the agreement with the buyer or seller that require the payment of a commission or other remuneration; and

    (b) the brokerage discloses at the earliest practicable opportunity to the buyer or seller, in writing, the terms of the agreement with the other person that require the payment of a commission or other remuneration.

Properties that meet buyer's criteria

19. If a brokerage has entered into a representation agreement with a buyer, a broker or salesperson who acts on behalf of the buyer pursuant to the agreement shall inform the buyer of properties that meet the buyer's criteria without having any regard to the amount of commission or other remuneration, if any, to which the brokerage might be entitled.

Seller property information statement

20. If a broker or salesperson has a seller as a client and knows that the seller has completed a written statement that is intended to provide information to buyers about the real estate that is available for acquisition, the broker or salesperson shall, unless the seller directs otherwise,

    (a) disclose the existence of the statement to every buyer who expresses an interest in the real estate; and

    (b) on request, make the statement available to a buyer at the earliest practicable opportunity after the request is made.

Material facts

21. (1) A broker or salesperson who has a client in respect of the acquisition or disposition of a particular interest in real estate shall take reasonable steps to determine the material facts relating to the acquisition or disposition and, at the earliest practicable opportunity, shall disclose the material facts to the client.

(2) A broker or salesperson who has a customer in respect of the acquisition or disposition of a particular interest in real estate shall, at the earliest practicable opportunity, disclose to the customer the material facts relating to the acquisition or disposition that are known by or ought to be known by the broker or salesperson.

Agreements with third parties

22. A registrant shall not, on behalf of a client of the registrant, enter into an agreement with a third party for the provision of goods or services to the client unless,

(a)   the registrant has disclosed in writing to the client the subject-matter of the agreement with the third party and the identity of the person responsible for paying for the provision of the goods or services;

(b)   the client has consented to the registrant entering into the agreement with the third party; and

(c)   the registrant has disclosed in writing to the third party the identity of the person responsible for paying for the provision of the goods or services.

Steps taken by registrant

23. A registrant shall inform a client of all significant steps that the registrant takes in the course of representing the client.

Conveying offers

24. (1) A registrant shall convey any written offer received by the registrant to the registrant's client at the earliest practicable opportunity.

(2) A broker or salesperson shall establish a method of ensuring that,

(a)   written offers are received by someone on behalf of the broker or salesperson, if the broker or salesperson is not available at the time an offer is submitted; and

(b)   written offers are conveyed to the client of the broker or salesperson at the earliest practicable opportunity, even if the broker or salesperson is not available at the time an offer is submitted.

(3) Without limiting the generality of subsections (1) and (2), those subsections apply regardless of the identity of the person making the offer, the contents of the offer or the nature of any arrangements for commission or other remuneration.

(4) Subsections (1) to (3) are subject to any written directions given by a client.

(5) Subsections (1) to (4) also apply, with necessary modifications, to,

    (a)   written amendments to written offers and any other written document directly related to a written offer; and

    (b)   written assignments of agreements that relate to interests in real estate, written waivers of conditions in agreements that relate to interests in real estate, and any other written document directly related to a written agreement that relates to an interest in real estate.

(6) Subsections (1) to (5) apply, with necessary modifications, if a brokerage and a customer have an agreement that provides for the brokerage to receive written offers.

(7) Subsections (1) to (5) apply, with necessary modifications, to brokers and salespersons employed by a brokerage, if the brokerage and a customer have an agreement that provides for the brokerage to receive written offers.

Agreements relating to commission

25. (1) If a brokerage has a seller as a client and an agreement between the brokerage and the seller contains terms that relate to a commission or other remuneration and that may affect whether an offer to buy is accepted, the brokerage shall disclose the existence of and the details of those terms to any person who makes a written offer to buy, at the earliest practicable opportunity and before any offer is accepted.

(2) Subsection (1) applies, with necessary modifications, to a brokerage that has a seller as a customer, if the brokerage and the seller have an agreement that provides for the brokerage to receive written offers to buy.

Competing offers

26. (1) If a brokerage that has a seller as a client receives a competing written offer, the brokerage shall disclose the number of competing written offers to every person who is making one of the competing offers, but shall not disclose the substance of the competing offers.

(2) Subsection (1) applies, with necessary modifications, to a brokerage that has a seller as a customer, if the brokerage and the seller have an agreement that provides for the brokerage to receive written offers to buy.

Written and legible agreements

27. (1) A registrant who represents a client in respect of a trade in real estate shall use the registrant's best efforts to ensure that,

(a)   any agreement that deals with the conveyance of an interest in real estate is in writing; and

(b)   any written agreement that deals with the conveyance of an interest in real estate is legible.

(2) Subsection (1) applies, with necessary modifications, if a brokerage and a customer have an agreement that provides for the brokerage to provide services to the customer in respect of any agreement that deals with the conveyance of an interest in real estate.

Copies of agreements

28. (1) If a registrant represents a client who enters into a written agreement that deals with the conveyance of an interest in real estate, the registrant shall use the registrant's best efforts to ensure that all parties to the agreement receive a copy of the agreement at the earliest practicable opportunity.

(2) Subsection (1) applies, with necessary modifications, if a brokerage and a customer have an agreement that provides for the brokerage to provide services to the customer in respect of any agreement that deals with the conveyance of an interest in real estate.

Delivery of deposits and documents

29. Except as otherwise provided by law, if a registrant is representing a client or providing services to a customer in connection with a trade in real estate, and the client or customer has entered into an agreement in connection with the trade that requires the registrant to deliver a deposit or documents, the registrant shall deliver the deposit or documents in accordance with the agreement.

Business records

30. In addition to the records required by Ontario Regulation 579/05 (Educational Requirements, Insurance, Records and Other Matters) made under the Act, a brokerage shall make and keep such records as are reasonably required for the conduct of the brokerage's business of trading in real estate.

Certificate of registration: broker or salesperson

31. Every broker or salesperson shall carry his or her certificate of registration and, on the request of any person, shall show it to the person.

Certificate of registration: brokerage

32. (1) A brokerage shall ensure that every certificate of registration issued to the brokerage is kept at the office to which the certificate relates.

(2) A brokerage shall, on the request of any person, show to the person any certificate of registration issued to the brokerage.

Certificates of registration for brokers and salespersons kept by brokerage

33. (1) A brokerage shall ensure that all duplicate original certificates of registration given to the brokerage in respect of brokers and salespersons employed by the brokerage are kept in a safe place.

(2) A brokerage shall, on the request of any person, show the duplicate original certificate of registration given to the brokerage in respect of a broker or salesperson employed by the brokerage to the person.

Current forms

34. A registrant shall ensure that forms used by the registrant in the course of a trade in real estate are current.

Financial responsibility

35. A registrant shall be financially responsible in the conduct of business.

Advertising

36. (1) A registrant shall clearly and prominently disclose the name in which the registrant is registered in all the registrant's advertisements.

(2) A brokerage that identifies a broker or salesperson by name in an advertisement shall use the name in which the broker or salesperson is registered.

(3) A broker or salesperson shall not advertise in any manner unless the advertisement clearly and prominently identifies the brokerage that employs the broker or salesperson, using the name in which the brokerage is registered.

(4) A registrant who advertises shall,

(a) use the term "brokerage", "real estate brokerage", "maison de courtage" or "maison de courtage immobilier" to describe any brokerage that is referred to in the advertisement;

(b) use the term "broker of record", "real estate broker of record", "courtier responsable" or "courtier immobilier responsable" to describe any broker of record who is referred to in the advertisement;

(c) use the term "broker", "real estate broker", "courtier" or "courtier immobilier" to describe any broker who is referred to in the advertisement; and

(d) use the term "salesperson", "real estate salesperson", "sales representative", "real estate sales representative", "agent immobilier", "représentant commercial" or "représentant immobilier" to describe any salesperson who is referred to in the advertisement.

(5) Despite clause (4) (c), a registrant who advertises may, before April 1, 2008, use the term "associate broker", "associate real estate broker", "courtier associé" or "courtier immobilier associé" to describe any broker who is referred to in the advertisement.

(6) A registrant who advertises shall not use a term to describe any registrant that is referred to in the advertisement if the term could reasonably be confused with a term that is required or authorized by subsection (4) or (5).

(7) A registrant shall not include anything in an advertisement that could reasonably be used to identify a party to the acquisition or disposition of an interest in real estate unless the party has consented in writing.

(8) A registrant shall not include anything in an advertisement that could reasonably be used to identify specific real estate unless the owner of the real estate has consented in writing.

(9) A registrant shall not include anything in an advertisement that could reasonably be used to determine any of the contents of an agreement that deals with the conveyance of an interest in real estate, including any provision of the agreement relating to the price, unless the parties to the agreement have consented in writing.

Inaccurate representations

37. (1) A registrant shall not knowingly make an inaccurate representation in respect of a trade in real estate.

(2) A registrant shall not knowingly make an inaccurate representation about services provided by the registrant.

Error, misrepresentation, fraud, etc.

38. A registrant shall use the registrant's best efforts to prevent error, misrepresentation, fraud or any unethical practice in respect of a trade in real estate.

Unprofessional conduct, etc.

39. A registrant shall not, in the course of trading in real estate, engage in any act or omission that, having regard to all of the circumstances, would reasonably be regarded as disgraceful, dishonourable, unprofessional or unbecoming a registrant.

Abuse and harassment

40. A registrant shall not abuse or harass any person in the course of trading in real estate.

Duty to ensure compliance

41. (1) A brokerage shall ensure that every salesperson and broker that the brokerage employs is carrying out their duties in compliance with this Regulation.

(2) A broker of record shall ensure that the brokerage complies with this Regulation.

Procedures of Discipline Committee and Appeals Committee

Composition and appointment of committees

42. (1) The discipline committee and appeals committee shall each consist of at least five members, at least one of whom has never been a registrant or a shareholder, officer, director or employee of a registrant or former registrant.

(2) A person may be appointed under subsection 21 (3) of the Act as a member of both committees.

(3) A member of the board of the administrative authority shall not be appointed under subsection 21 (3) of the Act as a member of the discipline committee or the appeals committee.

(4) An appointment under subsection 21 (3) of the Act expires at the end of the day on the day before the second anniversary of the day the appointment took effect.

(5) If the term of office of a member of the discipline committee or appeals committee who has participated in a hearing expires before the hearing is completed or a decision is given, the term shall be deemed to continue, but only for the purpose of completing the hearing and participating in the decision and for no other purpose.

(6) The board of the administrative authority may at any time terminate an appointment under subsection 21 (3) of the Act for cause.

(7) Subsection (5) does not apply to a member whose appointment is terminated for cause under subsection (6).

(8) The board of the administrative authority shall appoint,

(a) from among the members of the discipline committee, one person as chair of the discipline committee and one person as vice-chair of the discipline committee; and

(b) from among the members of the appeals committee, one person as chair of the appeals committee and one person as vice-chair of the appeals committee.

(9) Subsections (4) and (6) apply, with necessary modifications, to an appointment under subsection (8).

(10) The vice-chair of a committee may exercise and perform the powers and duties of the chair on the request of the chair or if the chair is absent or unable to act.

(11) Every person appointed under subsection (8) or under subsection 21 (3) of the Act as a chair, vice-chair or member of a committee shall, before beginning his or her duties, take and sign the following oath or affirmation in either English or French:

> I solemnly swear (*affirm*) that I will faithfully, impartially and to the best of my skill and knowledge execute the duties of .... and that, except as I may be legally authorized or required, I will not disclose or give to any person any information or document that comes to my knowledge or possession by reason of my being ....

So help me God. (*Omit this line in an affirmation.*)

Assignment of discipline committee panels

43. (1) When a matter is referred to the discipline committee, the chair of the committee shall assign a panel in accordance with this section to hear and determine the matter.

(2) The panel has all the jurisdiction and powers of the discipline committee with respect to hearing and determining the matter.

(3) Subject to subsection 4.2.1 (1) of the *Statutory Powers Procedure Act*, the panel must be composed of at least three members of the discipline committee.

(4) If the panel is composed of three or more members of the discipline committee,

(a) at least two of the members of the panel must be registrants;

(b) if a broker of record is the subject of the proceeding, at least one of the registrants must be a broker of record;

(c) if a broker is the subject of the proceeding, at least one of the registrants must be a broker;

(d) if a salesperson is the subject of the proceeding, at least one of the registrants must be a salesperson; and

(e) at least one of the members of the panel must never have been a registrant or a shareholder, officer, director or employee of a registrant or former registrant.

Parties: discipline committee

44. The parties to a proceeding before the discipline committee are the registrant who is the subject of the proceeding, the administrative authority and any other person added as a party by the discipline committee.

Notice of hearing

45. Subject to section 6 of the *Statutory Powers Procedure Act*, the discipline committee shall give the parties to a proceeding at least 45 days notice of a hearing by the committee.

Disclosure of evidence

46. (1) A party who intends to tender evidence at a hearing before the discipline committee shall, not later than the date specified by subsection (3), disclose the following to every other party:

1.   In the case of written or documentary evidence, a copy of the evidence.

2.   In the case of oral evidence of a witness, the identity of the witness and a written statement containing the substance of the witness' anticipated oral evidence.

3.   In the case of oral evidence of an expert, the identity of the expert and a copy of a written report signed by the expert containing the substance of the expert's anticipated oral evidence.

4.   In the case of evidence that is not oral, written or documentary evidence, a written description of the evidence.

(2) A party who intends to tender written or documentary evidence, or other evidence that is not oral evidence, at a hearing before the discipline committee shall give every other party a reasonable opportunity to examine the original evidence before the hearing.

(3) The date referred to in subsection (1) is,

(a)   in the case of evidence tendered by the administrative authority, the date that is 30 days before the date the hearing begins; and

(b)   in the case of evidence tendered by any other party, the date that is 15 days before the date the hearing begins.

Disclosure from closed hearing

47. If a hearing before the discipline committee is closed to the public, the committee may order that evidence given and submissions made at the hearing not be disclosed to any member of the public.

Notice of decision to complainant

48. If a proceeding before the discipline committee arises from a complaint by a person who is not a party to the proceeding, the committee shall send the person a copy of its final decision or order, including the reasons if any have been given, at the same time that it complies with section 18 of the *Statutory Powers Procedure Act*.

Notice of appeal rights

49. When the discipline committee sends a copy of its final decision or order to a party who participated in the proceeding, or the party's counsel or agent, under section 18 of the *Statutory Powers Procedure Act*, it shall also send a notice outlining the party's right to appeal under subsection 21 (5) of the *Real Estate and Business Brokers Act, 2002* and the procedures applicable to an appeal.

Commencement of appeals

50. (1) A party may commence an appeal under subsection 21 (5) of the *Real Estate and Business Brokers Act, 2002* by delivering the following to the appeals committee within 30 days after the discipline committee sends notice, under section 18 of the *Statutory Powers Procedure Act*, of the order being appealed:

1. A notice of appeal that,
    i.   identifies the appellant and the other parties to the appeal,
    ii. identifies the order being appealed,
    iii. sets out the grounds for the appeal, and
    iv. sets out the relief that is sought.
2. The fee for commencing the appeal, as set by the administrative authority under clause 12 (1) (b) of the *Safety and Consumer Statutes Administration Act, 1996*, payable to the administrative authority.

(2) The appellant shall, within the 30-day period referred to in subsection (1), deliver a copy of the notice of appeal referred to in paragraph 1 of subsection (1),

(a) to the other parties to the appeal; and
(b) to the discipline committee.

(3) When a party commences an appeal under subsection 21 (5) of the *Real Estate and Business Brokers Act, 2002*, the discipline committee shall at the earliest practical opportunity forward to the appeals committee the record compiled under section 20 of the *Statutory Powers Procedure Act*.

Assignment of appeal committee panels

51. (1) The chair of the appeals committee shall assign a panel in accordance with this section to hear and determine an appeal to the committee under subsection 21 (5) of the Act.

(2) The panel has all the jurisdiction and powers of the appeals committee with respect to hearing and determining the appeal.

(3) Subject to subsection 4.2.1 (1) of the *Statutory Powers Procedure Act*, the panel must be composed of at least three members of the appeals committee.

(4) If the panel is composed of three or more members of the appeals committee,

(a)   at least two of the members of the panel must be registrants;

(b)   if a broker of record is the subject of the proceeding, at least one of the registrants must be a broker of record;

(c)   if a broker is the subject of the proceeding, at least one of the registrants must be a broker;

(d)   if a salesperson is the subject of the proceeding, at least one of the registrants must be a salesperson; and

(e)   at least one of the members of the panel must never have been a registrant or a shareholder, officer, director or employee of a registrant or former registrant. O. Reg. 580/05, s. 51 (4).

(5) A person who was a member of the panel of the discipline committee that made the order being appealed must not be assigned to the panel of the appeals committee that hears and determines the appeal.

Parties: appeals committee

52. The parties to a proceeding before the appeals committee are the appellant, the other persons who were parties to the proceeding before the discipline committee, and any other person added as a party by the appeals committee.

Application of ss. 45 to 48

53. Sections 45 to 48 apply, with necessary modifications, to proceedings before the appeals committee.

INDEX

D

E

W